Stenhouse Publishers • Portland, Maine

**second edition**

# *Living the Questions*

## A GUIDE FOR TEACHER-RESEARCHERS

# Ruth Shagoury & Brenda Miller Power

*Credits*
Page 10: William Stafford, "Things I Learned Last Week" from *The Way It Is: New and Selected Poems.* Copyright © 1982, 1998 by William Stafford and the Estate of William Stafford. Reprinted with the permission of the Permissions Company, Inc., on behalf of Graywolf Press, Minneapolis, Minnesota, www.graywolfpress.org.

Pages 27–28: Mekeel McBride, "Inspiration's Anatomy" from *Dog Star Delicatessen: New and Selected Poems 1979–2006.* Copyright © 2006 by Mekeel McBride. Reprinted with the permission of the Permissions Company, Inc., on behalf of Carnegie Mellon University Press, www.cmu.edu/universitypress.

Page 120: William Stafford, "You Reading This, Be Ready" from *The Way It Is: New and Selected Poems.* Copyright © 1998 by the Estate of William Stafford. Reprinted with the permission of the Permissions Company, Inc., on behalf of Graywolf Press, Minneapolis, Minnesota, www.graywolfpress.org.

Library of Congress Cataloging-in-Publication Data
Shagoury, Ruth, 1950-
    Living the questions : a guide for teacher-researchers / Ruth Shagoury and Brenda Miller Power.—2nd ed.
    p. cm.
    Includes bibliographical references and index.
    ISBN 978-1-57110-846-3 (pbk. : alk. paper)—ISBN 978-1-57110-944-6 (ebook) 1. Action research in education—United States—Handbooks, manuals, etc. 2. Teaching—Research—United States—Handbooks, manuals, etc. I. Power, Brenda Miller. II. Title.
    LB1028.24.H83 2012
    370.7'2—dc23
    2011037286

Cover design, interior design, and typesetting by Martha Drury
Manufactured in the United States of America

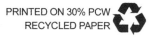
PRINTED ON 30% PCW
RECYCLED PAPER

18 17 16 15          9 8 7 6 5 4 3

For Heidi Mills, Amy Donnelly, and the entire community of learners at the Center for Inquiry (Columbia, South Carolina)—

May your garden of questions always bloom!

# Contents

*Acknowledgments*                                                                     *ix*

**Chapter 1:**  **Why Teacher Research?**                                               **1**
RESEARCH WORKSHOP
"Celebrating 'Things I Learned Last Week'"   9

FEATURED TEACHER-RESEARCHERS
"Teaching and Researching Riffs" by Jane A. Kearns   12
"Process Versus Product" by Jill Ostrow   15

**Chapter 2:**  **Questions Evolving**                                                 **19**
RESEARCH WORKSHOPS
"What's Coming Apart So It Can Come Back Together?" by Ruth Shagoury   26
"Strategies for Working Toward a Research Question" by JoAnn Portalupi   30

FEATURED TEACHER-RESEARCHERS
"Real Magic: Trusting the Voice of a Young Learner" by Susan Harris MacKay   33
"Real Teachers Don't Always Succeed" by Annie Keep-Barnes   40
"You Get What You Ask For: The Art of Questioning" by Heather Rader   45
"The Power of Wonder Questions" by Andrea Smith   49

**Chapter 3:**  **Research Designs**                                                   **53**
RESEARCH WORKSHOPS
"Hanging Around" by Brenda Miller Power   72
"Testing the Water with Mini-Inquiry Projects" by Jerome C. Harste and
    Christine Leland   74

FEATURED TEACHER-RESEARCHERS
Research Plans of Michelle Schardt, Emily Gromko, Sarah Christenson, Christina
    Wallace   76

**Chapter 4:**   **Harvesting Data**                                      **91**

RESEARCH WORKSHOP

"When to Write: Strategies to Find Time for Note Taking" by
    Brenda Miller Power   120

FEATURED TEACHER-RESEARCHERS

"Middle School Readers' Mid-Year Surveys" by Katie Doherty   124
"Focusing on Student Talk" by Sherry Young   127
"Assessment: Inside and Outside Views" by Andrea Smith   129

**Chapter 5:**   **What Likes What? Data Analysis**                       **135**

RESEARCH WORKSHOPS

"Language Patterns: Reflecting with Transcripts and Wordle" by
    Heather Rader   159
"The Draw a Reader Test: Informal Assessment Supporting Teacher Inquiry" by
    Suzy Kaback   162

FEATURED TEACHER-RESEARCHERS

"180-Degree Turn? Or Close to It?" by Audrey Alexander   167
"Simple Truths" by Ellie Gilbert   169

**Chapter 6:**   **Citing a Tea Bag: When Researchers Read**             **171**

RESEARCH WORKSHOPS

"You're Invited" by Kimberly Hill Campbell   178
"What's the Most Beautiful Thing You Know About . . . ?" by Melanie Quinn and
    Ruth Shagoury   185

FEATURED TEACHER-RESEARCHERS

"Writing a Literature Review: Joining a Conversation in Progress" by
    Jessica Singer Early   180

**Chapter 7:**   **Honest Labor: Writing Up Research**                    **187**

RESEARCH WORKSHOPS

"Seeing What Is Not Seen: Another Reason for Writing Up Teacher Research" by
    Ruth Shagoury   200
"Making Deadlines" by Julie Housum-Stevens   204

FEATURED TEACHER-RESEARCHERS

"5 Easy Steps for Starting a Blog" by Mary Lee Hahn and Franki Sibberson   205

**Chapter 8:** **Sustaining Research: Building and Extending Research Communities** **209**

RESEARCH WORKSHOP
"'A Secret Hidden in Plain Sight': Reflecting on Life Experiences" 223

FEATURED TEACHER-RESEARCHERS
"The Anticipation Guide: A Tool for Study Group Leaders" by Suzy Kaback 228
"To Fart or Not to Fart: Reflections on Boy Writers" by Jennifer Allen 231

**Epilogue:** **Why Not Teacher Research?** **235**

**Appendix:** **Teacher-Research Designs** **241**
Cathcrine Doherty, Bitsy Parks, Lara Murphy, Gloria Trabacca, Molly Taylor-Milligan, Laura Martinez, Saundra Hardy, Chrystal Freer, Gabi McGregor, Ellie Gilbert

*Bibliography* *269*
*Index* *281*

# Acknowledgments

Evelyn Beaulieu is a teacher-researcher in Maine. Her work involves building and sustaining networks of adult learners and educators throughout the state. When Evelyn began to integrate teacher research into her work among the adult education community, she found it almost impossible to express the place of inquiry in her life through words.

So she pulled out fabric, scissors, and thread, and began to cut and craft "We Are Each a Gem," the piece of fiber art about teacher research that is on the cover of this book. Each element of the artwork expresses a different aspect of becoming part of a research community. We find her metaphors are apt in describing our research community, too, so we will use them in thanking some of the people who are responsible for this book.

As you look at the art, the background fabric represents the Northern Lights. This is a symbol for how people are always changing and evolving. Our evolution as teacher-researchers came from apprenticing ourselves to near and distant teacher-researchers. Jennifer Allen, Andie Cunningham, Katie Doherty, Beth Lawson, Kelly Petrin, Heather Rader, and Franki Sibberson have been the teachers recently who welcome us into their classrooms most often. Allowing us to see their many "colors" as inquirers has stretched our own thinking about research immeasurably.

The center of the artwork is the "fire of knowledge," representing the fire of inspiration researchers receive from their closest colleagues. We thank Andie Cunningham, Maika Yeigh, Kimberly Campbell, Sherri Carreker, Jessie Singer Early, Melanie Quinn, Joan Moser, Gail Boushey, and Connie Perry for being those colleagues. Whenever the daily responsibilities of our professional lives become overwhelming, they give us the wisdom and compassion we need to renew our commitment to research and learning.

Every time you look at "We Are Each a Gem," you see something new, each stitch and bit of fabric contributing to the whole. We're grateful to the team at Stenhouse for their inspired work on this project. Philippa Stratton, our editor at Stenhouse, has challenged us again and again over the past three decades to think more deeply and differently about research. Her good humor and friendship mean the world to us. Martha Drury's lovely design, drawing on the work of Cathy Hawkes from the first edition, brings the concepts of the book to life. Jay Kilburn and Chris Downey have carefully shepherded the text through the production process, with an able assist from Chandra Lowe and Jill Cooley (the "Princesses of Permissions") and copy editor Laurel Robinson. We wouldn't have a new edition at all, if not for the marketing savvy of Nate Butler, Chuck Lerch, Rebecca Eaton, and Zsofi McMullin, who helped the first edition find a wide audience within a narrow niche.

Like Evelyn, we also find words fail us in expressing thanks to all the teachers in and out of these pages who have shaped our vision of teacher research. Robert Finch writes, "True belonging is born of relationships not only to one another but to a place of shared responsibilities and benefits. We love not so much what we have acquired as what we have made and whom we have made it with." This book has not been written so much as made, by a community that cares deeply about listening to and learning from students. It has been stitched together from bits and pieces of insight about research shared by generous teachers over many years. Those in this community know who you are—but you can never know how truly grateful we are for how your work has transformed ours.

*Be patient toward all that is unresolved in your heart and try to love the questions themselves like locked rooms and like books that are written in a very foreign tongue. Do not now seek the answers, which cannot be given you because you would not be able to live them. And the point is, to live everything. Live the questions now.*

—RAINER MARIA RILKE

# **Why Teacher Research?**

*Research is a high-hat word that scares a lot of people. It needn't. It's rather simple. Essentially research is nothing but a state of mind. . . . A friendly, welcoming attitude toward change . . . going out to look for change instead of waiting for it to come. Research is an effort to do things better and not to be caught asleep at the switch. It is the problem-solving mind as contrasted with the let-well-enough-alone mind. It is the tomorrow mind instead of the yesterday mind.*

—CHARLES KETTERING

Brenda's niece Julie is a born researcher. When she was four, her plans one summer morning included persuading her mother to take her and her two-year-old brother, Johnny, to the playground. All morning, as her mom worked in the kitchen, Julie kept asking, "Can we go to the playground this afternoon?" The first six lobbying efforts were met with the response, "I don't know." The seventh received the reply, "I don't know, but if you ask again, the answer is NO."

A few minutes later, Johnny toddled into the kitchen. Mom spied Julie hiding just beyond the kitchen door. "Momma, go playground?" asked Johnny. Mom replied in an exasperated tone, "I don't know—we'll see." Johnny toddled back out of the kitchen, to be met at the threshold by Julie. "What'd she say? What'd she say?!"

Johnny replied slowly, enunciating as clearly as he could, "She say, 'we'll see.'" Julie jumped up and down in glee. "Oh goody! 'Cause 'maybe' means 'no,' but 'we'll see' means 'yes'!"

After hearing this exchange, Julie's mom monitored her own speech for the next two weeks. She realized Julie was right. She discovered that every time she said "maybe," the answer was really no. And when she said, "we'll see," the children got their way.

Research is a process of discovering essential questions, gathering data, and analyzing it to answer those questions. Like Julie, we are all born looking for patterns in the world. These patterns unlock the secrets of how language works, of how affection is gained and lost, of how one piece of knowledge builds upon another. In its simplest sense, research helps us gain control of our world. When we understand the patterns underlying the language we use or the interactions we have with others, we have a better sense of how to adjust our behaviors and expectations. For four-year-olds, a critical goal of research might be to gain access to a playground. But for teachers who engage in systematic and thoughtful analyses of their teaching and students, the goals are diverse and complex.

Teacher research is research that is initiated and carried out by teachers in their classrooms and schools. Teacher-researchers use their inquiries to study everything from the best way to teach reading and the most useful methods for organizing group activities, to the different ways girls and boys respond to a science curriculum.

We began with the anecdote of Julie and her mom because it conveys the simplicity of beginning with genuine questions that are truly relevant to researchers. For many years, teachers have criticized education research as not being relevant to their needs, or written in a way that fails to connect with their classroom practice. We're not denigrating the value of traditional education research—we've completed many research studies ourselves as university professors. But there's little question that even the finest education research studies have failed to find a wide audience among K–12 teachers. It's no wonder that teacher research has emerged not only as a significant new contributor to research on teaching but also as a source of systemic reform within individual schools and districts.

We also began with Julie's story because much teacher research is rich in classroom anecdotes and personal stories. Although all methodologies are used for teacher inquiry, it is dominated by qualitative inquiry. In contrast to traditional education research studies, written in a distant, third-person voice, teacher research often has an immediate, first-person tone. Findings in teacher research are usually presented as narratives from the classroom, with metaphors a common means of highlighting key findings. As Jalongo and Isenberg note, "Stories are both mirrors of our own practice and windows on the practice of others" (1995, 174). In teacher research, stories are a critical tool for illuminating the deeper theories or rules governing the way a classroom community works.

As a teacher, it is natural to see research as "maybe" work—something that can be considered after the pressing needs of the classroom have been met. In this scheme, teacher research will never reach a high enough spot on the roster of duties in any classroom to be developed and supported.

But there are many ways to develop inquiry skills that are relevant to almost any teacher and classroom. Developing those skills, and seeing their place in teachers' lives across the country, is what this book is about.

# Little r and Big R

When we first talk with teachers about the possibilities for research in their professional lives, they often recount negative experiences with research, and stereotypical views of what researchers do. Teacher Julie Ford explains it this way:

> When I think of research, I think of the Big R type with long hours in the library, notes that could fill a novel, and a bibliography several pages long. I think of tension and stress lurking in the shadows. Feeling as I do about Research, the thought of conducting it in my classroom didn't curl my toes. But as I read the [classroom-based] research, I felt as though a door was beginning to open. My definition of research took a turn, and that familiar twinge of anxiety didn't come rushing forward. (Hubbard and Power 2003, xiv)

Teachers are surprised and delighted to realize that research can focus on problems they are trying to solve in their own classrooms, as Saundra Hardy, who teaches English language learners, discovered:

> I *am* a teacher researcher. I study students, and how they learn fascinates me. I am the one who desires to do what's best for students through my own classroom inquiry. I make informed decisions about curriculum and methodology based on my current student population and best practice.

At its best, teacher research is a natural extension of good teaching. Observing students closely, analyzing their needs, and adjusting the curriculum to fit the needs of all students have always been important skills demonstrated by fine teachers.

Teacher research involves collecting and analyzing data as well as presenting it to others in a systematic way. But this research process involves the kinds of skills and classroom activities that already are part of the classroom environment. As Glenda Bissex writes, a teacher-researcher is not a split personality, but a more complete teacher. Research is labor intensive, and so is good teaching. And the labor is similar for teachers, because the goal is the same—to create the best possible learning environment for students. We agree with Barbara Michalove that there is no real boundary between teaching and research within the real world of classrooms:

> When you teach a lesson and half the class gives you a blank look, you ask yourself, "How else can I teach this concept?" That's research. You observe, and respond to what you have observed. You begin to be aware of the intricate teaching and learning dance with your students. Researching took me a step further into my students' lives. The more I tune in, the better I become at knowing when to lead, when to follow, or when to play a sedate waltz or a lively rap. (1993, 33)

Barbara's words show how simple and immediate the research agendas of most teachers are—a kind of "dance" between teachers, students, and learning. Teacher-researchers rarely seek to initiate and carry out studies that have large-scale implications for education policy. Unlike large-scale education research, teacher research has a primary purpose of helping the teacher-researcher understand her students and improve her practice in specific, concrete ways. Teacher-research studies can and do lead to large-scale changes in education. But for most teacher-researchers, the significance of those studies is in how they inform and change teachers' own teaching.

Just as important for teachers, research can transform their understanding of students. This transformation can happen in a heartbeat, as it did for middle-school teacher Maureen Barbieri as she researched literacy in the lives of adolescent girls:

> The most exciting thing that happened with the research was the day a girl said to me, "You just don't understand," and she was ferocious when she said it. She looked at me, and I looked at her, and I felt like we really saw each other for the first time. I realized what she was saying. I did not understand their position. And there was this feeling in the classroom that I had to acknowledge that and in acknowledging it, then I was able to understand a tiny, tiny bit and then that grew. (Frye 1997, 52)

This notion of understanding learning from the students' perspectives is central to teacher research. Strategies for research emerge and evolve from these close, intense, shifting relationships between students and teachers. The research agendas of teachers can look nothing like "Big R" research, with objective, large-scale, and distant analyses of issues.

Comparing the value of large-scale education research and teacher research confuses the purposes of these different research agendas and devalues both types of studies. John Dewey was perhaps the first major figure in education to argue for teachers' entrée into traditional education research communities. In commenting on the large array of scientific reports on education and learning in 1929, he wrote the following:

> A constant flow of less formal reports on special school affairs and results is needed. Of the various possibilities here I select one for discussion. It seems to me that the contributions that might come from classroom teachers are a comparatively neglected field; or, to change the metaphor, an almost unworked mine. . . . There are undoubted obstacles in the way. It is often assumed . . . that classroom teachers have not themselves the training which will enable them to give effective intelligent cooperation. The objection proves too much, so much that it is almost fatal to the idea of a workable scientific content in education. For these teachers are the ones in direct contact with pupils and hence the ones through whom the results of scientific findings finally reach students. They are the channels through which the consequences of educational theory come into the lives

of those at school. [One questions] whether some of the incapacity, real or alleged, of this part of the corps of educators, the large mass of teachers, is not attributable to lack of opportunity and stimulus, rather than to inherent disqualification. As far as schools are concerned, it is certain that the problems which require scientific treatment arise in actual relationships with students. (Wallace 1997, 27–28)

Like other proponents of teacher research, Dewey chooses to emphasize the strengths that teachers can bring to research agendas (notably "direct contact with pupils" and their significant role as the "channels" for education theory). He looks at the potential of teacher research, interestingly, from the same place many teachers now look at the potential of each of their students—building from teachers' strengths rather than criticizing "real or alleged" deficiencies.

Lawrence Stenhouse noted that the difference between the teacher-researcher and the large-scale education researcher is like the difference between a farmer with a huge agricultural business to maintain and the "careful gardener" tending a backyard plot:

In agriculture the equation of invested input against gross yield is all: it does not matter if individual plants fail to thrive or die so long as the cost of saving them is greater than the cost of losing them. . . . This does not apply to the careful gardener whose labour is not costed, but a labour of love. He wants each of his plants to thrive, and he can treat each one individually. Indeed he can grow a hundred different plants in his garden and differentiate his treatment of each, pruning his roses, but not his sweet peas. Gardening rather than agriculture is the analogy for education. (Rudduck and Hopkins 1985, 26)

This view of the teacher-researcher as a "careful gardener" is the image we hold in our minds of the ideal teacher-researcher—not a scientist in a lab coat, staring down a "research subject" (a kid!), but a human being in the midst of teaching, carefully weighing the value of different ways of teaching and learning.

# Teacher Research: A Very Brief History

Although teacher research has reemerged recently as a significant kind of research in education, it is important to realize that the movement has deep and enduring roots. The two principles that define the teacher-research movement today have been used widely in different education contexts, at different times in history:

1. Teacher research is based upon close observation of students at work. Education historians (such as McFarland and Stansell 1993) have traced the roots of teacher research to Comenius (1592–1670), who

was a proponent of linking child psychology with observational data to develop teaching methods. Pestalozzi (1746–1827) and Rousseau (1712–1778) developed and advocated observations of children to understand learning. But it was Herbart (1776–1841) who applied these methods in a systematic way in schools to develop principles of curriculum development. At the turn of the century and beyond, the work of Montessori (1870–1952) emphasized the value of teachers using their observations to build systematic understanding of students.

2. Teacher-researchers depend upon a research community. There are examples of teacher-researchers doing fine studies without support, but usually sustained inquiry in schools or districts over time involves the development of a research community. One of the earliest proponents of teacher research was Lucy Sprague Mitchell. Mitchell, a close colleague of Dewey working in New York City, is famous for founding a consortium to support teacher research and the distribution of findings in 1916. This group, the Bureau of Education Experiments, became the Bank Street School of Education in 1930.

In England, Lawrence Stenhouse is widely credited with initiating an international teacher-research movement. His consortium for supporting school inquiry, started in 1967, was a sensation in the English teaching community. This initiative led many English educators to begin research projects in their schools and become part of school research communities that endure today.

Since the publication of *In the Middle* (1987) by Nancie Atwell, scores of books by teachers have been published that are infused with the power of "little r" teacher research.

Cynthia Ballenger has written three books about her classroom research, and the most recent is *Puzzling Moments, Teachable Moments: Practicing Teacher Research in Urban Classrooms* (2009). In her new book, she explores the intellectual strengths of students whom teachers find puzzling: poor, urban, immigrant, or bilingual children who do not traditionally excel in school. She challenges mainstream assumptions about both their backgrounds and their intellectual capabilities as she analyzes what the children said, what this indicates about their thinking, and how her dialogues with them informed her teaching. Thousands of teachers have been inspired by Debbie Miller's practical classroom research on primary children in *Reading with Meaning* (2002) and *Teaching with Intention* (2008). High school teacher Kelly Gallagher's classroom research with diverse urban adolescent populations are also best sellers (*Readicide* 2009; *Deeper Reading* 2004.) These books are rich with the stories of classrooms, the words of the students, and the insights of the teacher-authors, informed by their own classroom inquiries. These—and many more—are having a powerful effect on the profession.

Early teacher-research communities often evolved within lab school settings, but in the past two decades these communities have become more far-flung and diverse because of technology. Teacher-researchers gather in special-interest groups at the annual meetings of professional organizations such as the National Council of Teachers of English or the American Educational Research Organization, or at summer institutes such as Bread Loaf or those offered by the National Writing Project. They then stay connected through electronic forums that make sharing data and findings easier than ever. For more than a decade, the Teacher Inquiry Communities Network (sponsored by the National Writing Project) has also offered a four-day summer institute to support Writing Project sites that are new to the process of supporting inquiry communities or that want to revitalize their inquiry communities by taking a fresh look at how to work with them. (For more information, see www.nwp.org/cs/public/print/resource/3130.)

# Teacher Research Today: Will It Endure?

Given that the value assigned to teacher research has peaked and waned at different times, what evidence is there that teacher research will be a significant part of education reform in the coming decades? There are a number of differences between the teacher-research initiatives in previous decades and the current work of teacher-researchers that point to the movement's enduring.

Teacher research in recent years has received significant new support and validation from existing education research communities. In our own field, literacy education, teacher-research studies have emerged as a dominant research methodology during award competitions. Perhaps most important for teachers, we have reached a point where it is no longer possible to tackle one classroom issue or concern at a time. We face attacks in the media and at school board meetings over the quality of our work. But we also deal in individual classrooms with a science curriculum that needs to be rebuilt, or a literature circle format that works well in three groups but dismally in a fourth, or a very needy student who is disrupting an entire third-grade class. More and more, teachers depend upon using their reflective abilities to research these problems and then to build a corps of reflective learners in their schools who can work well together around tough issues.

This community of learners must have the ability to be those "problem seekers" Kettering praises in the epigraph for this chapter. It is a complex, complicated garden we are tending, and we need a diverse array of research tools and strategies to make it thrive.

If you are waiting for a "good" time to begin doing research in your classroom, give up! There is never a good time for research—and there is never a better time than now to begin. Every time a student stares you down and challenges your knowledge is an opportunity to begin. Every time a lesson falls flat is a chance to unearth a research question and start collecting data. Our days are full of opportunities for research, and all we'll be left with in the end is regret if we miss them all. In Elizabeth Berg's novel *The Pull of the Moon* (1997), the main character, Elaine, notes how much those missed chances nag at us later in life: "I am so often struck by what we do not do, all of us. And I am also, now, so acutely aware of the quick passage of time, the way that we come suddenly to our own, separate closures. It is as though a thing says, I told you. But you thought I was just kidding" (143).

So, start your research while you can, however you can. Follow Colette's admonition, "We will do foolish things, but do them with enthusiasm!" and take a few risks. Remember Diane Mariechild's advice to "trust that still small voice that says this might work and I'll try it," and believe in the many strong skills of observation and reflection you bring to your work as a novice researcher but veteran teacher.

And with those first small, tentative steps you take in becoming a researcher, you'll be joining a community of teachers throughout the world who are changing the way we think about teaching and learning—one classroom at a time.

# What's Changed in This New Edition

Perhaps our greatest challenge with the new edition of this book has been including new technologies. The emergence of digital cameras, recorders, and sophisticated low-cost services for posting and sharing media are transforming the way teachers collect and analyze data. These options are expanding research communities in ways we could only dream of when the first edition of this book was written more than a decade ago. Yet these new technologies are developing so rapidly, some that we mention may be nearly obsolete by the time you read our words. We've tried to acknowledge their importance throughout the text while being careful not to cite too many with specific brand names or Web addresses, given the fleeting nature of these changes.

We found in the thirteen years since we wrote the first edition of this book that classrooms have become ever more diverse. The examples from teacher-researchers in this book reflect this diversity in powerful ways—not just in language, but in income, class, and perspectives on teaching and learning.

The last change from the first edition reflects a more subtle shift: we eliminated many of the extended examples from teacher-researchers in favor of a greater variety of shorter pieces. One of the most popular features from the first edition was the section on research designs, or plans. We've included many more research design examples in the appendix.

The inclusion of many short pieces (both the research designs and featured teacher-researchers) stems partially from our desire to include as many diverse examples as possible of different grades, cultures, and possibilities for data collection and analysis. But we also think technology may be changing professional reading habits and preferences for many teachers. Professional books are getting shorter, and the daily reading diet of many teachers includes brief texts on the Web. The new edition includes more teachers writing about their research, in more succinct ways.

# How This Book Is Organized

Careful gardeners have their own preferences for their plot of earth. Some gardeners are crazy about tomatoes; others plant only flowers. And every gardener deals with constraints, too—the woodchuck who serves as a personal nemesis, the short growing season in some climates.

We can't anticipate your passions as a teacher or the constraints that you face in your research. But we can share the passions and constraints of teacher-researchers from throughout the world who have tackled all sorts of research projects and in the process developed creative methods for making research a vital part of their lives.

Each chapter of the book includes an essay in which we present snapshots of teachers doing research, presenting research, or musing about their research process. We distill their best advice about research methods and strategies into brief, practical essays. We then present a Research Workshop section—an opportunity for you to test out the methods and ideas of the section through some research activities of your own. Each chapter closes with a Featured Teacher-Researchers section, showing a range of strategies used by teacher-researchers in their work.

Although technology will make your work as a teacher-researcher easier, what matters most hasn't changed. Remember the importance of developing a research community. Try to find at least one other colleague willing to read and try the Research Workshop strategies with you. Many of them work best if you have a partner to test out the concepts with you and to sustain your motivation when it lags.

All careful gardeners begin from the same place. They plant seeds, they wait, and they hope. We hope this book plants enough seeds to allow some possibilities for teacher research to sprout in your own classroom, school, or district. Every teacher has wonderings worth pursuing. Teacher research is one way to pursue those wonderings in a thoughtful, systematic, and collaborative way.

---

## RESEARCH WORKSHOP

### Celebrating "Things I Learned Last Week"

In the pages that follow are examples from new and veteran teacher-researchers who explain how they dig into their data and cope with the messiness of their evolving research. Some of the advice deals with the little things we learn that can get us through the day, if we pay close attention to them, and help us reconnect with the research questions that intrigue us. It takes practice to notice the small details. It may involve looking through a new lens, readjusting our focus, and celebrating what we see as we document what we have learned.

The poet William Stafford believes that these details in life are the "golden threads" that lead us to what he calls "amazing riches." In his poem "Things I Learned Last Week," he celebrates the learning that comes from close observation, from reading, and from reflecting on his own actions:

### Things I Learned Last Week
William Stafford

*Ants, when they meet each other,*
*usually pass on the right.*
*Sometimes you can open a sticky*
*door with your elbow.*
*A man in Boston has dedicated himself*
*to telling about injustice.*
*For three thousand dollars he will*
*come to your town and tell you about it.*
*Schopenhauer was a pessimist but*
*he played the flute.*
*Yeats, Pound, and Eliot saw art as*
*growing from other art. They studied that.*
*If I ever die, I'd like it to be*
*in the evening. That way, I'll have*
*all the dark to go with me, and no one*
*will see how I begin to hobble along.*
*In the Pentagon one person's job is to*
*take pins out of towns, hills, and fields,*
*and then save the pins for later.*

When we take up William Stafford's challenge to look closely at "what we learned last week," what might we collect? After reading this poem, Saundra Hardy changed her lens and looked closely at her students for a week, and then wrote the following poem:

### Students Teach Me Things

*K'Moo Eh Paw talks less now*
*than the first few months of the school year,*
*but is writing more.*

*Andy needs to see in writing when it will be his turn.*

*Lucky eats crunchy, cheesy Cheetos in group*
*and doesn't seem to notice I know by the ring of cheese*
*around his lips.*

*Apoleen erases the whole sentence*
*when one letter doesn't match my printing style exactly,*
*and this annoys me.*

*Nai K'Ba May OO and Serlyanna are becoming leaders in their*
*English Language Development group.*

*Adrian has one great day to every four naughty ones.*

*Eyoub's goal is to keep his hands in his lap.*
*He does much better meeting this goal when given a hands-on project.*

*Eh Dah's real name is Eh Eh Dah,*
*but it was changed to Eh Dah after arriving in the United States*
*after someone said it was too hard to pronounce.*
*Nasteho responded by saying, "It's too easy, Eh-Eh-DAH."*

Saundra's insights about her Burmese student K'Moo Eh Paw led her to focus her inquiry into a case study of this young girl's growth as a writer over the year.

A group of experienced teachers, this time from Maine, did the same exercise together, focusing on their work with students to create a group poem, with one line from each teacher-researcher:

### Things I Learned This Week About Teaching

*There's a connection between watering the plant*
*on my office windowsill and paying*
*attention to the needs of my students.*
*Getting new braces is much more important*
*to talk about than acute and obtuse*
*angles.*
*When registering children for*
*kindergarten, you can't keep just the*
*well-behaved children and kind parents.*
*As much as I think I know about students,*
*they still surprise me with new insights,*
*and, this week, excuses.*
*Sometimes teachers who are innovative,*
*nurturing, and kind in their classrooms*
*do not treat colleagues the same way.*
*Teachers have to learn what to ignore.*
*A short piece of writing can unlock a big*
*hurt.*
*Sometimes you have to hold chuckles*
*inside, like when a second grader writes*
*about how he "knocked up" an alligator*
*instead of how he knocked it out.*
*Children know more than we give them*
*credit for. They let me know who the*
*great authors are and they're not the*
*ones I would have chosen.*

Setting these details down—recording and keeping track of them even for a week—helps us process the daily small moments that inform our lives. And hearing what others have learned motivates us to look closely at the small details that are the building blocks of our lives as researchers as well.

An Oregon group of teachers decided to extend their close examination and ask what they learned "last week" about their processes as teacher-researchers. This group poem summarizes those details they are learning about research:

### Things I Learned About Research

*The more I write or reflect,*
*the more questions I ask.*
*Some projects are like icebergs—*
*they look small on the top*
*and turn into monsters in the end.*
*Topics are subject to change and*
*events can enliven or*
*dampen my enthusiasm.*
*The computer is my friend.*
*I feel better about what I'm doing*
*and why I'm doing it*
*because I feel I can substantiate everything*
*with some kind of evidence and my own*
*personal thoughts.*
*I find I am researching when I'm not researching.*
*I'm starting writing more like a real writer,*
*mimicking writing I've read before.*
*Knowing there is an audience*
*helps me "toe the line."*
*I learn what I know by trying*
*to explain it to others.*
*Everyone's research informs my question.*

What will you learn this week? Try your hand at crafting your own "things I learned this week" poem about teaching or research, either alone or with your inquiry group. You may find yourself surprised at how varied the learning is.

## FEATURED TEACHER-RESEARCHER

## Teaching and Researching Riffs

*Jane A. Kearns*

"Are you still teaching?"
        I looked at my questioner.

"Are you still teaching?"

The tone of this question suggested that the speaker would have been pleased if I had moved into another field rather than still teaching. Do other professionals get asked that question: Are you still doctoring? Still lawyering? Are you still an architect?

No. They don't get asked those questions. So why do people ask teachers?

I think people ask us whether we are still teaching for one reason: they realize that teaching is an intense, complex, and stressful profession. They assume that teachers will burn out and change careers more than other professionals. And they imagine that no adult wants to spend all day with thirty children or preteens, and certainly not with teenagers.

Perhaps the questioners are in the vast majority of people who admit they just could not take the anxiety, the tension, and the challenge of dealing with thirty young minds in every class. Teachers are catalysts—doing so that someone else will learn. Our goal is to have ideas spring forth, like the mythological dragon-teeth warriors, to be conquered by the students' desire to know. The best days for teachers are those when knowledge filters in a new word or world or wonder.

Some days we knapsack thoughts in quiet, controlled classes; other times we choreograph spinning swoops and headlong leaps toward discovery. Eyes flicker, pencils roll, minds percolate.

It is difficult to explain to adults who ask questions such as, Are you still teaching? why we are still teaching. Their easy answer is that we must do it for the summer vacation. People who believe this will never understand teaching or teachers. Teachers love the exhilaration of the challenge, to get students to be curious. Most jobs lean on predictability; teaching leans on the improvised, based on knowledge and experience. And that is why many teachers are becoming researchers, to further hone their improvisational skills.

In this way, teaching and research are a lot like playing jazz, being in three places at once—many rhythms happening at the same time, playing together, going solo. Fluid blends of all the performers.

In both teacher research and jazz, you have a certain arrangement, a theme, a goal, but it is in the getting there that teacher research and jazz happen. The multiplicity of energies in the class and in the band balance and then sway, pitch, roll. From improvisation, the soul of jazz and of teacher research, comes the best—instinctive, being in the zone. Start with the basic guides and then go with the flow, react, extend, reach, and stretch.

Quiet one moment, then all out strummin' goin' to town, sweet clarinet together with funky keyboards. Listen and talk, talk and listen, and play.

A good class is like The Jam, a freewheeling interplay of improvisational riffs. Surprise. Point. Counterpoint. Point counterpoint. Spontaneous and effortless, with each participant growing and scaling new heights.

I love the passion of jazz. I love the passion of teacher research. Triple-time thrummin' and drummin', smoky and mellow, mellow and wry and wild.

Jazz has a sense of humor; you need one in teacher research, too. Both speak to me of the hope in our world. Upbeat. Heartbeat. Your own beat thumping, pounding high energy, entering unexplored space.

I love the pulse of each note alone or in raucous/smooth harmony. Jazz is straight from the heart. No two performances alike, each one full of surprises—funky and fun. Jazz struts and dances, careens. Just like a good class. Just like a good research project.

I bought my first jazz album when I was a teenager, captivated by the cover of a Dave Brubeck record—*Red Hot and Cool*. I played it all the time when I was alone. With friends, it was the new rock 'n' roll. I never shared my jazz because I didn't know how to explain the music or my soaring feelings.

Then I heard Sarah Vaughan in person. The Divine One. Her voice traveled places I didn't know any instrument could go. Into a different world, a different dimension of excellence. And freedom. And power and heightened awareness.

Preservation Hall Jazz, Dixieland, Creole, and Chicago. Scott Joplin. Bessie Smith. Billy Eckstine.

"Charlie Parker played bebop. Charlie Parker played saxophone. Never leave your cat alone" (Raschka 1992).

The Count, the Duke, and Jelly Roll Morton. Joe Williams every day; stompin' at the Savoy, striding, taking the A train.

The mellow tones of Mel Torme and Bobby Short, George Benson and Ella.

Errol Garner swinging on piano, BB King wailing on guitar; Kenny G sweet toning on clarinet. Louis. The new jazz of Pat Kelly, Gary Burton, and David Benoit, Pat Metheny and Harry Connick. Andy Narell making warm-weather jazz with steel pans and drums. In the zone.

I still can't find the words to explain why I like jazz. Leonard Bernstein's *What Is Jazz?* (1981) helps me understand what it is but not how it reaches me. Why does it reach me?

I can't explain the nuances of a good research project, either, "at once spontaneous and deliberate, passionate and controlled, controlled in ways that make its passion all the more convincing" (Williams 1993).

Jon Pareles (1993) wrote in the *New York Times* that jazz advances right through "a bewildering world." So does teacher research. Improvised jazz sits like a good research project—it can't be replayed in exactly the same way. Teacher research, like jazz, is a solo art even when completed in a group. Teacher research gets us involved to the point that we seem to all be working together, with the sum of the parts as great as the whole. Whether in isolation in our own classroom or teaming with others, a teaching moment, like a gig, brings out the best in each of us. Good teacher-researchers involve students in working things out together, like a jam session—individuals all, but building strength and risk taking from each other. Harmony.

A good research project is the result of knowledge and intuition. Our improvs are based on sound knowledge of the students and of our own craft. We assess what is going on as it is going on and build on that moment, in that moment. As teacher-researchers we know that the truth is often in the unexpected, not the planned. We wish for and wait for and relish those sidebars into new energies. In teacher research and in jazz, mistakes are not mistakes; they are calibrations for the mind.

Martin Williams in *The Jazz Tradition* (1993) writes about Louis Armstrong:

> And his genius is such that he can apparently take any piece, add a note here, leave out a note there, condense or displace this melodic phrase a bit, rush this cadence, delay that one; alter another one slightly, and transform it into sublime melody, into pure gold. He can turn something merely pretty into something truly beautiful and something deeply delightful. Conscious taste has little to do with such transformations; they are products of an intuitive genius, and of the kind of choice where reason cannot intrude. (15)

This defines every great teacher-researcher I have learned from, or observed, or worked with, or listened to, or read about. Good teacher research cannot be explained away in neat packages or labels. Good teacher research swings.

Jazz—and teacher research—affirms who we are, where we have been, and where we are going. This is why we teach. Why we research. And why, yes, I am still a teacher! I would not have it any other way.

## FEATURED TEACHER-RESEARCHER

## Process Versus Product

*Jill Ostrow*

I love buying new shoes. I don't often buy them anymore, so when I do, I try to keep them as fresh and clean as I can. But sooner than I'd like, they end up tossed in a heap in my rather embarrassingly disorganized and very small clothes closet. Dust settles on them, or a fallen sweater that I didn't hang correctly, but I'll dig them out and wipe the dust off with the arm of my shirt. Good as new. So often in education, those jargon-y words actually started off nice and clean, too. They've just gotten dumped in a heap and covered up by thick dust.

I imagine the term *workshop* as one of those dust-covered words. Back in the 1990s that word meant something much different from what it does today. When I listen to a new teacher use the term *writing workshop* quickly in a sentence, I often find myself blinking and shaking my head in confusion. I understand times change—that content, curriculum, and what we know and understand about learning has come a long way in the last twenty years. But the foundational principles of a *workshop*? I don't think so. What we know about *writing* might have changed in twenty years, but those principles certainly haven't.

Textbook companies love to basal-ize—to standardize—as much as they can. When *workshop* became a hot buzzword, textbook companies listened. When reading comprehension strategies became popular, those companies ate it up. Stupid, they're not. Jargon sells. It was hard not to find a first-grade classroom "using three sticky notes to comprehend." Heavy sigh.

As a higher education teacher I find it hard to infuse the idea of process over product. The *jargon* comes from something foundational—from teachers trying, learning, writing, and sharing. Instead of *leveling a child*, how about observation and figuring out what a child needs? In the climate of testing and standards and levels and benchmarks and scores and on and on and on, how do I teach my teachers to get back to that rawness of slowing down and letting their students show them what they know?

Taking a course titled Classroom Research strikes terror in many of my students when they first sign up. I am usually inundated before the term begins with e-mails asking such questions as, What should I be reading to get ahead? or Will this class be about data? or If I'm not in a classroom, what should I do?

Twenty years ago as a classroom teacher I didn't take a class specifically titled Teacher Research or Classroom Research or Action Research. But teacher research was infused into my thinking as a teacher. I don't remember learning how to *do it* formally. Granted, I presented my work, and yet what I am teaching now is difficult for me sometimes.

I find myself often needing to defend teacher research to my students. "This is what good teachers do all the time. All of those great books you read? Those were written by teacher-researchers." You have no idea how many times I've said that.

This year, I enlisted the help of Franki Sibberson and Suzy Kaback. I thought perhaps if I asked two other teacher-researchers what they do, I might learn something new, and my students would hear from someone besides me.

I asked Franki and Suzy to answer one simple question for me. They could send their answer back through either video or audio. I would edit their responses and create a new video for my online students. I purposefully chose these two for specific reasons. Franki is a well-known teacher-author. She has many publications, speaks around the country, has a blog, Tweets often, and works in the public schools. Suzy, also a published author, works in higher education. I wanted my students to know that, yes, even some of us in higher education consider ourselves teacher-researchers. Also, my students had just finished reading an article written by Suzy.

The question I posed to them was, How can I infuse the notion of *process* of teacher research into my graduate students, when they know they have a paper to finish at the end?

My students, and most students who take this course titled Classroom Research at my university, seem much more concerned about their final paper than they do with the actual process of teacher research. This has bothered me since I began teaching it. These aren't undergraduates. These aren't students new to education. The students in the course are teachers. Shouldn't they *want* to learn this?

And yet, I also understand that this is a course. Not just any course. This is their Masters Capstone course. It is important. They are nervous. So it is a battle between a passion of mine and their stress.

I decided to have them watch the video I created with Franki and Suzy (www.youtube.com/watch?v=jHqfSVH-buE) before I gave them their actual paper requirements. I'm sure they are still stressed.

I certainly feel better. I think I'll go buy myself a new pair of shoes.

# 2

# Questions Evolving

*What room can there be in that cramped skull for thoughts, imaginations, questions, wonders, for all that makes us human?*

—PETER DICKINSON

**W**here do our questions come from? It's a natural part of being human to look at the world around us and wonder. Peter Dickinson, in his novel *A Bone from a Dry Sea*, re-creates the world of our ancestors, who live between the land and the sea. Li, the main character, is a child. She is the "thinker" of her people, and it is her intelligence and imagination—her questioning stance—that holds the key to human evolution.

One morning, wandering off from her tribe, she catches a flicker of movement out of the corner of her eye:

> Inquisitive, she climbed down and crept across to see. The spider was crouched over its prey, bouncing gently on its springy legs. She wanted to see what the spider would do. She crouched and watched while the spider dragged the bug clear of the insect-sized track along which it had been scuttling. It climbed into the twigs above the track and rapidly wove a coarse, loose web, then returned to the earth and stretched a couple of threads across the path. It moved into the shadows and waited. So did Li.
>
> Every insect click, every faint rustle, might be a danger sound. She must go back. But first, she needed to know what the spider was up to. It was the mere knowledge that mattered. The excitement of her thoughts kept her awake. . . . There were pictures in her mind: the spider, the web dropping from the twigs. "What?" she wondered. "How . . . ?" (1992, 20)

Li's questions evolve from her interest in making sense of all that she is hearing, seeing, and noticing. She moves into the shadows, waits, watches, and asks "how." Her questions initially surprise her. From her continued observations and reflections, and ultimately the weaving of the first nets to catch fish, her questions work to change her whole tribe's way of life.

Teachers with a research frame of mind are open, too, to exploring the surprises that pop up in our teaching lives. We don't always start out with a specific, clearly formulated question. As observers of classrooms daily, we can unearth our questions by reflecting on what we see. Borrowing a term from pioneer teacher-researcher Janet Emig, Dixie Goswami reminds us that before beginning any kind of inquiry, it's important to identify what is "governing our gaze"; noting our tendency to "see what we elect to see" can help lead us to a deeper inquiry:

> Acknowledging that we have a governing gaze leads to an essential set of questions, for example, what influences the way we view our students? Their capacity to learn? Their use of language—first and second? Understanding the things that govern our gaze allows for positioning ourselves in relation to the research we are doing. Everything about governing gaze is specific to a certain time, place, and context, as well as to our identities and personal histories. A different time and circumstance would alter the gaze because we would be looking at different students, learning in different ways. (Goswami et al. 2009, 20)

Being mindful of our gaze helps lead us to surprising inquiry. Teaching is filled with researchable moments—those instants when a question suddenly snaps into consciousness. Questions may come from a teaching journal or a snatch of conversation with a colleague. For teaching intern Kelli Clark, a pile of student work was the catalyst for a research question. She recounts the experience in her essay "Harvesting Potatoes":

> My 70-year-old father astonished a young Girl Scout on a garden project by countering her assertion that potatoes come from Safeway. Her confident claim was met with a swift turn of the spading fork, unearthing a mound of potatoes at her feet. She was dumbstruck.
>
> The effect of my first encounter with teacher research was no less remarkable. Of course, I was impressed with the efforts of others and fully intended to implement a "system" for research in my own classroom. Like potatoes coming clean, sorted, and unblemished from the store, "good" teacher-research questions came from well-organized Über Teachers who pulled neat packages of insights from their classrooms. As a student teacher, I didn't know if I could evolve into one of these beings, but I harbored my fantasies. Someday I would get organized and begin my research.
>
> Imagine my shock to see eyes of potatoes staring at me from a pile of rough drafts on my first major teaching project. As part of the teaching team at Mount Tabor Middle School, we were investigating Ancient Rome, under the larger theme of Demise of Cultures. My class was composed of a mix of sixth, seventh, and eighth graders. Our goal was to examine why cultures failed and whether we could use that information usefully in the future.

To assess their learning, I asked students to assume the role of an emperor toward the end of the empire. Using their understanding of the reasons underlying the fall of Rome, they were to write a decree that issued orders that would effectively save the empire. I did a mini-lesson on the differences between a decree, a declaration, and a proclamation. We talked about establishing authority and the class role-played using authoritative language.

Teacher research was the farthest thing from my mind when I read the rough drafts of the decrees. Several students engaged in lengthy, grandiose descriptions of their personal authority and what might happen to their subjects if they did not comply with the decree. I read as the self-described "Supreme and Undaunted Ruler of the Universe," "Leader of the Assassins," and "John the Decapitator" blew up, savagely beat, and otherwise abused the unfortunate imaginary plebeians and patricians. These students engaged in this to the extent that they often neglected to discuss Rome, or issue any decree for which they'd described such detailed, severe penalties for noncompliance!

As I began to wonder if I'd overemphasized the authority issue, I started seeing papers that passively requested something be done. The "Most Superior Being on Earth" suggested that the people "do" something. "The Ruler Most High" said, "I think you should . . ."

Here it was: potatoes. No neat system or detailed notes caught the clear example of gender issues in student writing. Here were aggression and inappropriate levels of violence from my sixth- and seventh-grade boys. Here was Ophelia pleading for the salvation of Rome, even as she had been given complete authority and power to toss the populace a lifeline.

Overall, 35 percent of the boys and 30 percent of the girls showed these gender patterns in their writing. Not one boy wrote in the passive voice. Not one girl blew up a plebeian.

I responded to each of these papers. Their reactions to my comments, as seen in their final copies, gave me further reason to reflect. I reiterated the assignment to the boys and asked them to eliminate gratuitous violence and solve the problems of Rome. I reminded the girls of the lesson on authoritative language and urged them to use their power to command, order, and compel. Unlike the boys, however, not one girl corrected the problem. Though half of them altered the language, the change was to another form of passive voice.

Seeing these issues so starkly in such a short span of time has given me reason to reflect again on the challenges that each gender faces during the middle school years. Ophelia is no longer out there somewhere; she is clearly in my classroom. (1997, 182–183)

Like other teacher-researchers, Kelli noticed behaviors—leading to questions about gender-binding in early adolescence and what she could do to address it in her class. Her research question didn't emerge fully formed; she continued her observations and allowed her question to evolve.

Questions are often born of frustration. Ally Cross had started a "book talk" group with her kindergartners. But these conversations were not going as she hoped, and she was thinking of deleting the book talks altogether since "the books they were choosing didn't seem to provide much of an opportunity to dig deep, and I wasn't asking many higher-order questions about these books." She decided to gather more data by recording the conversations. When she listened to the recordings, she was able to hear her students talking in the background as they worked at their tables. "I was astounded at the types of conversations they were having with one another . . . and I decided to listen closely to the 'background noise' on my recordings and analyze the language of my students as they worked together," she said. Ally was stunned by what she learned:

> The students working at their tables were all doing one of three things: making connections with their current projects to another concept they learned inside or outside of school; helping each other finish work or find supplies; or playing with the sounds of language. What I heard was fascinating! Listening to these conversations made me think about the importance of opportunities to talk in the classroom. When I have been doing reading groups on the carpet, I have been shh-ing these conversations daily. About 90 percent of the time, the conversations were on topic and useful in helping others understand concepts they might not have grasped earlier in class. The students I listened to were trying out many different language uses and from this, they were receiving immediate feedback from their peers.

Listening to the "background talk" in her classroom created a new focus for Ally's inquiry. Rather than focusing only on the teacher-directed talk in her classroom, Ally is now more interested in the peer conversations the students have as she works with small groups of children.

In looking at the talk in her classroom, Ally found what Chip Heath and Dan Heath would call a "bright spot." In *Switch: How to Change Things When Change Is Hard*, the authors argue that understanding these bright spots is a key aspect of fostering meaningful change: "To pursue bright spots is to ask the question 'What's working, and how can we do more of it?' Sounds simple, doesn't it? Yet, in the real world, this obvious question is almost never asked" (2010, 45).

"While I am now confident that the conversations my students are having as they work at their tables are relevant and beneficial to their learning, I am intrigued to learn more," Ally explained. "Every moment in class, teacher-directed or not, is an opportunity to acquire and develop language. They are making rich connections, helping and encouraging other students, and playing with the sounds of words. What other language skills are they developing as they talk with each other?"

These and other teachers' questions are woven directly into the fabric of daily class life. And the questions are not neat and tidy—they evolved from what Kelli and Ally observed, and became more refined as they focused their attention on a particular issue.

# Mining Tensions

*Tension* is defined as both an act of stretching and a state of uneasy suspense. Each definition of tension applies to teaching and research. Often, the best research questions are in a taut spot between two points. We sometimes walk a tightrope between who we are as teachers and learners and who we want to be. Once you find a gap that needs to be traversed—between what you think will be learned in a math lesson and what is learned, between the calm, patient mentor you were yesterday and the abrupt, demanding authoritarian you were today, between your love of a book and your students' distaste for it—you have found territory in your classroom that is ripe for questioning.

There are always gaps between our expectations and those of students, misunderstandings born of cultural differences, and bureaucratic constraints, plus the frantic rush of the school day. In the midst of all these demands, miscommunications, and daily stresses of the profession, there is an oasis. Many teachers have found the process of generating research questions to be a healthy way to stretch toward new understanding and to avoid having the gaps become gulfs between students and colleagues. Turning tensions into a research question can be the best mental stress reducer at a teacher's disposal.

Maraline Ellis, a high school social studies teacher, was frustrated when a lesson she tried with her students worked really well in one class but failed to capture the interest of another class. She mused about it in her teaching journal:

> Fifth period rained on my parade. In fact it was a downpour. They went along with it, but without the interest my first period had shown. I don't think my presentation was any different. . . . I wonder, well, I wonder about a lot. I feel a brainstorm coming on. . . . I'm going to brainstorm what I wonder about—without censoring any thoughts:
>
> I wonder if the noise coming through the partition wall bothers the students as much as it does me.
> I wonder if my ninth-grade students know they have been placed in teams.
> I wonder how many of my students have parents in the penitentiary.
> I wonder how the ninth graders feel about participating in the service project.
> I wonder if their choices for work sites will be made based on what they really care about or what their friends signed up to do.
> I wonder how Kenny sees himself as a student in my class.
> I wonder if he is aware that he tried very hard to keep me from getting to the point in the lesson where he may have to write or read.

I wonder why he tried to get kicked out of his English class but not mine.
I wonder how sophomores feel about taking American Government when
       voting is still a few years away.
I wonder what students think is important/unimportant in what I teach.
I wonder what they think I think is important/unimportant.

At the end of her journal entry, Maraline concluded, "I think I will ask [the kids] to write about this tomorrow—tell me what they think." With her students' input, Maraline framed a research question that helped her continue to explore curriculum issues with more of a student-centered focus: What happens when I base my government curriculum on what is of concern to the students?

We don't always need a long list, like Maraline, to get to the heart of our teaching tensions. Sometimes our research questions begin with nagging worries about one student. Fifth-grade teacher Tonia Boyer's research question emerged from her frustration with Kenton:

Impetuous, impatient, impulsive, and impervious—nothing gets Kenton down for long. He is well aware of his limitations, of his impulses that often get him sent packing to another classroom for a large chunk of the day—and yet he seems unable to rein them in. Kenton lives life in a gush of lively activity. One never knows just what he might do or say. Despite his numerous misbehaviors, Kenton is always sincere in his apologies. It is obvious to anyone around him that his actions are of habit and circumstance rather than any truly deviant purpose. True to his nature, Kenton holds no grudges and willingly admits his mistakes—making it impossible to stay angry at him no matter the offense committed. He's just an all-around great kid, and it shows.

Why then, I wonder, is writing such a chore for Kenton? Is it just an issue of having to sit for such a long time? Is it a physical issue? Does it have to do with his prior writing experiences? Trying to persuade Kenton to write is like trying to get a guy to take out the garbage in the middle of the fourth quarter of the NBA finals—a long period of convenient deafness followed by procrastination and at times, stubborn refusal. When he does choose to write, it is usually stoic, boring, and safe. Why is Kenton somewhat trepidatious in his writing when it is so unnatural for his nature? Why isn't Kenton's attitude toward writing as impulsive, free, and fresh as he is?

I want answers. It is this inner turmoil that made me decide to take a closer look at Kenton's work, and to learn more about him as a writer.

# The Value of Subquestions

Tonia's reflections on Kenton led her to a research question. With this main question in mind, it may help her to think about the kinds of subquestions she wants to answer as she pursues her research. It can be extremely useful to list the follow-up questions that evolve from our initial research brainstorming.

Emily Gromko started with her primary research question, What happens when my tenth-grade language arts students set semester-long reading goals? This led to several subquestions:

> Will my students read more because they set their own goals?
> Will they enjoy reading more?
> Will it improve their reading comprehension?
> How will self-assessment and self-reflection affect reading in our classroom?
> Because they will be more accountable to themselves foremost, will they be more motivated to meet their goal?
> What kinds of goals will they set?
> Will their goals be related to quantity of reading, quality of reading, different genres? Place?

Another important aspect of these teachers' research questions is the focus of the study: their students. Often, questions in the initial raw stage center on our work as teachers. High school teacher Denise Sega warns against falling into this trap when she tells the genesis of her own research question:

> When I began the work that led to my article "Reading and Writing About Our Lives," my original research question asked how I could motivate a group of uninterested students to learn. What could I do to help them achieve? However, as my work progressed, I realized that I was not the center of the study—the students were. This sparked the concept of collaboration, refocusing my reflection to see how we—the students and I—could discover a new way to learn together, rather than my deciding on a way to teach. It was this idea of collaboration that led to more meaningful research and discoveries than I ever would have found alone. (1997a, 174)

Like Li's questions mentioned at the beginning of this chapter, your research questions may come from a glimpse of something out of the corner of your eye that intrigues you. They might burst forth from students who keep you up at night, observations that surprise you, tensions in your class, or individual students who just plain mystify you. Here is a list of questions that teachers we know are pursuing:

> How does imaginative play affect student writing?
> How do my students apply their knowledge about probability and statistics to other curricular areas?
> How does having a community meeting change daily communication between my students?
> What happens when students use self-reflection in science as a means of assessing growth?
> How does role playing affect first-grade writing?

How will home-school communication journals influence the student-parent-teacher collaboration?

What happens when I encourage Juanita to voice her opinions and insights?

How does math literature influence the oral and written communication of math concepts?

What are the outcomes for students with Asperger's in a fifth-grade classroom as they identify written and verbal language in relation to emotions?

How does the use of storytelling help students connect to historical information?

What effect do the artwork and other artifacts posted on the walls of my middle school art room have on my students' art literacy?

In my two-way bilingual class, what happens to Spanish language usage by my "English experts" when they have focused Spanish lessons for English-only speakers?

In what ways might participation in deliberately designed rites of passage provide teenagers a clearer passage into adult life?

How does incorporating writing and art into science instruction affect female attitudes toward science?

How does nightly reading and writing homework affect first and second graders' overall performance in reading and writing?

What happens when choice and collaboration become an integral part of the fifth-grade science curriculum?

What are the changing attitudes of my students toward Arabic language and culture as they acquire Arabic as a second language?

How does being involved in a school garden affect the nutritional, educational, social, and physical choices students make?

What questions do my first-grade students ask one another during writing time?

These questions show that any curriculum, grade, or concept is open to exploration by teacher-researchers. What matters isn't how experienced you are—it's how willing you are to ponder questions with no easy answers.

## RESEARCH WORKSHOP

# What's Coming Apart So It Can Come Back Together?

*Ruth Shagoury*

Turning your tensions into a research question can be the best mental-stress reducer at a teacher's disposal, whether you teach young children, adolescents, or new and veteran teachers.

Mekeel McBride's poem "Inspiration's Anatomy" provides a useful prompt for teacher-researchers to reflect on the underlying tensions in their classroom that might be fertile ground for research. The poem is especially useful to read aloud with a group of teacher-researchers, followed by time to write for five to seven minutes on "what's coming apart so it can come back together."

At a recent gathering with kindergarten through high school language arts teachers, I gave it a try, and we unearthed a range of tensions, along with possible "next steps."

Middle school teacher Carra realized that her tension was around her writing instruction:

> My writing program is coming apart. I used to teach sentence structure, good leads, paragraphing, and more as individual pieces that were then put together to create a nice piece of writing. I'm wanting to change this. It doesn't seem to be working, so what will? I've started with just getting words on paper.

Brittany also found a tension in her literacy program:

> My ideas about how spelling is taught have really been turned upside down. I loved spelling as a kid, mostly because I am very visual and spelling is like putting together a puzzle for me. I loved working through my spelling lists, and it's kind of hard for me to embrace new ideas for spelling. But when I see how kids struggle with spelling, I see my program coming apart. There must be more helpful ways to approach spelling instruction. I'm finding great ideas for a new way—and I'm going to pick up the pieces and refashion them into something useful for me and the kids.

Carra and Brittany have found a focus for their next steps, tensions worth pursuing as they see what happens in their classrooms as they pay attention to the tensions they've uncovered and begun to think about.

We shared our quick-writes with partners and found support and fresh ideas to help keep us going. Whether the tensions related to struggles with a colleague, frustrations with too much time on standardized testing, or issues with individual students, our group appreciated the chance to clear the air by looking at what was coming apart . . . so it could come back together in new ways.

### *Inspiration's Anatomy*
Mekeel McBride

> *Begins with the wishbone of a chicken hung with thread*
> *to dry in the kitchen. For weeks, it develops the invisible*
> *flesh of wish and desire. Sways, little divining rod, over*
> *the woman washing dishes, chopping onions, rinsing*
> *garden earth from her hands. When it is finally dry, it will*
> *weigh scarcely more than petals, drifted loose, from peonies*
> *on the kitchen table. Because the woman is alone, she must name*
> *one wish for her right hand, another for the left, then split*
> *the fragile bone to see which of the desires overrides.*

> *It is one of the conditions of inspiration that things must come apart before they can be put back together.*
>
> (2006, 82)

What's coming apart in your classroom, research, teaching . . . so it can come back together?

## H O W   T O

# Refine a Research Question

Start with four core principles:

1. Ask only real questions. Don't do research to confirm teaching practice you already believe is good or bad. Ask questions whose answers you are not sure about.
2. Avoid asking yes/no questions.
3. Eliminate jargon.
4. Avoid value-laden words or phrases.
   Teacher-researcher advocate Marian Mohr (2011) suggests that you "cast" your original question with these thoughts in mind:
   - What do I want to figure out?
   - What do I want to know about my teaching?
   - What do I want to know about student learning?
   - What classroom situation do I want to analyze?

For example, the question might begin as follows:

Will LD/ADHD students be more apt to read on their own after being taught from a reading workshop?

The final answer to this question, a yes or no, won't get at key issues of how/why/when these students are involved in their book reading and choosing. There is also the sense that the researcher is setting out to prove a preconception: either she supports certain students being in these reading workshops, or she doesn't.

Now is the time to "recast" the question. First, change the research question so that it is open ended:

What is the effect on LD/ADHD students when they are involved in a reading workshop?

Next, underline any words that are jargon and rewrite them so that any reader could understand what you mean:

What is the effect on <u>LD/ADHD students</u> when they are involved in a <u>reading workshop</u>?

The definitions of *LD* (learning disabled) and *ADHD* (attention deficit hyperactivity disorder) are debated even among educators and would likely be unknown to a lay reader. *Reading workshop* refers to a specific curricular innovation that is defined differently among teachers.

The revised research question becomes this:

> What is the effect on special-needs students when they are involved in a reading workshop where students are given the opportunity to choose their own personally meaningful reading materials during independent reading time?

Although the terms *special-needs students* and *independent reading time* are much broader, they are terms anyone can understand, and they can still be defined more specifically in the actual study.

Reading workshops contain many components; here, the teacher-researcher is limiting the material to a key aspect she wants to investigate.

Finally, underline and change any value-laden words that would require explanation for readers:

> What is the effect on special-needs students when they are involved in a reading workshop where students are given the opportunity to choose their own <u>personally meaningful</u> reading materials during independent reading time?

Part of the goal of this research will be to get at how the teacher and her students define *personally meaningful.* This phrase needs to be cut from the research question so that the values the researcher shares with her students, and the values that might divide the classroom community, can emerge from the study.

But it is a terrific exercise for any researcher to consider the ideals lying beneath value-laden words. When refining your research question, try to brainstorm on your own how you define words such as *meaningful,* and ask students to define what makes them likely to say a book they've chosen has been meaningful. By ferreting out value-laden words in your research question and subquestions, you can begin to get at your biases and preconceptions before the study begins.

The final refined research question, specific for this teacher-researcher, becomes this:

> What is the effect on fourth-grade special-needs students when they are involved in a reading workshop where students are given the opportunity to choose their own reading materials during independent reading time?

## Strategies for Working Toward a Research Question

*JoAnn Portalupi*

Several years ago, my nine-year-old son came home from school with an assignment to write a book report over spring break. The weekend passed into Monday. Tuesday and Wednesday came and went before I finally decided to ask him about his plans for completing it. I wanted to gently remind him that he wouldn't write it out clean onto the final draft paper the teacher had given him but would want to draft it first and work to bring it to its final form. He glanced at me impatiently and replied, "Mom, this isn't writing workshop!"

It is a sunny morning in a first-grade classroom, and the room buzzes with the noise of busy writers. Two boys decide to share their work with each other in the corner with the big stuffed pillows. I am interested in the kinds of response first graders give to one another. They agree to let me listen. First Jonathan reads his story about a visit to New York City. When he finishes, Brent says, "Good." He picks up his paper and begins to read about his cousin sleeping over during the weekend. When he finishes, Jonathan nods approvingly, picks up his story, and says, "Okay, my turn." Once again he reads about his New York visit. I leave a little later as Brent is starting in on the second reading of his story.

These are only two incidents among many that have caused me to wonder about the nature of work in classrooms and the nature of learning in general. When my son remarked, "This isn't writing workshop!" I wondered why the process he practiced during that particular time of the school day was not something he sought to employ during other writing experiences. It caused me to speculate about my work as a staff developer. Had I been negligent about helping teachers see writing workshop as connected to the rest of the time spent in school?

When I was listening to Jonathan and Brent, I was struck silly over the clash between my expectations for peer conferences and those of these first graders. It was clear they were getting the kind of "help" they had hoped to receive. I left the classroom wondering exactly what first graders expect to get out of conferences with their friends.

Asking questions of our classrooms is as natural as breathing. Teachers who conduct classroom-based research turn those wonderings into research questions they can systematically pursue. Those who continue to incorporate research into their teaching know two things. They understand research to be an integral and energizing aspect of teaching. They have learned how to streamline their research questions so they fit into both the dailiness of teaching and the long-term learning goals they hold for their students.

A colleague of mine hangs a sign on her classroom door: "The first real step in learning is figuring out the question." For teachers wanting to do research, this is often the first struggle encountered. Framing the question can feel like a "chase in the dark" game. The teacher-researchers I've worked with over the years have expressed a wide range of response to this frustration. Some see too many questions to ask, yet when they try to single one out, they find themselves holding a tangled knot of questions. Others wonder when the process of framing a question ever really ends. Just when they think they have the elusive thing pinned down, it shifts before their very eyes. Question posing can at times present a conundrum—many teachers report their ability to frame the question only after they get a glimpse at the answer. Nonetheless, the process of articulating a question is an important one. Not only does it initiate the research, but it plays an important part in the research process itself.

There are a number of strategies you can use to guide yourself through the process of "figuring out the question." I'll explore some of these with attention toward helping you integrate your research and teaching.

***Tap your available resources—your daily work and the wonderings that arise from it.*** Though questions are informed by the theories we bring to our work—personal theories and theories we've read from others—they are most commonly born from our day-to-day experiences with students. Glenda Bissex (1987) writes that teacher research begins not with a hypothesis to test but more with a wondering to pursue. Begin by paying attention to these wonderings. Adopt your first research tool—a journal—where you can record the queries that arise during the day. Don't worry that they are always framed as questions. Include the things that surprise, concern, or delight you. After a week or two, go back and reread your jottings. Are there themes of interest that emerge?

***List questions about the area of interest you discovered.*** You'll probably find it easier to generate a list of related questions before writing one inclusive one. I have a general interest in how teachers learn to teach writing. In thinking about that broad question, I wrote a series of smaller questions. How does a teacher's own writing affect his or her teaching? How does a teacher's history of learning to write affect his or her development as a teacher? What do the shifts look like in teachers' thinking as they make pedagogic changes? What supports teachers' growth as they implement a new approach? What hinders it? What kind of talk do teachers trade about the teaching of writing? How does it affect their daily actions? Why do some teachers make the shift to a process approach more easily than others?

***Examine your list of generated questions.*** In generating this list of questions, I'm careful that each one is genuine. I don't want to ask a question that leads me to document something I already know to be true. For instance, I can pretty much answer the question, What happens when a writing process approach is mandated in a school? My experience leads me to a fairly knowledgeable hunch about the answer. There is, however, much I can pursue about the topic. I am genuinely interested in understanding what conditions support teachers' implementation of a mandated approach.

I also want to read my questions to see if they can be answered. The best research questions often begin with the words *what* or *how*. *Why* questions ask you to trace the source of a phenomenon. You can develop a hypothesis about why something occurs, but to conclusively identify the source is virtually impossible. By contrast, *what* and *how* questions lead you toward descriptions of phenomena. These are more easily documented and identified.

You can work with a *why* question to envision the *what* and *how* questions that compose it. Consider my question, Why do some teachers make the shift to a process approach more easily than others? This requires me to look at teachers who have made the shift. What specific changes have they had to make in their practices to do so? What problems do they encounter? How do they work through these problems? I may also want to look at teachers who have not made the shift. What factors contribute to their rejection of the approach? What do teachers say in defense of making change? If I can begin to describe the actual process teachers take either toward or away from a direction of change, I may be able to speculate about why some teachers make the shift and others do not. Then again, I may not. Regardless, I will have some interesting descriptions to inform my future work.

**Force yourself to write a succinct what *or* how question.** I've chosen this one: What are the stories teachers tell about their own experiences learning to write? I'm not sure the question is just right yet, but it points me in the direction I want to go. I want to explore the effect of a learning history on a teaching present. So I'm beginning small. This question allows me to start at a decisive point, gathering stories from a selected group of teachers. As they tell their stories, I suspect they will reflect on the meaning they bring today and the ways in which the stories affect their teaching. Beginning with a small focused question will often lead you toward a bigger one. The data I uncover from this question will likely lead me to understand other factors that have an effect on how teachers learn to teach writing.

**Practice tunneling in on your question.** Don Graves (1994) used the term *tunneling* to describe the process of anticipating the kinds of data you will need to answer the question. This procedure can help you fit your question to the natural structures of your classroom.

One teacher-researcher phrased the question, What is the effect on student writers when their teachers publicly demonstrate their own literacy? In order to answer that question a series of smaller questions will need to be addressed. Notice how each of these questions is written to point exactly to the place she will look to gather the data.

What literacy demonstrations does the teacher present in the classroom? (This involves observing and recording visible acts of literacy.) What student perceptions exist about the teacher's use of writing? (You can get at this by talking with students. Some of this talk will naturally occur during writing conferences.) What literacy acts do students engage in? (Again, this information can be collected through observation and gathering actual products. If you have the task of taking surveys on your class job chart, students can share the responsibility of documenting the kinds of reading and writing that occur throughout the day.)

This teacher will need to define for herself exactly what constitutes an act of literacy. Since she is looking at the effects on writers, not simply writing, she will also want to understand the ways in which students define literacy. This process of tunneling is another way to test the feasibility of pursuing the question. If it is difficult to see where the data to answer a question lie, then you can be fairly certain the question will be difficult, if not impossible, to pursue.

***Be aware of the effect a research question will have on your students.*** I remember Nancie Atwell sharing the effects her interest in journal writing had on her students' work. She describes the scene in September when she was eagerly writing notes of interest about the thinking students recorded in their reading journals. By June students were beckoning her with reading journal in hand: "C'mere. This is really interesting!"

Students will inevitably pay attention to whatever you're choosing to attend to. If you are looking at the way in which students are affected by a teacher's own literacy, you can be certain that your question will ensure they pay attention to that literacy. My question about the stories teachers tell is bound to orient a teacher toward the histories she brings to her teaching.

Think of your question as a grow light. When shined upon your students, you should see them flourish. Here is where the potential effect of teacher research on student learning is made most visible. Capitalize on it when you decide your area of inquiry. If you want to see improvement in peer conferences, ask a question that will allow both you and the students to pay attention to this aspect of the day. If you want more successful writing in science journals, shine the grow light in that direction. One teacher-researcher I know did just that with the questions, What kinds of writing do eight- and nine-year-olds write in science learning logs? And in what ways do their entries change when they are shared in large class-size groups and small response groups? Research should not be an appendage to your teaching. When carefully thought through, it can be a teaching strategy that helps you realize the learning goals you and the students have set for the year.

One way to ensure that your research supports such learning is to spend ample time in the process of question posing. Don't rush to form a question so your research can begin. Figuring out the question is an important part of the research. Once you've arrived with a question ready to pursue, you will look back and see that you are already deeply involved in the work of conducting a classroom-based inquiry, one that will guide the learning of both you and your students.

## FEATURED TEACHER-RESEARCHER

# Real Magic: Trusting the Voice of a Young Learner

*Susan Harris MacKay*

*Editor's note: In this case study of Eric, a kindergartner who speaks Vietnamese at home, Susan Harris MacKay shows how research questions serve as the impetus for a study but also evolve and change as the research continues. She starts with the simple question, What are the connections between home and school learning for Eric? A home visit produces new subquestions about Eric's family and learning: How must it feel to be ultimately responsible for a child enmeshed in a system totally foreign to you? How must it feel not to be able to ask any questions? What happens to your concern for the well-being of your child? Does it consume you, or do you have to let it go a little? Working with Eric in the classroom led to further questions about his language learning and traditional ways of teaching kindergartners.*

I think good research questions are found in the unexpected. Only when I look back over my notes, lists, and questions do I begin to see the interesting patterns that help me form the Research Question. I certainly couldn't have known what Eric would teach me until after I had the opportunity to work with him. In fact, every time I try to set up questions beforehand, I seem to be distracted by questions I find more compelling as time goes on. What I thought would happen is always less interesting than what actually happened. This parallels everything I've learned about teaching, too. Good teacher research is exactly like good teaching. It requires careful listening, observing, and a good idea of where you want to go—combined with a focus on what is happening right now and a knowledge of how it all connects to what happened yesterday. Most important is the determination, in the midst of all this, to remain open to possibility.

I had never made a home visit before, and I was nervous about arriving unannounced. I was going to teach a kindergarten/first-grade multiage classroom, and I wanted Eric, a kindergartner in my classroom the year before, to continue with me into first grade. I walked slowly down the passage between the two short rows of dingy one-story apartments while the bright, late August sun beat down.

I lack any ability at all to imagine the homes from which my students come. So it is at once unsettling and relieving for me to cross over into this other world that belongs solely to them. The tension caused by simply not knowing is relieved, but at the same time, it feels strange to find someone so familiar in a place so unfamiliar. In the classroom, we are very much entangled with each other's lives.

Eric's family lived behind the last door on the right, and I knocked. Not realizing that the sun had blinded me, I was surprised when the door opened inward on complete blackness. I smiled, knowing whoever was there could see me, and was trying to introduce myself when his familiar, happy voice yelled, "Hi, Teacher!" I relaxed and was invited in.

My eyes adjusted to a small, dark apartment full of smiling, friendly people. Because none of them except Eric spoke any English at all, I was pulled and pushed into a chair, and patted and grinned and nodded at. I was hoping with all my heart that my six-year-old friend would be able to translate as they all waited for me to explain the reason for my visit. Not knowing yet how I would explain the situation to them, I made small talk with Eric. I asked him about his summer vacation while I glanced around the living room. I saw the version of "The Important Book"—an idea I borrowed from

Bobbi Fisher (1991)—that our class had written the previous year. Eric's page stated clearly, "The important thing about Eric is that he is Eric." Seeing this somehow bridged the gap a little for me between home and school. I felt more sure that Eric's family would support what I was there to propose to them.

Slowly and seriously, I gave small pieces of information to Eric and asked him to translate. It was very important to me that his family understand that Eric would not be repeating kindergarten—that I would be his first-grade teacher. Without any discernible enthusiasm or concern, they quickly agreed. How must it feel, I wondered, to be ultimately responsible for a child enmeshed in a system totally foreign to you? How must it feel not to be able to ask any questions? What happens to your concern for the well-being of your child? Does it consume you, or do you have to let it go a little?

I left Eric's house happy that I would be able to work with him for at least another year, and frustrated that I could not tell his family so.

Eric's immediate family consists of his grandmother, grandfather, and himself. They are Mien people. Eric's school registration form says he was born in Thailand, in November 1988. His older brother has finished high school. Eric mentions him more this year than he did last year, but I have never met him. I have been told that Eric's parents are both dead, but I do not know the whole story. I keep hoping that someday Eric will be able to tell it to me.

Eric is one of the most energetic, wide-eyed little boys I have ever had the pleasure to know. Everything seems exciting and interesting to him—most especially, dinosaurs, sharks, the X-Men, and recently, swordfish and frogs. The first notes I have about him are dated September of last year: "English is very limited." I had just been hired for my first full year of teaching, and my first responsibility as the kindergarten teacher was to assess all incoming students with the Early Screening Inventory (ESI). I was unprepared for, but generally unconcerned about, meeting a child who couldn't speak English. My first meeting with Eric only served to reconfirm my dislike and distrust of the ESI.

I wondered what would have happened to Eric if he had landed in the hands of a teacher who relied heavily on the scores of the Early Screening Inventory and set her expectations for children accordingly. I could have decided right then that Eric was "at-risk." But I didn't. The ESI told me little enough about any of the children, but for a child who did not speak English, I was sure it could tell me nothing at all. I knew that Eric would be immersed in English in his new classroom. I would try never to separate language from context—never to isolate skills or drill him on anything. He would allow me the privilege, for the first time, to observe someone in the process of acquiring English as a second language.

I haven't been disappointed. Over the past year and a half, Eric has undergone a transformation. The once shy, limited speaker of English has become one of the most dominant members of our classroom. He has proved himself to be a kind person as well as a wonderfully independent and creative learner.

For me, Eric has come to represent all the reasons for student-centered, constructivist classrooms. My perception of his experience has made me less tolerant of teachers resisting change. The more success Eric has, the less tolerant I become. What if Eric had been subjected to "letter of the week" activities and worksheets in kindergarten? What if Eric's teacher had spent twenty minutes or more of precious time each day drilling him on letter names and sounds out of context? Twenty minutes that he could have spent finding a reason to use language, and using it.

As early as November of last year, I noted that Eric was writing and sharing stories that he had written with the class. "I can't believe the growth this child has undergone—he writes and shares stories! He participates!" The next day I noted that he was "making predictions during story reading." Eric was learning English and becoming literate. One of my favorite memories of Eric comes from January of last year, when I was reading *Millions of Cats* (Gag 1928) to the class for the second time.

Eric's big, silver-toothed grin stretched wide across his face as he bounced on his knees and chanted along with me enthusiastically, "Hundreds of cats, thousands of cats, millions and billions and trillions of cats!" I remember being struck by his attempts to recite the whole book along with me, and his obvious pleasure in having at least mastered the repetitious lines. He was oblivious to the others around him. His world was the story and the story was his world in that precious moment.

A year later, there remain few stories about which Eric is unenthusiastic. And he is absolutely irrepressible about the rest. During shared reading, it is nearly impossible to keep him in his seat. He'll cry out, "Teacher! I notice something!" and almost without fail, my impending reprimand—the one that would implore him to wait his turn—is rendered soft with a look at the excitement in his face. He is bursting with ideas and observations that simply will not be contained. This year, he has become as excited about facts as about fiction, although the line between the two remains blurred (as it always is in first grade). In January of this year, while we were studying the water cycle, I happened to ask the class if anyone knew the word that meant water was being taken back into the air. Eric's immediate reply was a self-confident and emphatic "Abracadabra!" Proof enough of this child's magic in the surest sense.

As I marvel over this incredible child who can turn a big, flat piece of cardboard into a pretty blue tractor for his classmates and him to ride in, and who can teach a younger child to apologize to another for unkind words, I can't help but wonder what it would take to strip this little boy of his powers. What if we concentrated for a moment on what Eric can't do—or at least by some standards, doesn't do very well? If we were to return to September of his kindergarten year, we would see a child who spoke no English, couldn't write his name, knew no letter names, and couldn't count with one-to-one correspondence. He was quiet and seemed reluctant to play with the other children except for the two Mien girls. He was not read to at home. His guardians spoke no English at all.

By midyear of first grade, Eric is only beginning to grasp letter-sound associations. He is only recently able to read a simple pattern book using one-to-one correspondence. His math computation skills are below grade level. He continues to confuse the pronouns *he* and *she*, even with constant correction from the other students and occasionally from the teacher. He cannot seem to remember to put up his hand before he speaks. He tends to stutter.

I am frightened and saddened by how easily Eric is reduced to this list of deficits. I am angered by how difficult it is to find room in this list for Eric's fluent and elaborate ideas. For his sharp eyes and quick memory. For his intense interests, his independence, his creativity, his love of learning. For the responsibility he takes in doing his homework every night—checking a book out from our classroom library, doing his best to read it at home with no one to help him, writing in his journal about his favorite part, and showing it proudly to me every morning. For his concern the day the book had accidentally fallen out of his bag onto the classroom floor and he didn't know what had happened. For the time he built the set for the Frog and Toad puppet show—claiming his form of participation in the response to a book that was too hard for him yet to read but that his friends had read to him.

As his teacher, I can choose to kindle these flames or snuff them out—depending on the lens through which I choose to see him. As Herbert Kohl (1990) has said, "Any limit on expectations will become a limit on learning" (83). It is my responsibility to expect and hope the world for Eric, and I do. My very conscious decision has been to encourage everything I see he is capable of, and to provide an environment where he has the opportunity to discover for himself everything else he can do. There simply isn't room to see the things he can't do. Eric is proving to me, without question, that he knows what he needs as a learner better than I ever will. If I allow him the opportunity to show me what he needs, and I am prepared to see, he will share with me the things I need to be a good teacher.

Above all, I think, Eric is teaching me the importance of time. As I have witnessed his growth, I have learned to trust all the children I teach as competent proprietors of their own learning. This year, my palms have sweated and my heart has raced as I have tried to find balance in a negotiated classroom (Ingram and Worrall 1993). I have tried to find out what would happen if five-, six-, and seven-year-olds were given the responsibility for planning and organizing the majority of their time at school. What would they choose to do? What would my role be? How flexible could I be in valuing different methods of "performance" or representations of learning? What I have learned from Eric is indicative of the whole process. One particular aspect of his writing development provides a helpful illustration. It has been obvious for some time that Eric values reading and writing. During our extended, twice-daily workshop times, he chooses writing first, almost without fail. At the end of kindergarten, I interviewed Eric about his developing literacy. I asked him how he learned to read, and he simply answered, "Try." He told me that he believed himself to be a capable reader and writer. More recently, when I asked him what his favorite part of school was, he said, "Writing, and reading to you." This year, Eric has worked hard to develop his concepts about print and phonological awareness. In the past month, the school ESL teacher asked him to tell her the sounds associated with the letters of the alphabet she had printed on a sheet. She told me she was struck by how Eric associated whole words with each letter, and not just isolated sounds. When she pointed to *O*, Eric said, "Cheeri-os!" (This is a child who knows what letters are for!)

Although Eric has not been any more or less exposed to Wright Group pattern books than any other child in the class, he has been the only child to use those patterns consistently in his own writing. He used the pattern in *The Ghost* (Cowley 1990)—"I see the _____"—for many of his books early this year. Eric's pattern in his first few books, however, was written "I C the _____." It was a wonderful moment when I finally asked Eric to compare the pattern in *The Ghost* with his own book. I asked him to find the word *see* in *The Ghost* and then look at it in his version. In his face, I saw that flashing moment of disequilibrium of which learning is made, and he diligently went about the task of correcting his error throughout his book. If I had corrected it for him, would the moment he discovered his mistake have been as powerful?

Similarly, I wonder if his learning would have been any more or less efficient if I had told him to use these pattern books as models for his writing, or discouraged him from doing so. These patterns seem to be very important for him. On February 15, Eric wrote a story about taking a boat ride with me and some other kids, and having to kill a shark that attacked us. He first shared the book with me in its wordless state—five or six pages of his wonderfully elaborate drawings, which showed the progression in which we boarded the boat, the detail of his own "mad" face when the shark attacked, and the problem solved as Eric harpooned the shark. After drawing a harpoon in his picture, he pointed to it and asked me what it was called. When he finished telling me the story, he returned to the writing table to add the words. I was excited because, for the first time in a long while, Eric had not used a pattern to tell me this story.

A few minutes later, Eric brought me the finished product. He read, "Eric came to the boat. Ms. MacKay came to the boat. Tyler came to the boat. The shark came to the boat." I'm afraid I wasn't terribly successful at hiding my disappointment. "Eric," I said, "that's great, but what happened to all that cool stuff about how you were mad at the shark, and how does it end?" He looked at me seriously and said, "I need to write that." And I thought, "Well, good."

After lunch, Eric brought the revised edition to me. He had crammed a string of letters on the page where the shark appears, but when he tried to read it to me, he got stuck. In frustration, he erased them and rewrote new letters until it was impossible to see what was what. He wasn't nearly as pleased with this new version, and I was sorry. I had asked Eric to give me what I wanted, and it didn't work. Using those patterns had been extremely important to Eric. He wasn't ready to let go of them, and he knew it. But how easily he was persuaded to do what the teacher wanted him to do.

In early March, Eric broke out of the patterns on his own, with a book titled "Fishing." It reads, "I didn't catch a fish. I caught a fish. I went home. I cooked it to eat." Now I see why those patterns were so important to him. They were giving him a foothold—allowing him a comfort zone. He knew exactly what he was doing. When I stepped in his way, I confused and frustrated him. But because he respected me and knew I cared for him, he was willing to do as I asked. It is possible that Eric broke out of the patterns because I had made that earlier nudge. But it is equally possible that he would have done so on his own anyway.

As the teacher, I need to remain constantly aware of my opportunities to learn from the children I teach. In the kindest way possible, Eric has shown me the importance of being in control of and responsible for one's own learning. His face beamed at me as he held his rough draft high and announced, "I want to publish this book, Teacher!" He knew an accomplishment when he felt one, and I only needed to be there to congratulate him. Eric and the other children have shown me that my role is much larger than and much different from directing each and every child's learning through assignments. It is to provide the tools (such as pencils, mini-lessons, tape recorders, Legos, and handwriting practice) and the environment (both physical and social), demonstrations, expectations, time, and opportunity for engagement by loving all the children enough for them to see themselves as members of the "club" (Frank Smith 1986)—as potential doers of literate activities. And then I need to step out of the way.

In February, I had the opportunity to return to Eric's home—this time with a translator. I wanted Eric to go through the testing process for the Talented and Gifted (TAG) program, and I needed his grandparents to sign the consent form. I was very excited about the opportunity to tell them, finally, how proud I was of Eric, and how much I enjoyed him. For a second time, I was received warmly into Eric's home. In the tiny, dark apartment, his work still hung prominently on one wall. As the translator presented the TAG form to Eric's grandfather, and he agreed to sign, I was reminded that Eric will be one of the first in his family ever to read and write. Eric's ancestors did not use written language. As I watched his grandfather write his signature, I could see that learning to use a pen had come very late in life. It was a painfully arduous task. Shaky lines slowly formed the letters of his name.

We talked for half an hour about Eric and school. They were mostly pleased to know that he was a "good boy" and that he was staying out of trouble. They said they regretted that they could not help him with his homework, and I told them how impressed I was that he worked so hard on it. I had brought Eric's portfolio along with me and tried to encourage Eric to share it with them. Although he happily pulled out the photographs and shared those, he seemed reluctant to share his writing.

I was confused by this until I realized that the books and the writing weren't meaningful to them, except in the sense that they were Eric's, and Eric knew that. Why would he bother to translate his stories for his grandparents, when writing was not something they valued or used? Eric's grandparents made a point of sharing with me the importance they placed on Eric's understanding of and feeling good about "where he came from." And I could see, in the midst of all my excitement about Eric's success in my culture, their concern that he retain theirs. Humbled again by the experience of this child, I reconsidered my perspective.

It is easy for me to see why, as a teacher, I am responsible for respecting the voices of the children I teach. To hear those voices clearly, Eric and the other children have taught me, this year particularly as we practiced the art of negotiation, the importance of choice in the daily life of school. If I had made all, or even most, of the decisions for them, I would have denied them the opportunity to learn what it means to be responsible for their own learning. By implication, I would have taught them that their voices aren't important or right. Eric would have begun to learn that there is no way to reconcile the culture he was born into—which has given him his voice—with the culture in which he lives now. Forcing him to choose between the two would cause him to reject one, to live either on the fringe of American society or on the fringe of his own family.

It is difficult, but possible, to bridge this gap, and it is the responsibility of his teachers to help him learn how. Eric's polite refusal of my idea for him to share his writing with his family in his home is, I think, evidence of beginning success. Eric will need to continue to be comfortable with and increase his ability to be critical of situations that affect cultural aspects of his family life, or face the risk of ostracism. He will also need to experience continued success in a classroom where his voice is valued. He will need to feel justified and comfortable in saying, as he did yesterday both gently and sincerely, when a fellow classmate started sharing a poem that sounded too much like a story, "Hey! That's not poetry!"

And if "poetry" is what we hope for all the children we teach, we will need to listen.

## FEATURED TEACHER-RESEARCHER

# Real Teachers Don't Always Succeed

*Annie Keep-Barnes*

Did you ever read any of those "Teacher as Savior" books? You know, the ones where the teacher meets the troubled learner, sees what needs to be done, and then in a nine-month span (often less) she saves him? Well, I read way too many. I came out of my undergraduate program with an imaginary *S* emblazoned on my chest. I was not just a teacher—I was a special ed teacher. I was going to fix kids. I've been teaching for eleven years. I should know better by now.

When I met Robert, a virtual nonreader/writer and victim of overprogrammed instruction, I assumed that, armed with my understanding of language and my strong theoretical background, I would fix him. Well, the reading is finally happening, but it looks like writing will be a long time coming.

His mother came in today. She called yesterday just before a staff meeting and said she had just found Robert's reading journal. "Ms. Keep-Barnes," she said, "I can't read this! Angie does better than this in first grade. What's my boy doing up there?"

She blew into my room armed and dangerous. "Ms. Keep-Barnes, what has my boy been pulling on you?"

I smiled, although inside I was sick. This wasn't just any child; this was a child I have taught in special education for almost three years. Not only that, this was a child I agonized over and read books over and watched and studied. This was a child I loved. This was my glorious failure.

"He hasn't been pulling anything on me."

"Oh, Ms. Keep-Barnes," she cried. "I know my boy. He can do better than this! He's a smart boy. My boy has you exactly where he wants you. 'Oh, Ms. Keep-Barnes,' he says. 'I just love her.' You're so sweet to him. When we go shopping, he'll see some pretty flowers and say, 'Mama, I want to get those for Ms. Keep-Barnes.' He's got you exactly where he wants you."

"Do you think I'm too easy on him?"

"Yes! I do. My boy should be doing better than this. I guess I'll just have to do it myself. I'll need to make a new strategy."

"Mrs. Johnson, I'm not too easy on Robert. I know he can't spell. I've been beating myself over the head for three years. I teach him strategies. When I'm hanging right over him, he does very well. When I turn away, I can't read what he's written. I believe that writing is for communication. I give it back to him and say, 'I can't read this. Write it over.' You saw that in his journal. I'd write, 'Robert, I can't read this.' When he turns in a paper that's indecipherable, I say, 'Now, rewrite it so I can read it.'"

"Well, I know my boy. He's lazy."

"I'm not going to disagree with you. I feel that sometimes he just can't be bothered, but he also has a lot of trouble understanding written language. I don't know why it's so hard for him, but he has a huge struggle. Robert has a learning disability."

"He's lazy and he's got you just where he wants you. He thinks you've got this little soft heart and he won't have to try."

I was fascinated at this portrait of me with the little soft heart. I do love my students, but I can't believe that I have ever not expected things of them because I was "soft." Which of course, is the bottom line here. If I weren't such a soft, undemanding teacher, Robert would be fixed.

In eleven years of teaching special education, I can count on one hand the number of kids I've taught who were truly learning disabled in reading and writing. Usually, I explain to parents, a child qualifies as learning disabled if there is a significant difference between aptitude and achievement. But generally, I see it as a developmental issue or poor instruction or something else rather than assuming the child is neurologically impaired. Most kids have been behind or confused or slow. Very seldom have I come across a child who is completely perplexed by print. Robert is one of them.

I have clung tenaciously to my understanding of the developmental nature of language. Fragmented print never crossed his path, whereas grapho-phonemic, syntactic, and semantic strategies were religiously coached, in balance and in the context of real reading events. His retellings have been supported and his responses respected. I have helped him in his writing, encouraging fluency while following his leads in ideas, celebrating meaning while suggesting strategies to use while spelling. When he failed to meet his communicative intent, he was advised to rethink and revise.

His reading has improved, although nothing miraculous has occurred. As a matter of fact, the first story I was going to tell you is one of simple, patient victory. How after nearly three years, he is finally reading—tentatively, with fear, but still reading. Though wildly overpredictive, he catches himself eventually. When I read aloud, he can follow along. He takes his turn in a partner situation and can sneak into the back of the room and read into a tape recorder, finally staying engaged for the entire sustained silent reading period. He's going to be okay.

I wish I could say the same about his writing. After almost three years of process writing instruction, he still can't spell. He'll sit down and write madly for fifteen minutes. I'll come by and look at what he's written and, except for a very few high-frequency words, be completely unable to read what he's written. When I ask him to read what he has written, he will confidently rattle off something, yet what he says does not match what he has written, not graphically, not even structurally. I ask him to point while he reads. He can't do it. He has no idea what those words on the page are.

A few weeks ago, we had a school spelling bee. It's something that must be endured. The kids like it, but I hate it, for it seems that spelling is always harder when done out loud. After all, spelling is for writing, not for speaking. Robert entered. I was sick. Here this boy, who is such a problem speller, was going to go up in front of the school and embarrass himself.

The students were getting knocked out right and left. As many as ten sat down in succession in the first round. It was Robert's turn. The word was *numeral*. He started in: "Numeral. N, u, m, e, r . . . , numeral." Good grief! He was so close! He could never come that close in writing. What could it mean? It should be easier to spell when you can see the writing on the page.

That's why spelling develops along with reading, right?

So, I did an experiment. I extracted words he had spelled from his writing, and I dictated to him one word at a time and had him spell them orally as I wrote them down:

| First Spelling | Oral Spelling | Actual Spelling |
|---|---|---|
| cald | calld | called |
| thed | shuod | should |
| alled | old | old |
| aet | out | out |
| sand | soud | sound |
| cand | came | came |
| sade | sead | said |
| nane | name | name |
| salva | slave | slave |
| at | that | that |
| akict | asx | ask |
| sater | streg | strange |
| hes | his | his |
| hin | him | him |

He spelled more than half the words correctly. The other half were much more similar to the actual spelling than his written version of them.

Somehow, his auditory channel is stronger than his visual. This confirms my suspicion that if he just slowed down and vocalized, he might be able to communicate better. Or, if he went back over every draft and labored out the spelling once he got his thoughts down, his drafts would make more sense.

I have been asking him for more than a year to vocalize when he spells. I see the first graders doing this all the time. They're writing and talking continually. I feel this is important for him. He says the other kids will laugh at him, that I don't know what it's like. I say I've never seen him try.

Which brings me to this. Why hasn't he been trying? His mother says she knows her child and that he's lazy. Well, I think she's right. Special educators always see that as the first line of accusation from teachers and parents: "This kid would be doing more if he [or she] weren't so lazy." This assumes the child is to blame for failure. I have always looked elsewhere. It's too easy to say that and then not assume any responsibility. That is not my way.

And perhaps this, too, is my failing. This child has not taken responsibility for his learning. I cannot make him vocalize. I cannot put his eyes to the printed page. All I can do is provide the context where these things happen. And he really is lazy; I have to admit, sometimes kids are lazy. Instead of accusing him of laziness, I have focused very closely on making sure that every writing act is enjoyable, that he not become frustrated. My belief has been that when it does finally happen for him, he'll understand that literate acts are positive, fulfilling experiences, not chores that need to be endured.

But should I have pressured more? Should I have told him early on that it was his life and I was there to help, but that he needs to choose his level of commitment? I think so. It has been his responsibility all along, but I never wanted him to hate the written word by applying too much pressure.

I've been successful. He said only last Friday that he wants to be a writer when he grows up. I tried to help him celebrate the writer within, even when I couldn't see it on the page. The problem is, I still can't see it.

This isn't so much Robert's story as it is mine. Mrs. Johnson said to me, "You've got a job. You'll be here next year and next. But my boy, he's got no time. Every year matters."

I know that. I do understand her panic. Yet I want to ask her why she just now noticed. Haven't I sent her updates on his progress and samples of his work? Haven't I begged her to read and write with him at home?

Yet in her eyes, his failure is my fault alone. If I were a better teacher or less "softhearted," he would not be such a failure. And truthfully, my self-esteem as a teacher is tied up with his success. I want him to succeed not just for him, but for me as well. And I feel like a failure.

When she left, I wanted to lay my head on my desk and cry, but I had a ten-year-old friend waiting for a ride, so I swallowed the lump in my throat and left the school. I feel like crying now as I write this, because I'm scared I did blow it for this boy who has so little time. Do kids leave school illiterate even when someone has done all she can imagine to prevent it? Should I leave my job so someone else can try with him before he goes on to junior high? If I can't teach him, shouldn't I find someone who can?

I have failed. I failed Robert not by neglecting his learning needs, but by not trying harder to connect with his family. I've known from the start that this child was one of the truly disabled. Because I inherited him having been in special education for three years, I assumed they knew. I should have looked them in the eye the first time I met them and said, "Your son has a serious problem. I cannot help him on my own. You must be committed to reading with him every night, to writing with him daily. You must be responsible for looking over his work." Although I advised these things regularly, I did not really tell them straight out. Perhaps I enabled their denial and ultimately brought this down upon myself.

And I failed Robert by not making it more clear to him that it was up to him to try. I mean really try. It's important to keep learning stress-free, but it is equally important to know how to gauge and engage a child's commitment.

Since my meeting with Mrs. Johnson, it looks like Robert has shaped up somewhat. He is taking more care in writing. He's trying to make his writing resemble words more closely, if not grapho-phonemically, then at least in spacing and neatness. This actually helps a great deal in understanding what he is trying to say. He will go back over his drafts and vocalize to closer approximate spellings once he's got the ideas down. All this is progress toward personal ownership.

As for Mrs. Johnson, she did not come in for conferences; I guess she'd said all she'd wanted. None of the notes I've sent home have been responded to in any way. We had a very important celebration last Friday for my troubled learners who have mastered the multiplication table. I planned to take the five boys dog mushing, something they'd never done. Robert was one who was scheduled to come. His mother did not bring him, although she had promised him she would and he wanted desperately to go. That, too, is part of his problem.

I'm muddling through this so you can help me find what it means. As I examine the idea of moving on to give him a chance with someone else, I realize that I still have ideas for him. There are visible cornerstones upon which to build. I want to keep trying.

I need to see my encounter with his mother as a blessing. It is not an easy thing to have someone think you have let another down, especially when the life of a child is at stake. I'm hurt. That's me, however, and my pain is nothing compared with hers and the knowledge that her child is at risk for failure in life if he cannot become literate. And hers is nothing compared with the anger and disappointment that Robert must feel now and will feel forever if the two of us do not help him.

As I said before, this is not the story I set out to tell. I was delighted with Robert's growth as a reader and wanted to share that with you, but reading in school is only part of becoming literate, and I was tempted to tell you a partial truth. A more complete truth is that I have succeeded as well as failed with this child. And yet, by examining my failure, I find ideas. So, I submit this to you as a report and proposal. I am asking now:

How can I help this boy take responsibility for his learning?
What is motivation for the chronically unmotivated?
How can I work as an ally with his mother rather than as an adversary?
How will Robert learn to fit his ideas into the standard lexicon?

I'm not superteacher and he's not superstudent, and she's not supermom, but we're all this boy has. I'd like to have been the one who saved him—that was part of the fantasy. But this is the real world; real teachers keep trying.

---

## FEATURED TEACHER-RESEARCHER

# You Get What You Ask For: The Art of Questioning

*Heather Rader*

When I pick up my children from school and ask, "How was your day?" 99.9 percent of the time I get the f-word: *fine.* However, when I noticed the green outline around my fifth grader's hand and said, "What did you trace your hand for?" she told me about writing a five-W (*who, what, where, when, how*) summary for an article on cockroaches in her handprint.

My youngest daughter, a kindergartner, works with different students during reading time, and she mentioned Elizabeth recently. After our hug and kiss I asked, "Did you get to sit by Elizabeth again today during reading?" She thought for a moment and said, "No, because we didn't have reading, because a policeman came to school, because, did you know he lost his dog in his divorce?" A specific answer follows my explicit question, even if it's not the one I expected. With their responses, my children have taught me how to ask better questions. "How was your day?" yields a one-word response. "What did you trace your hand for?" or a query about a specific friend opens the door to a genuine conversation. I use these lessons from my children about specificity in my coaching work with teachers.

## Neti Neti: *What Is and Isn't*

I became aware of the term *neti neti* through yoga and meditation. My understanding is that it's a Hindu mantra meaning "neither this, nor that." It is essential in understanding a concept or skill to know both what it is and what it's not. To create the following vignette I've combined transcripts of my own coaching questions with those of other coaches to look at some of the questioning pitfalls it's helpful to avoid.

**Coach:** Thanks for taking the time to debrief with me.
**Teacher:** Sure.
**Coach:** So how did you feel that lesson went?

**Teacher:** Well, I'm not sure. I mean, it was okay. I hadn't realized that some of the kids had already read the book, so that made predictions difficult. Some purpose was lacking, but they loved the book—this is a class that loves read-aloud. It seemed like they were distracted by having a guest and were a little off but not too bad. Some of them seemed to get antsy toward the end, but that's pretty typical of right after lunch. Overall, I guess it was fine.

**Coach:** What are the implications of the text choice, and did it enhance or detract from your differentiation?

**Teacher:** I'm not sure exactly . . .

**Coach:** What I mean is, what might be a way to take today's lesson and think about future lessons? [*Less than half a second pause.*] What will happen the next time some students have seen text and you need them to predict? I guess I mean, What are the requirements for text you'll use with prediction?

**Teacher:** Well . . .

You don't have to be a literacy expert to see that that exchange didn't go so well. Why not?

## *Too Open?*

I know some coaches like the opener "So how do you think the lesson went?" From the responses I hear, I wonder if it's too open-ended. My thinking was piqued by an article by Amy Noelle Parks in the March 2009 issue of *Teaching Children Mathematics* where she posed the question, Can teacher questions be too open? Parks defines explicit questions as "questions that direct students to focus on specific ideas and answer in a particular way" and inexplicit questions as ones that "often provide no clues about the kind of answer desired." Although as a coach, I don't have a "desired" answer in my head that I want to hear from the teacher, I've found better opening questions to be more explicit. For example, I might say, "I know your objective was to have kids use evidence to support their predictions. Which students were able to do that?" Another one might be, "I remember in our initial meeting you talked about how choosing texts with this new reading program is a struggle. How did the text fit your purpose today?"

## *What Is the Question?*

Then there are the questions I couldn't answer myself without some serious sentence diagramming. Even though there are only a couple of multisyllabic words in the question, What are the implications of the text choice, and did it enhance or detract from your differentiation? (and I've heard it phrased in even worse ways), that question is still a stumper. I believe the role of a question-asker is not to sound über-intelligent, but to allow the responder to make meaning.

## *Spray and Pray*

Another rut is having a high number of QPM (questions per minute). If one question is met by any more than a second or two of silence (otherwise known as think time), there is a tendency to rephrase, add on, and offer options. More noise than inquiry. Just like in the classroom, I've learned to ask one question and say, "Please take your time." And then I sit. Quietly. If they ask me to rephrase it, that's fine, I can do that. But I don't need to pepper them with questions until in desperation they grab one to stop me from firing at them.

In the book *Good Questions for Math Teaching* by Pat Lilburn, Peter Sullivan, and Toby Gordon, I'm reminded that "good questions . . . have the potential to make *us* more aware of what *we* do know and what *we* do not know" (2002, 4). One good question that gets us talking about what we don't know is far superior to five questions that get us talking like know-it-alls.

## *If Not That, Then What?*

In the practice of neti neti, asking a question that is too open or overly complex or rapidly fired follows the mantra "neither this, nor that." As my colleague Cristina Charney says, "If not that, then what?"

Good question.

I started out as a question collector. I used questions from the University of Kansas, Cathy Toll, and every coaching article I put my hands on. I typed every word that came out of literacy coach Katherine Casey's mouth during trainings. I thought that somehow if I collected enough good questions, I would know what to ask and how. The truth is that although the list focused my attention on questioning and I have kept a couple of gems, I didn't really get good at it until I started paying more attention to the responses from teachers. My inquiry skills didn't come from a list or my mouth; my questions came from my ears.

Below I've dissected an abridged debriefing showing the connection to what the teacher is saying in italics. I've also broken it into three phases: the *So . . .* phase is about setting the context, the *So What?* phase is about the purpose, and the *Now What?* phase is about the action.

### So . . .

**Coach:** You talked about "just-right" books. What instruction have the students already received around choosing one?

**Teacher:** I did some mini-lessons in September. I taught them the Rule of Five and we practiced it. I also taught them how to preview the title, blurb, and take a quick picture walk.

**Coach:** *With the Rule of Five and previewing,* if a student isn't sure, or doesn't remember what to do, what would they do?

**Teacher:** I was going to say they could ask another student, but I do expect it to be quiet. I used to have an anchor chart up, but I took it down because it seemed like they all got it.

## So What?

**Coach:** *And maybe they do have it.* When you look at the titles I recorded for the two groups I observed, do they seem just right?
**Teacher:** No, that's what I'm thinking. *Superfudge* is not a good fit for Angelica, and Tre is reading *No, David!* for the second week . . . so it doesn't really help him apply the skill of predicting.
**Coach:** *To have them use the skill of predicting,* are you wanting more than a "just-right" book then?
**Teacher:** Yes, because I want it to be new content so they can predict. I have to be more explicit about that.

## Now What?

**Coach:** Those anchor charts?
**Teacher:** I think we need to refresh how to choose a "just-right" book—specifically, what kind of book would help them apply predicting as we work on that standard. Could we plan to do that the next time you are here?

## *Ask the Right Question or Ask the Question Right*

Although it's powerful to start off with a good question that focuses the teacher and coach right at the heart of student learning, it doesn't always happen. Luckily teachers are both resilient and forgiving. I've found that even if I bumble through a couple of questions, as long as I'm operating from a place of curiosity and not judgment, I eventually find my way. Tools such as waiting three to five seconds before I respond, nodding encouragement, paraphrasing, and encouraging phrases such as "talk to me more about that" help set the tone for asking questions right.

I'm still a work in progress. Even today, I opened a spontaneous debriefing with the question, How did you feel the mini-lesson went? and got exactly what I wrote about at the beginning of the article. The teacher gave me superficial responses like "good" and "students seemed to be getting it" and of course, she ended with the f-word: *fine.* Later during my after-school professional development I asked two-and-a-half questions right in a row without pausing for a breath. I had to laugh at myself. Neti, neti, I thought. Try it again tomorrow, this time with more patience.

## The Power of Wonder Questions

*Andrea Smith*

"Do you know what I've been thinking and reading about?" asked Will as we settled into an out-of-the-way spot in my grades three–four multiage classroom. It was time for reading workshop, and the room was quietly buzzing as students gathered books and other resources and settled into their places, and the hum of engaged learners slowly crept across the room. Will's green eyes were sparkling with excitement as we began our reading conference.

"What's on your mind?" I asked, sensing that he had big things to tell me.

"I'm studying the creek for my micro-habitat study, right?" he said, referring to our ongoing science unit, "Reading and Writing Like a Scientist." "Remember how I found the raccoon tracks by the creek? Since then I've been reading a lot about raccoons."

He showed me two books and an article printed from a Web site.

"So what's your plan for today?"

"I want to use my time today to answer a few of my wonder questions about raccoons. Since raccoons show up to find food in the creek, I think I need to know more about raccoons if I'm going to really get how the creek life works as a system. Don't you think that's a good idea?"

"Tell me more," I added, starting to jot notes in my conference notebook. "Show me what you are thinking about."

I was eager to see what Will had to share. During the first weeks of this science unit, my students were eager to explore and learn in our outdoor learning lab. I took advantage of their enthusiasm, planning a series of exploration lessons that captured their wonder questions. As the children explored the outdoor lab, I recorded the group's questions and "wonders" in my notebook. After the exploration period that lasted several days, students were asked to thoroughly explore one micro-habitat and generate their own wonder questions about it.

After posting their micro-habitat questions on our Wonder Board, students worked with a partner and selected at least three of their wonder questions to answer. It was important for them to continue their outside observations while learning how to use a variety of books and Web sites to answer their questions. Writing like a scientist was inseparable from reading like a scientist. During science time, I presented a critical set of mini-lessons on using research organizers, such as two- and three-column charts with headings, webs, and other info-graphics for gathering dash notes. I was eager to see how our science work would affect students' thinking during reading workshop.

## Wonder Questions Lead to Independent Learners

Wonder questions are a critical part of my students' nonfiction reading. Debbie Miller has written and talked extensively about these questions in *Reading with Meaning*. Rooted in a respect for each individual's learning and interests, wonder questions honor the fact that each person views the world differently. Given time and support to identify interests and the freedom to consider "What do I want to learn?" children naturally understand how to create authentic, thought-provoking questions. Wonder questions help a teacher consider that fragile balance of support—knowing when kids need us, and letting them discover when they can move ahead in their learning without us.

Will opened his notebook to a tabbed page labeled *raccoons*. He showed me a list of wonder questions he'd developed and recorded on a two-column table across two pages in his notebook. One column listed his questions, and the other column provided a place for his future dash notes once he begins his research.

"You have big plans," I said as I proceeded to read aloud his questions about raccoons.

*Why is the raccoon usually the top of the food chain and not eaten by predators? Do they taste bad?*

"What made you think about this?" I asked.

"Well, just look at them. . . . For some reason they don't look tasty and they eat odd things, so maybe they just taste weird. Or are they just good at keeping themselves safe?" he said with a very earnest look.

"I don't know," I answered, now wondering about the same question.

*Raccoons' front paws are useful for catching and eating food. Why are the back paws shaped differently? How do they help the raccoon?*

"I never thought about this before when considering raccoons," I answered, looking at a picture of a raccoon and a diagram of raccoon tracks Will had marked in a book.

He looked at me, puzzled. "Well, our hands are different from our feet, so doesn't that seem like a good question to ask about another animal?"

"Absolutely," I answered while I moved to his next question.

*What creatures in the soil will break down the raccoon's dead body so it rots back into the soil?*

"I think I just need to know this," said Will. "I really want to understand the last part of the food chain and the last part of the raccoon's life. I know some about vultures . . . And it's weird. Now that I've been thinking about raccoons, I see so many dead raccoons on the roads. My mom even lets me move dead raccoons to the ditch when we see a dead one when we're driving.

. . . Ever since I started studying raccoons, I notice them."

"Really?" I commented, making a note about his serious intentions to understand food chains.

"Don't worry—we keep a box of those plastic gloves in the car so I'm not touching the dead body . . . and I only move them when cars aren't coming . . ."

"Aren't moms great?" I smiled, adding a side note to e-mail this amazing mom who was supporting her child's fascination with animals to the point that she took the time to let him examine "roadkill" whenever they came across it.

And so unfolds our conference. I learned a lot about Will as a reader, thinker, and person during those few minutes of our conference. I discovered what he was thinking about beyond reading workshop. I saw how our science work was influencing his ability to identify his interests. He demonstrated how he had taken charge of his learning and reading by drafting such thought-provoking wonder questions.

"I think we can try to identify the living and nonliving things in the soil that will help decompose the raccoon someday when it dies. We should talk to Dr. Languis about this and get you two together. . . . He knows so much about the role of soil and decomposition because he is such a composting expert. He might know some things about the decomposing of animals after they die."

I wrote a reminder on a sticky note to e-mail Dr. Languis, a retired professor who works with our school in our outdoor learning lab, to see if he could meet with Will during the coming week to discuss decomposition.

"I better write that word down," said Will as he wrote *decomposing* at the top of the page. "That is a better word than *rotting*."

"Are you ready to get back to work?" I asked, already knowing Will's answer. "You can just keep this spot. . . . I'll move along to my next conference now, okay?"

"Uh-huh," he mumbled, already flipping through his book to begin his work, almost unaware that I was leaving him (for now).

My time with Will strengthened my confidence in my decision to introduce wonder questions during the first weeks of reading workshop.

Through mini-lessons, guided experiences, and then opportunities to try wonder questions in a supportive workshop community, Will's conference comments and reading plans documented how he had adopted a vital learning strategy that could support him as a learner now and in the future. I reconsidered his opening words today:

"Do you know what I've been thinking and reading about?"

Now my conference notes would bring mental snapshots of Will discovering raccoon tracks by our school's creek, his carefully crafted questions, and how he moves a dead raccoon to a safer place to decompose into the soil. The word *wonder* sanctifies the art and science of learning, reminding me to begin each conference with a quiet reverence for my students' thinking. Wonder brings respect, energy, and determination to our work. How might your students answer this question: What have you been reading and thinking about?

# Research Designs

*Design is the application of intent—the opposite of happenstance, and an antidote to accident.*

—ROBERT L. PETERS

As you move from putting your research intentions into action, you need a plan. We like the term *design*, with the key notion of intent at its heart and the artistry it implies. The best designs are often simple, putting your inquiry plans into a form that will give you—and your curriculum—direction.

The notion of inquiry at the center is crucial, as literacy researchers Jerry Harste and Christine Leland remind us:

> [I]nquiry is the only sure way for students and teachers to find and maintain direction. Education really is inquiry—at every level. We see curriculum as a metaphor for the lives we want to live and the people we want to be. . . . We believe that there are really three curricula. The *paper curriculum* is the document on paper, your official plans. The *enacted curriculum* is the curriculum that results from your putting those plans into practice. The *real curriculum*, however, is what happens in the head of the learner. The tension among these curricula is what fuels teacher inquiry. (Harste and Leland 2007, 9)

Research is a fragile enterprise, easily disrupted by our needs and those of our students. The research design is a kind of backbone for your study—a skeletal frame on which to hang all your emerging thoughts about your research question, data collection, and how you might sustain your research. When it feels like your research is falling apart, a glance back at your original design can be the glue that holds your work together. A plan, like writer Annie Dillard's schedule, is "a net for catching days."

Teacher-researchers we work with swear by the power of a research brief—a detailed outline completed before the research study begins. In designing a research brief, researchers work their way through a series of questions to develop a plan for their study. The brief often includes these topics, derived through these questions:

**Research Brief Guidelines**

Research purpose: Why do I want to study this?

Research question: What do I want to study? What subquestions do I have?

Data collection: How will I collect data?

Data analysis: How will I analyze my data?

Time line: When will I complete the different phases of my study?

Support: Who will help me sustain this project?

Permissions: What permissions do I need to collect? Are there ethical issues to consider?

It takes time to develop a strong research design. Many teachers we've worked with keep a journal or notes for weeks or months, highlighting emerging questions or issues before they begin to draft a research plan they can frame into a design. They might test out a data collection strategy or two, audio- or video-recording a few discussion groups or taking notes during a science activity to rev up for generating a research brief. We've found that summer is often the best time for teachers to develop a full-scale research design. Teachers can be too immersed in the back-to-school rush in September to think through all the logistics of gathering and analyzing data.

The following research designs by teachers at a variety of grade levels and with a variety of student populations show the range of ways in which you can develop a plan. You might be surprised at how unique each one is. Even though researchers are working with common headings and steps, their interests and personalities shine through.

# Drawing a Fish Tail: Patrice Turner's Research Plan

Although the plan is a blueprint for your research, it's important to realize that it will change as you begin your research and discover what works and what doesn't. That was exactly the case for Patrice Turner, a kindergarten teacher who studied kindergartners during writing time. Figure 3.1 shows the research brief she wrote in the summer before the school year began.

In October, six weeks into the research process, Patrice took the time to reflect upon her original plan. She discovered that her plan, and her view of herself as a researcher, had changed:

Planning to do research in my kindergarten classroom was exciting and fun, but I found myself getting really nervous as the new school year approached. I have taught for twelve years but have never been a teacher-

Figure 3.1

---

### Patrice Turner's Research Plan

**Research Purpose**

As a kindergarten teacher, I am intrigued by the process young children go through as they begin to write. I am curious about their needs as writers and what they want to know about beginning writing. I hope that through this research I can discover more of what they need and immediately begin to offer mini-lessons to help satisfy that need, so the children will feel more confident as we work through the process of writing together. I also hope to encourage and model the importance of asking questions to learn from one another.

**Research Question**

What questions do my kindergartners ask one another during writing time?

**Subquestions**

Do certain children ask more questions than others?

Do certain children get asked more than others?

Does gender play a part? Who asks more questions: girls or boys?

Are more questions asked directly of another student or in a way that's open to anyone at the table?

Do children direct certain questions at some children and other questions at other children?

Are there children who never ask questions?

Are any children ignored when asking a question?

Do children give examples when they answer a question?

Do the questions change over time?

I have a lot of subquestions (maybe far too many), but I am hoping I can manage them. If I find I can't, I will simply let a question or two go. The data should be very explicit, so I should be able to answer many of my questions by doing a lot of tallying.

**Data Collection**

- I will tape the children at the writing table once a week for about twenty minutes. Because of the placement of outlets in my room, I will need to keep the tape recorder at one table. I will keep track of the children I tape, and tape a wide range of children. If things go smoothly, I certainly can increase the number of times I tape the children. I plan to do this throughout the school year.
- I will try hard to keep a teacher journal and do some note taking.
- I may even attempt a little video-recording during writing.
- I will survey the children with a brief interview later in the year. I am thinking about January, because we will have had more exposure to writing by then. An example of the survey follows:

    Do you ever ask other people at your writing table questions?

    What do you ask for help with? or What kinds of questions do you ask? (I need to decide between the two, but I'm leaning toward the second one.)

Whom do you ask for help?
Do people ask you questions?
Do you like to ask questions?
Do you like to answer questions?

The last two questions are not a part of my research, but I'm curious. I could make them into yet another subquestion.

- I may try to have an adult/teacher/principal come in to take notes on any questions that the children ask one another during writing time. I wonder, though, whether or not having an adult present will influence their questioning. Will the children ask the adult more questions than they do each other?

## Possible Codes for Types of Questions

Ideas
Illustrations
Letter formation
Sounds
Punctuation
Capital letters
Spaces
Left to right
Direct/open

I will need to revisit these after two or three weeks.

## Data Analysis

- I plan to listen to the audio recordings at home, where it is quiet and I can focus on listening while relaxing. I have a small room at my house with the computer and a daybed. I have found that I do the majority of my reading and writing for my courses in this room. I feel very comfortable picturing myself listening to the recordings in the evenings. I think this can easily become a ritual without interrupting my school or family life. I plan to listen to the tapes on a weekly basis. I will transcribe the questions asked on the tapes and tally them.
- I plan to read over my teacher journal on the same night I listen to the tape.
- I plan to create a sociogram each quarter. I will focus on who asked questions of whom.

## Tentative Time Line

*September*
- Talk to principal.
- Send permission slips home.
- Explain to kiddos what I'm doing.
- Model asking questions in mini-lessons.
- Discuss with children the importance of asking questions and learning from one another.
- Start recording during the very first week. (Even if they're just drawing at the writing table, it will be considered writing.)

*Two or Three Weeks into Research*
- Revisit list of potential codes.

*September–May*
- Continue to record once a week or more, transcribe and analyze the recordings, and cook my teacher journal entries.

*Twice a Month*
- Meet with my inquiry group at Timberhouse [a local restaurant].

*November*
- I will share my research process with the parents during conferences.
- I may share my research process at a kindergarten meeting.

*January*
- I will share my midpoint findings with my inquiry group.

**Reflections Before Beginning**

I think this is doable. I feel focused and ready. I'm ready for the learning that will go with this project: the unexpected, the questioning, the thrills, the letdowns (what if they don't ask questions?). I will seek help and encouragement. I am excited about the insight I will gain as I analyze my data. As I discover patterns, I can adapt my teaching to the needs I have discovered.

researcher before. The label scared me at first, but the thought of actually doing research in my room was even scarier. Even though I had my research design, my notebook, and my special pen, I was shaking in my new school shoes!

In the first few weeks I discovered some great surprises and some new beliefs about my research. One wonderful surprise was the excitement that Jeanne, our kindergarten aide, had when she read my research brief. She literally got goose bumps. I was thrilled to have discovered an unexpected research partner.

I had planned to use audio recorders and clipboards to collect data on questions children ask each other during writing time. I didn't really know what to expect at all. I was standing there thinking about what was going to happen, and the kids started right in asking questions as they worked. Jeanne and I each grabbed paper from the recycle box because it was the closest paper. In my excitement I folded my paper crookedly and had no sturdy backing to write on as I recorded my first piece of data: one of my students looking up at me seriously and asking, "Do you know how to draw a fish tail?"

Jeanne and I were like two buzzing bees. We recorded questions that the children asked one another and wrote down who was asking whom. I had planned to be neat, serious, and very professional with my work. Well, that crooked paper worked just fine, and I didn't have time to be really professional about it. It was all in a rush, and I was almost frazzled, but in an exciting way. These emotions just weren't in my original plans.

I discovered, too, that I was not going to make my kids do things just for my research. My kindergarten program comes first, although I hope my research will help me improve my program. With that in mind, I relaxed a little about my informal collecting of data. This made the research more fun for me, and Jeanne and I could get the bigger picture by watching and scripting, instead of using the tape recorder.

Being a teacher-researcher is more enjoyable and less stressful than I thought. I also find that I am more involved in the process than I thought I was going to be. Taking pressure off myself about what I thought I should be has paved the way for a more meaningful experience.

And, by the way, Ronnie and I made an awesome fish tail together!

Patrice had to let go of the formality of her original plan in order to be comfortable in her research. But she was able to gather a surprising amount of data right from the start of the year because she had a clear focus and a research partner as eager as she was to learn from the children.

Patrice also gave herself permission to find her own style and rhythms as a researcher. She knew she was trying on the cloak of teacher-researcher at the start of the year, wondering if it would be as comfortable as those new school shoes. It was a fit because Patrice allowed the research to be a wedding of her questions, her research partner's questions, and the needs of the children. Dewey's ideas about planning research from decades ago echo in Patrice's work:

> The plan, in other words, is a cooperative enterprise, not a dictation. The teacher's suggestion is not a mold for a cast-iron result, but is a starting point to be developed into a plan through contributions from the experience of all engaged in the learning process. The essential point is that the purpose grow and take shape through the process of social intelligence. (1938, 72)

Like Patrice, all teacher-researchers work through issues of how their research fits in the classroom and how they will balance their research and teaching responsibilities. Research is a mold with a shifting form—and it is the social relationships in the class that will teach you how your plans need to change.

# Baby Steps Are Still Steps—and Should Be Celebrated: Audrey Alexander's Research Plan

Grappling with curriculum change can be difficult and soul-searching work. Special education teacher Audrey Alexander found that her research design (see Figure 3.2) was a format to help her examine and frame her changes in practice, to make plans to document her process as well as her students', and

Figure 3.2

---

## Audrey Alexander's Research Plan

### Origin of the Question

As an elementary special education teacher, I am interested in the process students with disabilities go through as they learn to read. I have used a scripted reading program for the past three years with my students in special education. I have noticed an increase in their decoding and comprehension skills, but I have not noticed a joy for reading. They love when I read picture books orally to them but are not willing to pick up a book on their own. This year, as I have combined the scripted reading program with choice reading, I have noticed an increase in my students' enthusiasm for reading. I hope that through this research I can increase my students', especially my fourth graders', joy for reading through a reading workshop model. I also hope to learn more about their individual needs as readers.

### Questions

What is the effect on fourth graders who are at least two years below grade level in reading when they are in a reading workshop where students are given the opportunity to choose their own reading material(s) during independent reading time?

> Do students' perceptions of their reading skills change when they choose their reading materials?
> Will students be more apt to read on their own after being taught from a reading workshop?
> How do district-mandated monthly reading scores change?
> How do other staff members' perceptions of students in special education change?

### Data Collection

- Observations: I will take observation notes during reading workshop on the engagement and enthusiasm I see from students. I will also take daily notes on any progress I observe in my students.
- Conferring/Interview: I will confer with and interview selected students throughout the research project to see how they are responding to the reading workshop.
- Student Work Samples/Journals: I will have the students keep a journal to reflect on their reading and also to reflect on their skills and perceptions of themselves as readers.
- Field Notes: I will keep field notes of conversations or comments I hear from general education teachers in regard to our students' reading skills.
- Running Records: I will keep running records on students' reading skills.

### Data Analysis

- I will review my observations, field notes, and student work samples/journals. I will compare and reflect on any patterns I notice.
- I will confer with and interview each student and take notes on the conversation and comments.
- I will compare and contrast student work samples/journals and look for trends within individual students and the whole class.

- I will review running records and keep a table of miscues and patterns I notice for individual students.

**Time Line**

1. I will continue to conduct my research for the spring trimester.
2. I will analyze my data and write memos of patterns I notice twice in the spring: in March and May.

**Support/Resources**

1. General education teachers of students in special education
2. Colleagues at work
3. Principal
4. Teacher research support group (meets monthly)

**References**

Boushey, Gail, and Joan Moser. 2006. *The Daily Five*. Portland, ME: Stenhouse.
———. 2009. *The CAFE Book: Engaging All Students in Daily Literary Assessment and Instruction*. Portland, ME: Stenhouse.
Calkins, Lucy. 2000. *The Art of Teaching Reading*. Portsmouth, NH: Heinemann.
Miller, Debbie. 2002. *Reading with Meaning*. Portland, ME: Stenhouse.

to celebrate the successes, small and large, they were all experiencing. As the special education teacher, her work with students had been one-on-one or in very small groups in scripted programs. Pulling together a larger group of her students for a reading workshop would allow her to work with them for more sustained periods of time, and in more authentic reading situations, but the idea was daunting.

In early October, she wrote a memo for her teacher-research group to share some of her reflections:

I have now sat in front of the computer for almost thirty minutes trying to figure out where to start. I feel as though much has happened since our first meeting in September, but at the same time, I feel as if not much has occurred in terms of student progress. Now that I'm taking some time to reflect, I think part of why I'm beating down on myself is that I don't talk much with my coworkers about what I'm doing. I'm actually surprised my principal approved my work with the fourth graders because I am not using the district-required basal reading curriculum at all. I am having students read books of their choice during the ninety minutes of core reading instruction, which is a big "no-no" in my district.

On the good days (which are just about every other day) I force myself to take a deep breath and remind myself of what it was like on day one and how thankful I am that we are not there anymore.

Things I did not consider that have become very prominent:
- How disproportionate my group is: eight boys and only four girls!!! (Yes, I realize I used more than one exclamation mark, and that was intentional.)
- Finding enough space in my classroom to spread twelve students out so that they aren't close enough to talk with each other during independent reading
- How frequently the students are absent (No wonder some of them are so far below grade level.)
- How exhausted I am after only an hour of these twelve students!
- How quickly the students have picked up on key comprehension and accuracy strategies that they have never used before (such as checking for understanding, going back and rereading, and skipping the word and then coming back)
- The little effort I needed to exert to find books the students can read AND love (Fox series, George and Martha, Mr. Putter and Tabby, Eric Carle books)
- How quiet the room gets while I'm doing a read-aloud (which brightens my day)

Things that need some tweaking or are not working well:
- Students reading both the books I select for them and the books they select for themselves
- Lance and Isaiah fighting over the purple-and-green pillow on a daily basis (until Lance puts himself in the "Thinking Spot")
- Reminding myself that it is important to keep a research journal and write in it daily (I do, but it is not automatic or fully enjoyable yet.)
- The students self-assessing their use of comprehension, accuracy, and fluency strategies on a daily basis
- It is getting better, but strategy groups, and more specifically, having the students read independently while I'm working with other students
- Putting a sticky note on the "Please Come See Me" sign only when they have tried at least three strategies on their own (Within five minutes of reading, at least five names are on the sign.)
- Talking and not reading the entire time
- Building our stamina past fifteen minutes of independent reading

Things that are going well or small accomplishments:
- The students and I seem to have built a trusting relationship.
- Students feel very proud when they have read an entire book without needing my assistance.
- Students are eager to share with the entire group the strategies they tried in their reading.
- Making predictions is a comprehension strategy that almost all the students are good at.
- Jessica and Koral (the lowest readers) have chosen to stay in during their afternoon recess every day this week to read!

- The students seem to enjoy working in small groups with me during strategy group time.
- I love listening to students read every day.
- Kids are laughing out loud while reading.
- The daily journal reflection is a nice glimpse into their reading and incorporates writing skills.
- The students are asking me to get certain books they enjoy from the library for them.
- Just this week I tightened my schedule to make the pace a little faster, and I feel like I'm getting more accomplished.
- Despite being hard on myself, I am enjoying the hour the fourth graders and I share together every day.

Working through the issues of carrying out her research required Audrey to reflect and to grapple with problems in her original plans. Her reworking involved making changes in the setup in the classroom, adjusting curriculum, and thinking through relationships with students.

Audrey's research plan is not a dry, distant recitation like a grocery list, but a melding of mind and heart, intellect and affect.

As she continued on her inquiry journey, Audrey zeroed in on her readers' workshop through the eyes of one student, Jessica. Noting progress after three months of school allowed Audrey to see her classroom through a new lens:

> Jessica began the fourth grade as a nonreader. She did not have any comprehension or accuracy strategies that she used while reading. Her beginning running record in September was at a kindergarten level, and she read it with only 65 percent accuracy. She could not read three-lettered CVC words. She was not using the pictures as cues for words. Most of the time, she could not retell a story she had just read. She appeared to have little or no confidence in reading and did not like attempting to read a book. After only three months, things have changed for Jessica!

Going through her notes, Audrey found and recorded two pages of bulleted data that showed Jessica's growth as a reader. She shared anecdotal data. ("Can I read this book to the class today?" Jessica asks the twelve fourth graders; she pulls out a chair for me and invites me to stay and read with her. "You, sit here. Read with me," she says as she opens a book and begins reading.) She showed documented growth on assessments. ("On 11/12 during a running record, Jessica self-corrected for meaning!") Finally, she noted Jessica's growth within classroom activities. ("Her stamina has built to reading for twenty minutes.")

Audrey's ongoing data analysis through one student allowed her to see the growth in all her students. "I realize all of their confidence has grown drastically. They are all real readers! This is why I became a special education teacher and love working with struggling readers; small successes—hardly anything to others—are huge monumental moments for me and my students. Baby steps are still steps—and should be celebrated!"

Not all research briefs include lists of books to read, as Audrey's does. For some researchers, this additional reading is integral to the research process. But for others, the main "texts" read in their work will be observations of students and artifacts collected—field notes, audio and video recordings, and work samples.

# Reflections on Reflection: Wally Alexander's Research Plan

Research at the college level involves constraints and opportunities that make it different from research in elementary or secondary classrooms. Professors work with students over a shorter period of time, and there are even more concerns about ensuring that the research be a natural fit with the goals of the course.

But at the same time, research at the college level can focus and energize teaching. That was the case with Wally Alexander as he used his research to question some basic assumptions about the role of reflection in learning (see Figure 3.3).

Wally had a keen sense of the ethical issues inherent in this study. He wanted to enlist his students as coresearchers. At the same time, he realized that young adults who are "adept at playing the game" might feel coerced to participate, or give answers they thought would please him rather than being honest. Because he had a detailed plan, he was able to think through these issues in advance and consider a range of strategies for dealing with his concerns.

# Permissions and Ethical Issues

Wally confronted the subtleties of ethical issues right in his research brief. The ethical issues inherent in your study will become apparent when you begin to plan your study and think about getting permission to do your research.

As you make your plans to do research, you will need to think about permissions and notifications. As a rule, we encourage all teachers to get signed permission forms from parents of students involved in their research, or from the students themselves if they are over eighteen years old. Your research likely won't involve any data collection or work on the students' part outside of normal classroom expectations, but it's still helpful to let parents know what you are studying in the classroom. It also helps give parents a different perspective on what teaching is, and how much of it involves understanding and analyzing students as they work.

Figure 3.3

---

## Wallace Alexander's Research Plan

### Purpose

Self-reflection is critical to the learning process. It is important that we be able to relate our work to that of others, and that we can connect it to what we did yesterday and see possibilities for where it may take us in the future. All of this depends on our ability to step back from our work constantly, look at it carefully, and assess and refine it, gleaning new insights about ourselves as learners in the process. Self-reflection is fundamental to authentic assessment, yet this vital element is largely overlooked in most classrooms.

Considering the important role reflection plays in learning, it seems that development of reflective behaviors should be a goal of our work with undergraduate students aspiring to teach. Becoming more aware of what reflective practices students bring with them and determining what activities promote self-reflection are among my goals for this study.

### Assumptions

- These students are reluctant to believe their thoughts will actually be valued. Why? Where did this come from? Issues of trust?
- Different events are paradigm breakers for different people. Gender may be an issue. People jump aboard at different times.

### Research Question

What happens to undergraduate education students when they engage in self-reflection activities that are valued?

### Subquestions

What are their past experiences with self-reflection?
How do they define self-reflection?
Are they reluctant to believe that their reflective thoughts will be valued? If so, why?
Do they see self-reflection as important to learning?
Can we identify "aha" moments when the value of reflective behaviors becomes self-realized?
What can we learn from students who value self-reflection and already have self-reflective behaviors?

### Data Collection

*Survey of baseline data: where are they starting from?*
This survey will try to identify reflective behaviors in these students. I'd like to do this at the beginning of Week 2. The survey will be completed in class. Compiled results will be shared. Possible survey questions include the following:

How are you more comfortable with grading? Grading self? Teacher grades? Combination?
Are there people you use as a sounding board? Who?
How do you feel about revising your writing?
Do you ask for feedback on your work?
Do you talk over your plans with others?

Do you discuss schoolwork with classmates or friends?

Do you carry on conversations with yourself about your work?

How do you get good (better) at something?

What does self-reflection mean to you?

When you complete a project, do you think about what went well with it and/or what you would change if you had it to do over again?

*Observational notes of students during "shining moments" activity*

This is a very reflective activity that we'll probably do on the second day of class. Observer notes might produce more baseline data (maybe an observer in the back of the room?).

*Weekly reflective responses from students*

- I'll keep copies.
- Responses will be analyzed for evidence of presence/evolution/valuing of reflective behaviors.
- Responses will be analyzed for evidence of "aha" moments.

*Notes from reflective assessment conferences—midterm and final*

- Main topics for conferences will be brainstormed with the class.
- Students will be prepared with written notes, which I'll keep or copy.

*Reflective freewriting (periodic)*

- I'll keep copies for analysis and coding.

*My anecdotal notes from observing cooperative teams at work and other activities*

- Possibly their notes too, which I'll copy.

*Interviews with students who value self-reflection and already have self-reflective behaviors*

- Students who appear to have effective self-reflective behaviors will be interviewed to attempt to find out how they got where they are.
- Protocol for interview will be open ended, aimed at getting their story.

**Data Analysis**

- Compile and code survey results.
- Code anecdotal notes, weekly student reflective responses, and reflective freewriting, looking for trends, evidence of reflective behaviors, and changes in students' perspectives on the value and usefulness of self-reflection.
- Compile and code assessment conference notes (mine and students').
- Compile and code interview results.

**Time Line**

*Week 2 of Class (mid-September)*

1. Survey and discussion of project with class
2. Compile survey results.
3. Permission/releases

*Late September*

1. Code notes from "shining moments" and survey results.

*October*
1. Begin analyzing student weekly responses, anecdotal notes, and freewriting.
2. Midterm assessment conferences

*November*
1. Analysis of information from conferences
2. Continue coding weekly responses, anecdotal notes, and freewriting.

*December*
1. Final assessment conference
2. Work on final analysis.

*Semester Break*
1. Write.

*Support/Collaboration*
1. Bimonthly meeting and frequent e-mail with Julie, Patrice, and other members of our newly established, as yet unnamed, teacher-research network
2. Connect with teacher-research electronic mailing list discussion group.
3. Semiregular meetings with Kelly [another college instructor and potential collaborator] to plan, analyze data, and write

### Issues I'm Struggling With

- How and when do I inform the students about this project? I'd like them to know what I'm doing and why, but I don't want them to artificially become self-reflective because that's what I'm looking for. Undergrads are very good at playing the game. This question really has me stumped at the moment. Maybe it isn't a big deal. They'll soon know what I value anyway. Even as I'm writing this, I'm thinking that I need to share my question with them.
- Can I enlist them in note taking in their cooperative teams?
- When do I get permissions/releases? If I fill them in early, could I ask for blanket releases?
- More work is needed on identification of reflective behaviors.
- What will be the best format for the initial survey?
- What in my data is going to show presence, evolution, and valuing of reflective behaviors?

Even when you use pseudonyms for your students, there are ethical issues involved in writing about children's actions. Karen Gallas wrestled with this when she wrote about the themes of power and gender in her classroom:

> Well, there's always issues when I write about children who are doing things that could be hurtful to other kids. I have to think hard about, "How do I write about these children?"—children who I don't want to present as bad people, because they aren't bad people. The ethical issue for me there is accurately presenting them from a number of dimensions. Their behavior should be seen within the context of their whole way of acting in the world rather than just isolating this one thing and saying, "Look at what this child did here!" and assigning it "X, Y, or Z." So, when

I'm writing about unpleasant things, I feel it is my obligation to find ways to present children as part of a larger picture.

I have to say, I wonder if this is going to come back at me. Especially with my "bad boy" work. You can imagine the parents who had those little boys. They know who I'm writing about. But what I tried to do was to create a broader picture of both the child and the behavior. So they could see their child in all his glory as well as his . . . struggle. So that's the trick. So far, those parents know their children and they've appreciated those descriptions. (MacKay 2002, 149)

Karen's words show how complicated a researcher's work is—the task is to show how complex and varied students are yet still find ways to respect everyone in the classroom community. Teacher-researchers live daily with the consequences of their work, and how they represent students, colleagues, and themselves can affect relationships (positively and negatively) for years to come. Developing a permission form is the first step in sorting through these issues of representation, honesty, and respect.

Sometimes, it's clear from the beginning that the research will be focusing on aspects of children's work that doesn't require confidentiality.

Teacher-researcher Bridget Justiss sent the permission form shown in Figure 3.4 home to the parents of her students. Though your research may be very different, you can adapt this format to meet your needs. For example, if you are planning to publish your work, you would substitute Bridget's statement that no one but her classmates and professors in her graduate program will view student work with a sentence such as this: "I would appreciate your permission to include copies of your child's written work and art work in the articles or chapters I may write for publication."

Some teachers ask to use their students' real names in their permission form. In this case, you would frame your request something like this: "I am planning to use your child's real name in my writing, since all examples I use will be a celebration of what children can do. I have spoken with the children, and that is what they prefer. (However, if you would prefer that I use a fictitious name to protect your child's privacy, please write your name choice here: _____.)"

Any permission form should include the following:

1. A brief explanation of the research project.
2. Request to use student samples or other artifacts in publishing.
3. Explanations of confidentiality.
4. A clear description of how students will not be hurt in any way if they do not participate.
5. An e-mail address, phone number, or other forum for parents to discuss the project with you.

Figure 3.5 provides a template of a permission form that teacher-researchers might adapt for their student permission forms.

Figure 3.4  Bridget Justiss's Permission Form

Dear Parents,

I am currently conducting research on how literacy is integrated inside and outside the classroom. I would love for you to be involved in this research. I am interested in learning how I can better serve families and support you outside of school with your child's education. I am in the early stages of my research and would like to begin surveying parents, collecting student work, and taking photographs for documentation. I will also be providing resources, games, and workshops in the months of March and April.

At this point, I do not know what I will include in my final report, but I would greatly appreciate your permission to reproduce your child's work and/or photographs in the research. My classmates and professors at Texas A & M University-Commerce will be the only ones to view the student work and photographs. I will not be including any personal or identifiable information about your student, such as names or phone numbers. If you are willing to participate, please sign this form and return it to school. I will send you a copy of the form for you to keep for your records.

Please know that whether or not you give your permission for your child to participate in my study, his/her grade will not be affected nor will the amount of attention your child receives change. Your participation is completely voluntary. If you are not interested in granting permission, you will still be able to attend the literacy workshops.

I am more than willing to answer any other questions or concerns you might have. You may contact me by e-mail at [e-mail provided] or by phone [phone provided] after 3:10 p.m.

Sincerely,
Bridget Justiss

Please check one of the following:
_____ I grant permission for the use of my child's work and/or photographs.
_____ I do not grant permission for the use of my child's work and/or photographs.

Date: _____
Child's Name: _____
Parent's Name: _____
Parent Signature: _____

What if a child or parent chooses not to participate? We like the writer Lillian Ross's advice: "Do not write about anyone who does not want to be written about" (Murray 1990b, 47). At the same time, a refusal to participate can be a red flag—it may signify other concerns the parent has about your classroom and teaching that are worth exploring before misunderstandings escalate.

We also encourage you to share your research plans with administrators in your school and district. Rarely is an administrator anything but enthusiastic about a teacher's willingness to tackle a new project. But again, concerns can point to potential future conflicts if they aren't resolved in the planning phase of your work.

Figure 3.5 Template for Permission Form

Dear _____,

    I am . . . [add concise but specific description of what you are writing; for example, "working on my master's thesis and also writing an associated article that I hope will form a chapter in a professional book for teachers" or "starting to write a book for other teachers on teaching first grade, based on the work we do in my classroom here at . . . school."]

    The project is in the early stages of development, and one of the things I am doing is collecting samples of children's work for possible inclusion in the [thesis/article/book]. From time to time I may also be taking photographs of the children.

    At this point I don't know exactly what I will and won't be able to include, but I would very much appreciate having your permission to reproduce your child's writing, drawing, or photograph in the publication. Would you please sign both copies of this form and return one to me, keeping the other for your files?

If you would like to discuss this further, please e-mail me at _____ or call me at school any morning/afternoon between _____ and _____.

Your name: _____
I grant permission for the use of the material as described above.
Child's name: _____
Parent or guardian's signature: _____
Name and address: _____
_____
Date: _____

The two statements of ethics shown in Figure 3.6 can be helpful guides in thinking about the ethical issues of your research. The National Writing Project will also provide readers with the *Guide to Ethical Issues in Teacher Research.*

# Planning and Pleasure

Planning your research design can give you lots of insight and joy if you accept it for what it is: a starting point for your work, not a rigid summary of what must be done when. Research is a cyclical, not a linear, process. Throughout your research, you'll want to circle back to your original plans, revising, extending, and abandoning parts of the design that don't represent the actual work of your research. Researchers are sometimes discouraged in their work when they don't see the plan as something that can be altered, as a team of teachers completing a long-term study in Georgia discovered:

> Probably our most serious mistake as novice teacher-researchers was to
> commit ourselves to a two-year research design before we had any experience

Figure 3.6  Ethics Statements

**Statement of Ethics**

The Teacher Research Special Interest Group
American Educational Research Association
Drafted by Marian M. Mohr

1. The Teacher-Researcher Role: Teacher-researchers are teachers first. They respect those with whom they work, openly sharing information about their research. While they seek knowledge, they also nurture the well-being of others, both students and professional colleagues.
2. Research Plans: Teacher-researchers consult with teaching colleagues and appropriate supervisors to review the plans for their studies. They explain their research questions and methods of data collection and update their plans as the research progresses.
3. Data Collection: Teacher-researchers use data from observations, discussions, interviewing, and writing that is collected during the normal process of teaching and learning. They secure the principal's permission for broader surveys or letters to solicit data. They also secure permission to use data already gathered by the school to which they would ordinarily have access as part of their teaching responsibilities (such as standardized tests) or for school information that is not related to their assigned responsibilities (such as protected student records).
4. Research Results: Teacher-researchers may present the results of their research to colleagues in their school districts and at other professional meetings. When they plan to share their conclusions and findings in presentations outside the school or district, they consult with the appropriate supervisors. They are honest in their conclusions and sensitive to the effects of their research findings on others.
5. Publication: Teacher-researchers may publish their reports. Before publishing, teacher-researchers obtain written releases from the individuals involved in the research, both teachers and students, and parental permission for students eighteen or younger. The confidentiality of the people involved in the research is protected.

**Ethical Responsibilities of Researchers**

Clayton Action Research Collaborative
Clayton, Missouri

Participating in a research project requires that some attention be paid to the ethical responsibilities of researchers. We have adapted the following five rules that Hitchcock and Hughes (1989) recommend:

1. Establish whom you need to get permissions from.
2. Be clear and straightforward in articulating the nature and scope of the research.
3. Anticipate potentially sensitive areas or issues the research may focus upon.
4. Be sensitive to the hierarchy of the school or district.
5. Be aware that the aims and objectives of action research are to make changes. Recommendations for practice in a particular direction may challenge colleagues.

Before you begin to collect data, think through how you intend to make use of the data. If you intend to quote sources by name, the sources should know this in advance of participating in the project, and permission to do so should be obtained in advance of any data collection. Share your plans for shielding identities and maintaining confidentiality with those you might use as sources of data collection.

Action research is aimed ultimately at helping students. You would never want to do anything as a researcher that would impede or jeopardize that process.

at research. We stuck doggedly to the two-year design even when it wasn't working because we thought we had to. We didn't realize that a written design is seldom the lived design of classroom research. More experienced teacher-researchers might have cautioned us to be prepared to adjust our plan, to speed it up, slow it down, change its emphasis, or abandon it mid-stream. (Keffer et al. 1998, 30)

The time you spend planning your inquiry should be some of the most enjoyable time you spend as a researcher, especially if you realize that your final research project may end up looking very different from what you had originally envisioned. In the busyness that is everyday life for teachers, we rarely give ourselves the gift of stepping back and creating a larger portrait of what we know and what we want to learn more about. In talking about teacher research, Deborah Meier notes the power of enjoying those moments of insight:

This is the sustainable thing: the pleasure we can take from the imperfect instrument that we've created, and the imperfect kids we have, and our imperfect selves. If we're only looking at ourselves as something that we're going to like later on, then we're not going to like who we are now, either. I think there's a lot of that happening now. We're under such pressure to produce results—outcomes—we don't allow ourselves a lot of enjoyment in the here and now. (Campbell 1997a, 23)

The research design is a snapshot of the here and now of you as a researcher—what you care enough about to study, what strategies you've developed to answer your questions, which colleagues can sustain your growth as a researcher. Take time to enjoy the researcher you are now, and use your research plans to chart the researcher you hope to be one day.

## RESEARCH WORKSHOP

# Hanging Around

*Brenda Miller Power*

There are many variations on the "hanging around" activity, which is a terrific way to help novice researchers go through all the phases of research design and implementation in a short period of time. More important, it exposes researchers to the concept of understanding others through understanding their cultures. Any place people meet and interact is a potential research site. As Mary Catherine Bateson writes, "Participant observation is more than a research methodology. It is a way of being, specially suited to a world of change. A society of many traditions and cultures can be a school of life" (1994, 27).

This activity will get you started as a researcher in that "school of life." You will need the following:

- One or two research partners
- A good people-watching spot at a mall, a restaurant, or a retail store

Begin at your school or at a central meeting spot before you go to the "hanging around" site. After you've identified where you want to do your research, answer these questions individually (from Kirby and Kuykendall 1991):

- Considering what you know about this place, product, or service, what do you expect to find?
- How do you expect the place to be organized?
- What type of clients/customers would you expect? Would one age group or sex predominate? Would you expect a certain income or educational level to predominate?

You and your partners then compare notes, highlighting differences in expectations. You then go to watch people in the location of your choice. Your goal is to describe fully the scene, events, actors, and interactions.

Once there, start with the basic components of understanding the site by answering more of Kirby and Kuykendall's questions:

- How many cars are in the parking lot?
- What are the "arrival behaviors" of the customers? (For example, Do they pause to look in the window or rush in? Do they speak to other people, and if so, what greetings do they use? Do they ask for information?)
- Note the number of customers arriving alone and the size of groups. Keep a running tally of customers by age group, sex, and ethnicity.

- If possible, talk to one customer who doesn't seem to be in a hurry. What brings the customer there? How often? What does he or she think of the placc? Ask similar questions of an employee about the clientele of the place.

Set aside at least fifteen minutes to write down random observations of the site. Ask yourself these questions as you take notes:

- Who's in charge? How is power gained or lost as the actors interact?
- Who controls conversations? What are the topics of conversation?
- What are the key elements in the scene?
- What are the relationships of the actors?
- What language or actions seem culture- and scene-specific?
- What ethical concerns arise from the assignment?

You and your partners should take notes separately and then compare them. This activity should be repeated the following week, with at least a couple of hours set aside for discussion of notes. Your final collective analysis should describe the scene, events, actors, and interactions fully in any form—narrative, poem, fiction, role play. You should also include a detailed map of the scene. It's best to do this activity with groups of researchers going to different sites. You can then share your findings at a final meeting and discuss how what you've learned transfers to your classroom research planning. We have done this activity many times with students and colleagues and are amazed at the range of research design issues that emerge as people work in teams to understand a place outside of school.

For example, one group decided to hang around at McDonald's. They were surprised at the differences in the behaviors of customers who seemed to be "regulars" and those who seemed to be making a quick stop for food. Their final write-up of their research was a poem, describing with spare, clean phrases the routines and rituals. They used the hanging-around experience to think more about the rules and routines in their classrooms—and what role they played in establishing these routines.

Another group spent time at a large chain bookstore coffeehouse. They catalogued all the differences in cultures present, from the youths with pierced noses to the dapper retired professors in tweeds. These researchers learned the importance of noting the most telling details to describe members of different social groups, knowledge they would use to explore the more subtle differences between students in their classrooms.

The team of researchers who observed customers at the local Department of Motor Vehicles found it was essential to include the snippets of conversations, both from those waiting in line and between clerks and customers. Their observations led them to include more tape recording and transcriptions in their research studies, because they saw that research informants come to life on the page when their lives are presented in their own words.

A trio who observed at a local restaurant found that sketches of where customers sat and how space was used by customers were most helpful in understanding their site. They decided to collect more visual information in their research project, including photographs and daily charts of where children chose to sit and whom they chose to work with.

As you have insights about what you're seeing, keep returning to your research plan. How does this change the way you'll want to collect data? What is most helpful to you in understanding this site with others, and how can that understanding inform the way you analyze your data? How do your teammates support you? When do they get in the way of your work? How can you use this knowledge to find the research partners who will be able to help with your classroom project?

We've had findings presented as poems, songs, want ads, original art, plays, pantomime, and narratives. The final presentations may be the most important part of the activity. Researchers see that they can take a small amount of data and still have insights about how people interact and cultures form.

## RESEARCH WORKSHOP

# Testing the Water with Mini-Inquiry Projects

*Jerome C. Harste and Christine Leland*

Engaging teachers and undergraduate interns in mini-inquiry projects is an effective way to encourage classroom-based research. Mini-inquiry projects are just that: quick investigations of issues that get raised through professional reading, conversations, or occurrences in classrooms. Some of the questions and comments that led to mini-inquiry projects and were subsequently investigated by teachers and interns at the Center for Inquiry in Indianapolis follow:

> "I think *The Witch's Broom* is too hard a book for first graders."
> "I don't think children can correct their own spelling errors; if they could, they wouldn't make them in the first place."
> "I think kids like books that are concrete (about things they have had experience with) rather than abstract (fantasy)."
> "Are manipulatives as important for older kids as they are for the younger ones?"
> "Instead of focusing on the elements of literature—characters, setting, events, main ideas—as we talk about books, will an open conversation lead to coverage of these same topics?"
> "If I get Terrance to talk about the successful strategies he uses when reading, will this make him a better and more confident reader?"

Each of these musings has been the basis for a mini-inquiry project at our school. Although questions might provide the most direct route into the inquiry process, statements that are shared in collaborative settings become inquiries when the speaker is asked, "How do you know that?" In our combined group of teachers and interns, for example, it was one of the interns who originally commented that *The Witch's Broom* was too hard a book for first graders. Others in the group immediately asked, "How do you know that?" and "How can we find out if that's true?"

The formulation of questions leads to hypotheses and plans for gathering classroom data that will test them. More often than not, these plans are generated through collaborative discussions. In our case, teachers and interns worked together to figure out the best ways to collect appropriate data for the various mini-inquiries that members of the collaborative were interested in pursuing. With concrete plans in mind, teachers and interns now saw their classrooms as places for doing research as they went about their teaching. They agreed to gather data for a specified period of time (a week, in this case) and to come together again to discuss, interpret, and analyze what they had found.

Sometimes the discussion with others led participants to revise their plans for data collection or to conclude that they had not collected enough data. In addition, we frequently found that new questions were generated before the original ones had been answered, causing inquiries to take sharp turns in new directions. In most cases, the final result was a one- or two-page write-up that was shared with the whole group.

Mini-inquiry projects, we believe, have done more to establish an attitude of inquiry among our community of teachers, undergraduate interns, and university faculty than anything else we have tried. Although we also engaged in some larger inquiry projects such as a "sense of place" study that focused on Indianapolis, we found that these required significant investment in terms of time, travel, trips to the library, finding people to interview, and so on. These projects were beneficial in many ways, but we all felt that the mini-inquiries provided easier access to a greater variety of explorations into various aspects of teaching.

We see mini-inquiry projects as a low-stress way to start messing around with inquiry. Their inherent simplicity helps to ensure that inquiry is seen as a way of life rather than as a big deal. Philosophically, education-as-inquiry is meant to suggest that the whole of education is inquiry—everything from building curriculum according to the personal and social interests of children to seeing teaching as inquiry and ourselves as teacher-researchers. When paired with opportunities for systematic collaboration, mini-inquiries can be powerful curricular invitations that do much to support us all in becoming more reflective practitioners.

We also think that there is something to be said for the idea of venturing slowly into unknown territory. New Englanders, for example, know that the idyllic beauty of their rocky coast needs to be juxtaposed with knowledge of the frigid ocean water that can literally take one's breath away if approached without due restraint. Visitors who wish to swim there soon learn that they experience less of a shock when they test the water with their toes and wade in gradually. We think there's an analogy here to teacher research. Mini-inquiries help us test the water before plunging into something that might otherwise be pretty scary. Doing teacher research (like swimming in cold water) doesn't have to leave us breathless if we start small. We might even be surprised to find that once we're used to it, the new perspective is quite refreshing.

## FEATURED TEACHER-RESEARCHER

## Research Design

*Michelle Schardt*
Elementary Bilingual Teacher

### *Research Purpose*

Bilingual education was developed after so many language minorities were found to be failing in regular education programs. By teaching subject matter and literacy in the first language while the student is acquiring English, we can help him or her be more successful. Two-way bilingual education programs developed when schools realized they could use the language minority population to help English-only speakers acquire a second language, too. This is the type of program I have been involved in for five years at various schools in California and Oregon, with Spanish and English being the languages. One aspect of all the programs that has bothered me is the English-only students' lack of Spanish proficiency. As we try to "sell" these programs to parents, I am feeling more and more dishonest saying that our goal is for all the children to be bilingual. It seems the focus is still on the language-minority children. Although we are having a lot of success in this area, we have to put more energy into Spanish language development. My research will see if I can do just that.

### *Research Question*

In my two-way bilingual class, what happens to Spanish language usage by my "English experts" when they have focused Spanish lessons for English-only speakers (without "Spanish experts")?

### *Subquestions*

Will English experts play and work with Spanish speakers more frequently?
How will the English speakers use their acquired language?
Will they enjoy Spanish more?
Will they take more risks?
Will they ask Spanish experts for help?

## *Data Collection*

- Starting at the beginning of the year, three times a week I will take running notes during "Big Workshop" (free-choice time), recording which children choose to work together. I will make record sheets with each area of the classroom and fill in names to make it easier.
- I'll code the language users with S or E. I'm sure a few will want to take over this job soon after I begin. I will also record what subject is being discussed.
- During different group work times (patterning, free exploration, journals) in which students choose whom they work with or sit by, I will take photographs. Later I can show the students the pictures and ask them why they chose to work with that person. I think it will be interesting to have the students be a direct part of the observation.
- With a tape recorder, I will bug the playhouse, reading corner, and math center once a week to capture which languages are being used and which books are being chosen.
- I will initiate a dialogue with the parents in our interactive homework journal to see how the children's attitudes about Spanish change over the year.
- I will do surveys with all my English experts at the beginning and end of the school year. Possible questions:
  - How do you feel on Spanish days?
  - Do you understand Spanish?
  - Do you want to learn Spanish?
  - Do you like Spanish?
  - How much Spanish do you know? A little, a lot, or a medium amount?

## *Data Analysis*

I will look through my notes once a month and count up the interactions lasting more than ten minutes with a Spanish expert and an English expert. I will record what language was used and make it into a ratio (for example, out of twenty-five encounters, nine were in Spanish in September).

The photographs will provide a visual record of the children and the partners or groups they are choosing to work with. They will also be good springboards for conversations among the students involved about why they are choosing to work with the people the pictures show them working with. I will record our interviews the week I do them instead of bugging the room, and then transcribe when I do the other tapes. Once a week in my morning prep, when it's nice and quiet, I will transcribe the tapes I collect with my kindergarten partner for the next year. She will be collecting tapes, too. This will tell me what the kids are actually saying (if anything!) in the target language. I will be able to hear what they are getting out of their Spanish language instruction.

The dialogue journals will provide me with individual accounts about the students' attitudes. I'll put copies of pertinent information in their files to follow the phases of their feelings toward Spanish. I will triangulate the findings from the different forms of data and see if they are congruent. I will report the results in narrative form as an overall evaluation. I will share this information with students and parents.

When discussing language, I will use a code system to record what type of language is used. A possible system might look like this:

> D: directing, telling what to do
> H: asking for help
> VH: help on vocabulary
> WH: help on work being done
> L: labeling, naming objects, colors, numbers, and so on
> S: social

## Support/Collaboration

I plan to do this project with the other kindergarten teacher, who will be teaching the English language development part of the program. We will be pooling our kids and planning our lessons together, so it will be natural for her to follow along with the research with her English experts. Heather will be professional and motivating, even though she is new at all this. I also plan to use a group of teachers I've met through my course work and with whom I'm in a new writing group. They will question me about my research every time we meet! I want them to expect to read the transcripts and the results of my surveys. Maybe I'll pick one to really watch me and my progress!

## References

Cummins, Jim. 1997. "Metalinguistic Development of Children in Bilingual Education Programs." In *The Fourth Locus Forum*, ed. M. Paradis. Columbia, SC: Hornbeam.

Diaz, Rafael M. 1983. "The Intellectual Power of Bilingualism." Paper presented at the New Mexico Humanities Council, Albuquerque, NM.

Edelski, Carole. 1996. *With Literacy and Justice for All*. Bristol, PA: Taylor and Francis.

Fergusen, Charles. 1978. *Talking to Children: A Search for Universals.* Stanford, CA: Stanford University Press.

Freeman, D. E., and Yvonne S. Freeman. 1994. *Between Worlds: Access to Second Language Acquisition.* Portsmouth, NH: Heinemann.

Hakuta, Kenji. 1986. *Mirror of Language: The Debate on Bilingualism.* New York: Basic Books.

Halliday, Michael A. K. 1977. *Exploration in the Functions of Language.* New York: Elsevier North-Holland.

Krashen, Stephen. 1982. *Principles and Practices in Second Language Acquisition.* Oxford, UK: Penguin.

## FEATURED TEACHER-RESEARCHER

## Research Design

*Emily Gromko*

### Research Project Plan

*Origin of Question*
After reading Nancie Atwell's book *The Reading Zone* (2007) a few years ago, I wanted to delve deeper into pushing my students with their reading work-shop and choice books. Last year, at the semester break, the students were asked to give a book talk about one of the books they read first semester. As they did this over several days, I asked them to keep track of the names of books their peers talked about that sounded interesting and that they might want to read for the second semester. After having them list books they'd be interested in for next semester and why, my thoughts turned to *The Reading Zone* and how Atwell's students set goals for themselves with reading. I started to wonder about choice, in terms of standards. I wanted to research goal setting and reading.

### Research Question

What happens when my tenth-grade language arts students set semester-long reading goals?

### Subquestions

Will my students read more because of the goals?
Will they enjoy reading more?
Will they improve their reading comprehension?
How will self-assessment and self-reflection affect reading in our class-room?
Because they will be accountable to themselves foremost, will they be more motivated to meet their goals?
What kinds of goals will they set?
Will their goals be related to quantity, quality, genre?

### Data Collection

Student surveys: At the beginning of this second semester, the students will complete reading surveys that ask their opinions on reading and how much they already read, and generally, take their reading temperature. At the end of the year, I will give the surveys back to the students and have them assess and reflect. What changes do they see in their reading? Did they meet their goal? If not, why? What got in their way?

Journals/reading logs: At intermittent times throughout the semester, especially at the quarter, students will write and reflect on their goal and how they are striving to meet it, and whether they are meeting it or not.

The students' goals: The actual goals the students set will be important for the research. I will learn what kinds of goals they are setting and what areas they want to achieve in. This will tell me the areas in which they want to improve.

Interviews: Talking to the students about their goals and their progress will also be a source of data. I'll be able to hear how their progress is coming and what might be getting in their way, if anything.

My observational notes: I will take notes when students are conferring with each other and reading and writing about their reading during reading workshop.

## Data Analysis

- I will read the initial reader's surveys within the first week of the new semester and take notes. I will write about their thoughts and ideas about reading during the semester.
- Once the students set their goals, I will create a code sheet for the different sorts of goals they set to create categories or track trends.
- I will interview students at least once a quarter to talk with them about their progress. I will take notes during the interviews.
- I will write narrative and journal entries once every two weeks.
- Each month, I will review the data I collected and trends I am seeing.
- Once a month, I will review the students' reading logs and reflections on their progress.
- At the end of the semester, I will give students their reader's surveys and guide them in self-assessment; this will be an important piece of data because they will reflect on their goal, whether they met it, and how it changed reading for them.

## Time Line

*January/February (start of new semester)*
1. Administer reader's surveys.
2. Students set their new semester goal.
3. Start my journal.
4. Code and chart their goals.

*March, April, May*
1. Conduct at least two interviews with each student.
2. Keep teaching journal twice a week.
3. Check reading log at least once a month.

*June*
1. Students assess themselves and whether they are meeting their goals.
2. Students get reader's surveys back from the beginning of the year and write reflections about how their relationship with or thoughts about reading has changed.

## Support/Resources

1. Fellow teachers in English department
2. Independent study group
3. Texts for ideas and guidance
4. Resources: file folders, papers, more books to replenish my classroom library, time for my students to use the school library

## References

Atwell, Nancie. 1998. *In the Middle.* Heinemann: Portsmouth, NH.
———. 2007. *The Reading Zone.* New York: Scholastic.
Gallagher, Kelly. 2009. *Readicide: How Schools Are Killing Reading and What You Can Do About It.* Portland, ME: Stenhouse.
Hubbard, Ruth Shagoury and Brenda Miller Power. 1999. *Living the Questions: A Guide to Teacher-Researchers.* York, ME: Stenhouse.
Miller, Donalyn. 2009. *The Book Whisperer: Awakening the Inner Reader in Every Child.* San Francisco: Jossey-Bass.
Rief, Linda. 1992. *Seeking Diversity.* Portsmouth, NH: Heinemann.
Tovani, Cris. 2000. *I Read It, But I Don't Get It.* Portland, ME: Stenhouse.
———. 2004. *Do I Really Have to Teach Reading?* Portland, ME: Stenhouse.

## FEATURED TEACHER-RESEARCHER

## Research Brief

*Sarah Christenson*

## Research Question

How does nightly reading and writing homework affect first and second graders' overall performance in reading and writing?

## Alternate Questions

How does doing partial homework affect overall reading and writing performance?

How does doing reading homework instead of writing homework affect overall reading and writing performance and vice versa?

How does the amount of time spent doing reading and writing homework affect overall reading and writing performance?

## Background

Each year in late August as I am putting together my classroom I vow to
myself and my students that this year homework will be different. I will not
only come up with meaningful homework that meets the needs of all students, but it will not be time consuming and it will not teach new concepts.
As the school year starts, I end up tweaking the homework slightly, but never
really end up making a big change. Each year I vow to make a change, and
each year I fail to follow through.

I have always believed that homework is important for children of all
ages, whether it be five minutes a night or half an hour. For first and second
graders I believe that homework should meet many different requirements.
First, homework should not be used to teach new concepts, but instead rein-
force concepts that have already been taught. Because of this, homework
should be able to be completed independently. Second, homework should
not be time consuming; after all, these are first and second graders. The last
thing most of them want to do after spending six and a half hours in school
is go home and do more schoolwork. Next, homework should be used to
teach students responsibility. As students get older, they will be expected to
do and turn in homework. If we can establish good work habits now, it will
be a lot easier for students in the future. Last, homework should be meaningful and not busywork.

The intention of my research question is to find out if those students who
read and write nightly turn out to be better readers and writers by the end of
the year than those who do not do nightly reading and writing homework.

## Data Collection

*Reading*

Method 1
Students will be asked to complete at a minimum ten minutes of nightly
reading Monday through Friday. Five nights a week, students will take home
a book that is at their independent reading level to practice. On a reading log,
like the one below, parents will record the number of minutes their child
reads each night along with their initials.

| Reading Log | | | | |
|---|---|---|---|---|
| Monday | Tuesday | Wednesday | Thursday | Friday |
|  |  |  |  |  |

Method 2
Using our required district assessment, the DRA (Developmental Reading Assessment), I will formally assess students four times a year. To collect baseline data I will first administer the DRA in September. Then I will use the DRA to assess students in December, March, and June.

Method 3
Students will interview each other four times a year (a baseline in September, and then one in December, one in March, and one in June) about their reading habits outside the classroom. Students will fill out the following form during each interview:

| **Interviewer's Name:** | **Interviewee's Name:** |
|---|---|
| 1. Do you like to read at home? | Yes          No |
| 2. How many days of the week do you read or get read to at home? | 1   2   3   4   5   6   7 |
| 3. What is your favorite book? | |

*Writing*

Method 1
Five nights a week, Monday through Friday, students will be asked to complete a minimum of five minutes of free-choice writing. Using Aimee Buckner's idea of "daily pages," students will keep their writing organized in a writer's notebook. Students will return their writer's notebooks daily so we can use them in class.

Method 2
I will collect four writing samples throughout the year and then score them using our district scoring guide. I will collect a baseline sample in September and then three more samples, one in December, one in March, and one in June.

Method 3
Students will interview each other four times a year (a baseline in September, and then one in December, one in March, and one in June) about their writing habits outside the classroom. Students will fill out the following form during each interview:

| **Interviewer's Name:** | **Interviewee's Name:** |
|---|---|
| 1. Do you like to write at home? | Yes          No |
| 2. How many days of the week do you write at home? | 1   2   3   4   5   6   7 |
| 3. What's your favorite thing about writing? | |

## *Data Analysis*

*Reading*

Method 1
On a class roster I will record the number of days each student reads for the assigned week of homework. Students can earn a score of one through five, depending on how many days they read. If they read five days, they will score a five, if they read four days, they will score a four, and so forth. At the end of each trimester, and the end of the year, I will total up each person's scores. Students with higher scores will have completed more homework than those who have lower scores.

Method 2
I will use the DRA to score students in the areas of accuracy, comprehension, and fluency. I will keep a master list of each student's DRA scores throughout the year and save each student's DRA in their portfolio.

Method 3
After each student has been interviewed, I will save his or her interviewing sheet in a portfolio. I will look to see if there is any correlation between each student's answers and the other two forms of assessments.

*Monthly Memo*

During the last week of each month I will look at all of my data and write a memo detailing what I have learned thus far.

## *Writing*

Method 1
Each day I will use a class roster to check off if students wrote the night before. An *X* will indicate that a student has written the night before and a zero will indicate that they didn't write. At the end of each trimester, and the end of the year, I will total up each person's *X*s. Students with higher numbers of *X*s will have completed more homework than those with lower numbers.

Method 2
Using the district scoring guide I will score four samples of my students' writing in the areas of conventions, organization, and ideas and content. (These are the three areas my district focuses on for first and second graders.) I will then keep their writing samples in their portfolios.

Method 3
After each student has been interviewed, I will save his or her interviewing sheet in a portfolio. I will look to see if there is any correlation between each student's answers and the other two forms of assessments.

*Monthly Memo*

During the last week of each month I will look at all of my data and write a memo detailing what I have learned thus far.

## *Time Line*

*Second Week of September*
1. Implement reading logs and "daily pages."
2. Collect baseline DRAs and writing samples.
3. Students administer interviews.

*Fourth Week of September*
1. Write memo.

*Fourth Week of October*
1. Write memo.

*Fourth Week of November*
1. Write memo.

*First Week of December*
1. Calculate at-home reading and writing participation.
2. Administer DRAs and collect and score writing samples.
3. Students administer interviews.

*Fourth Week of December*
1. Write memo.

*Fourth Week of January*
1. Write memo.

*Fourth Week of February*
1. Write memo.

*Second Week of March*
1. Calculate at-home reading and writing participation.
2. Administer DRAs and collect and score writing samples.
3. Students administer interviews.

*Fourth Week of March*
1. Write memo.

*Fourth Week of April*
1. Write memo.

*Fourth Week of May*
1. Write memo.

*First Week of June*
1. Calculate at-home reading and writing participation.
2. Administer DRAs and collect and score writing samples.
3. Students administer interviews.

*Second Week of June*
1. Compile data.
2. Write final memo.

Weekly: Record scores for reading logs.
Daily: Check off "daily pages."

## Support/Resources

1. I plan to send home a letter getting parents on board with my research so they will be sure to fill out the reading log weekly.
2. My team of teachers
3. Our teacher-research support group (League of Teacher Researchers)

## References

Bennett, Sara, and Nancy Kalish. 2007. *The Case Against Homework: How Homework Is Hurting Children and What Parents Can Do About It.* New York: Three Rivers Press.

Buckner, Aimee. 2005. *Notebook Know-How.* Portland, ME: Stenhouse.

Cooper, Harris. 2006. *The Battle Over Homework: Common Ground for Administrators, Teachers, and Parents.* Thousands Oaks, CA: Corwin Press.

Hubbard, Ruth Shagoury, and Brenda Miller Power. 1999. *Living the Questions.* Portland, ME: Stenhouse.

Kohn, Alfie. 2007. *The Homework Myth: Why Our Kids Get Too Much of a Bad Thing.* Cambridge, MA: Da Capo Press.

Vatterott, Cathy. 2009. *Rethinking Homework: Best Practices That Support Diverse Needs.* Alexandria, VA: Association for Supervision and Curriculum Development.

## FEATURED TEACHER-RESEARCHER

# Research Brief

*Christina Wallace*

## Research Purpose

> *I learned how to write from writers. I didn't know any personally, but I read . . . .*
>
> —Cynthia Rylant

I've been thinking a lot about my writing class—what I teach and how I teach it. Technically, it's a writer's workshop, where choice and independence should come first and collaboration is appreciated and respected. However,

I've been feeling more and more pressure to teach children specific skills and formats in order to boost scores on the state writing prompts. Aimee Buckner (2005) writes, "[S]tate standards demand that students write and try out different kinds of writing for different purposes. Yet as teachers have come to rely more heavily on the state or district curriculum, a sense of independence has been lost" (15). What happens to students as writers when their choice and independence is taken away? Many teachers say they want to create lifelong readers, but what about lifelong writers? My research will focus on what happens to students when they participate in a writer's club, similar to a book club, in which they meet weekly to talk about their writing. By having them see each other as writers, I hope to bring the sense of choice, independence, and collaboration back into my writer's workshop.

## Question

What is the effect on emerging writers when they take part in a writer's club?

## Subquestions

What growth did students have in their writing skills?
How have student attitudes toward writing changed?
How are my teaching practices affected by student attitudes, participation, and growth?
How do students perceive themselves as writers?
Are students more willing to revise when getting feedback from peers?

## Data Collection Strategies

- Taped recordings (video or audio) of writer's club groups, sampling different groups throughout the year. To keep things manageable, I plan to tape at least once a week, but I can increase the frequency if needed.
- I will keep a teacher journal to record observational notes "in the midst" and "after the fact"—I can peek in as a casual *observer* of groups (not participant) and write down what I see and hear.
- I will ask students to complete attitude surveys before the project begins and after it ends. This survey will ask students about their attitude toward writing, their self-efficacy, and so on.
- I plan to do open-ended interviews with students at the start of the year. This will take place during individual conferences. My goal with this is to follow up on any questions I have from the attitude surveys, as well as to get a better idea about their writing lives in and out of school.
- Conference notes. During individual writing conferences, I will write down any references children make to their time in writer's groups. These will be incidental notes, rather than from any direct questioning on my part, although I might nudge or follow leads. I'm hoping to see that kids are making connections between what happens in writing groups and what happens in class.

## *Data Analysis*

- I plan to listen to the tapes either at home or at school once a week. Since transcribing takes so long, I am going to have a loose goal for transcription: transcribe any conversations that seem critical, instead of transcribing *everything*.
- I will review my teaching journal and conference notes. The best way to do this is to integrate it into my daily routines, by spending probably five to ten minutes of review during planning time. I would also like to dedicate an hour or two, either monthly or weekly, to reviewing my notes in more depth.
- I will compile and code attitude surveys and student interviews. I will look for any patterns or themes that emerge. I will do the same thing at the end of the year and compare results.

## *Time Line*

*September*
1. Meet with principal. Align professional development goal with research.
2. Send out letters of intent and permission (for names and video) to parents during back-to-school night.
3. Administer writing surveys.
4. Conduct student interviews.
5. Do a fishbowl writer's club with other adult volunteers.
6. Start mini-lessons that model listening, how to give feedback, and other appropriate behaviors.

*October–December*
1. Start writing unit based on "ideas" for writing. Students will form groups based on choice.
2. Start taping writing groups.
3. Cook and code notes from attitude surveys and interviews.
4. Share progress with parents during conferences.

*January*
1. Start genre or author study writing unit. Students will form groups based on genre or author.
2. Continue taping and observing.

*Monthly*
1. Cook and code notes.
2. Meet with colleagues.

*March*
1. Administer second attitude survey.

*April-May*
1. Write.

## Resources

- Digital/video recorder
- Smock!
- Writer's notebook (personal and for students)
- Research toolbox

## Support

1. Colleagues—enlist fellow teachers (at least one, I hope!) to try this out with me or at least do their own research project, so we can talk about ups and downs
2. Write letter to Aimee Buckner—and ideally, get a response!

## References

Cruz, Colleen. 2004. *Independent Writing*. Portsmouth, NH: Heinemann.

Dorfman, Lynne.2007. *Mentor Texts: Teaching Writing Through Children's Literature*. Portland, ME: Stenhouse.

Kempton, Sue. 2007. *The Literate Kindergarten*. Portsmouth, NH: Heinemann.

Ray, Katie Wood. 1999. *Wondrous Words*. Urbana, IL: National Council of Teachers of English.

———. 2004. *About the Authors: Writing Workshop with Our Youngest Writers*. Portsmouth, NH: Heinemann.

———. 2006. *Study Driven: A Framework for Planning Units of Study in the Writing Workshop*. Portsmouth, NH: Heinemann.

For more examples of teacher-research designs, see the appendix, p. 241.

# **4**

# **Harvesting Data**

*Some say it is no coincidence that the question mark is an inverted plow,*
*breaking up the hard soil of old beliefs and preparing for new growth.*
—SAUL ALINSKY

Saul Alinsky's notion of question marks as inverted plows brings us back to the metaphor of our classrooms as garden communities. Equipped with our questions and our research designs as tools of our trade, we are faced with the task of harvesting the rich crop of data that surrounds us in our classrooms.

The harvest is most fulfilling when we connect it to practices that are already a part of our teaching lives. Many teachers rely on their observations and reflections to help them make sense of their students' learning and to make their teaching plans. As teacher-researchers, we just record these observations and reflections in a more systematic way, building on existing skills.

## **Journals and Notes**

With so much going on around us, it can be easy to overlook the little things that add up to the big things—the chance observations that might lead someday to breakthrough findings. Slowing down and being open to our impressions, living in the moment with a mindful stance—being ready to take in the world around us—is the starting place in collecting data. This is the stance that teacher-researchers such as Jessica Singer Early describe as essential in their ability to harvest large crops of data:

> I wanted to find a way to begin to understand and examine more clearly
> what was taking place each day in my classroom. My goal was to become
> more conscious of what was happening in my teaching in order to
> improve my practice. The decision to begin to write daily in a teaching

journal felt like a manageable step toward participating in a written inquiry process. . . . I filled my journal with pages of unpolished thoughts, questions, reactions to conversations, and wonderings. All of this writing was rough. Some days I wrote lists and other days I wrote long reflections in response to a class or a conversation. Students came to expect that I would grab my journal in the middle of heated conversations in order to jot down ideas or quotes from their discussions. (Singer 2005, 147)

Taking notes is one of the main tools in teacher-researchers' repertoire. As teachers, we have long relied on our memory for details and history in our classrooms. But some of this must make its way into recorded writing, even very brief jottings. Looking back on those written notes and elaborating on them can provide a bridge between what you are experiencing in the classroom and how you translate the experience into larger meaning.

Educational ethnographer Harry Wolcott reminds beginning note takers that observation is "a mysterious process":

At the least, it is something we do "off and on" and mostly off. A realistic approach . . . is to recognize and capitalize on the fact that our observations—or, more accurately, our ability to concentrate on them—are something comparable to a pulse: short bursts of attention, followed by inattentive rests. Capitalize on the bursts. Be especially observant about capturing little vignettes or short (but complete) conversational exchanges in careful detail. (1995, 98)

One of the mysteries for many novice teacher-researchers is how teachers find time to observe and take notes in their classrooms. When you see experienced teacher-researchers at work, the process isn't too mysterious at all. Veteran teacher-researchers rely on those "short bursts" of time. They may take notes for only ten minutes during any teaching day, but they really focus their attention for that period. What matters is not how much time you spend taking notes, but how consistently you make focused observation a regular part of your day.

Kim Stafford (2003) writes in *The Muses Among Us* about listening to the world around us, writing what we see, note, and overhear, one step at a time. His advice to writers applies to teacher-researchers writing in their classrooms and schools.

The writer's prerogative is to take small things seriously: A glimpse, a flicker of recognition, an evocative phrase of a few syllables spoken by someone near you. Take down observations and ideas in the moment they arrive. (4–5)

If you look back through the research designs in Chapter 3 and in the appendix, you'll notice that the main data-collection strategy teacher-researchers rely on is collecting and recording these observations:

"I will keep field notes of conversations or comments I hear from general education teachers in regard to our students' reading skills." (Audrey Alexander)

"I will take notes when students are conferring with each other and reading and writing about their reading during reading workshop." (Emily Gromko)

"I will keep a journal noting lessons, as well as comments, discussions, attitudes, and writings about in-class reading, including whole-group, small-group, individual, and read-aloud experiences. I will be especially interested to 'listen in' on novel group discussions, to note any changes that may occur." (Gloria Trabacca)

"[My conference journal and chart] will give me a place to take notes about the reading behaviors I am noticing in each student. It will be a place to reflect on particular students, conferences, and my perception of the strategy as a whole. The conference chart is a class list on a spreadsheet where I record the date each time I meet with a student. The chart gives me a quick reference for how often I confer with each one." (Bitsy Parks)

"[I will rely on] my anecdotal notes from observing cooperative teams at work and other activities." (Wally Alexander)

"I will try hard to keep a teacher journal and do some note taking." (Patrice Turner)

Patrice set out to record her data with some uncertainty and trepidation. Like many beginning teacher-researchers, she wondered, "What will my notes look like? How will I manage to collect them?"

Several years ago, when Susan MacKay was a beginning teacher-researcher, she wrote about her own uncertainty and how she found a way to build on her "kid-watching" strategies in her essay "Breaking in My Research Tools":

Since I am a beginner at teacher research, my research tools are mostly new. None of them tucks neatly behind my ear or rests comfortably in my hand. None of them feels soft and broken in.

I'm most at home with my anecdotal notes—the kid-watching tool I learned to use in my teacher education program. After playing with different kinds of notebooks, sticky papers, and grids, I've settled on a red three-ring binder with a divided section for each child in my class. I record various notes at various times on a few sheets of loose-leaf paper in each section.

On the first day of school, and periodically throughout the year, I run through all the names of my students and write down the first things that come to mind. Other times, I flip through slowly and jot down the important things that bubble up in my memory as I think carefully about each child. On some days, things happen that just beg to be recorded right away. I note connections children make—between books and life, between their stories and other stories, between math and reading, between a new problem and a problem solved.

I record anything that helps make the familiar become unfamiliar. I look for that all the time. I want the unexpected to occur. It's no great surprise that these themes run central to all my questions about teaching and learning. My anecdotal notes have become a place to chart paths toward the answers to my questions—and the asking of more.

Various teaching journals go hand in hand with the anecdotal notes. The red notebook works well as an assessment and research tool, but the journals have turned me from a good kid-watcher into a beginning teacher-researcher. In the teacher journals, unlike the anecdotal notes, my plans and questions get muddled with the kids' plans and questions, and the questions become much clearer. I also have a legal pad on which I am constantly writing. I note kids' choices, plans for later, things that must be finished. I jot down pieces of conversations, questions, ideas—both mine and theirs. This pad of paper is helping me to integrate my research with my teaching and helping them become seamless.

I usually write in the other journals after school, although, I admit, without any degree of consistency. I take them with me when I work with other teachers or go to a staff meeting or development opportunity. I list questions I have and processes I observe. I quote other people. I jot down the titles of good professional books and children's literature. I sometimes also take the messy thoughts written on the legal pad and straighten them out on a clean page in another journal. More questions, thoughts, and connections always follow. (1997, 154–155)

Susan doesn't rely on one strategy to record her observations. Legal pads, three-ring binders, journals, sticky notes, clipboards, and index cards are all part of her toolbox. She documents some notes "in the midst" of her teaching, and others "after the fact," depending on the nature of her task, the information she needs, and her own writing preferences. Susan adopts a strategy common to many novice teacher-researchers: she tries a range of note-taking materials, forms, and times for writing, experimenting to find the style of notes and observations that best suits her needs as a teacher-researcher. Many teachers begin like Susan with a wide array of notebooks, sticky notes, labels, stickers, and journals—keeping the methods that work and discarding those that don't.

Like Susan, Title I teacher Carey Salisbury relies on various note-taking strategies, recording her anecdotal notes on clipboard sheets (see Figure 4.1). In her very brief jotted notes, she captures a phrase or two that she can flesh out later. She uses her teaching journal to fill in more details of encounters and to reflect on them. For example, on the day she recorded, "Billy: looked up at clock once—wandering—looked for book George and he talking

Figure 4.1
Anecdotal Notes
Sheet

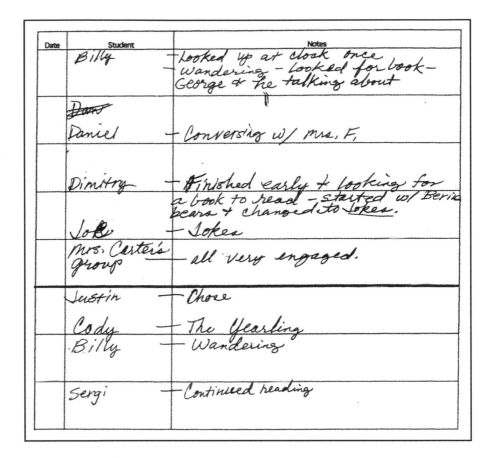

| Date | Student | Notes |
|------|---------|-------|
| | Billy | Looked up at clock once Wandering – looked for book – George & he talking about |
| | ~~Daniel~~ Daniel | Conversing w/ mrs. F, |
| | Dimitry | Finished early & looking for a book to read – started w/ Berin bears & changed to Jokes. |
| | Joke | Jokes |
| | Mrs. Carter's group | all very engaged. |
| | Justin | Chose |
| | Cody | The Yearling |
| | Billy | Wandering |
| | Sergi | Continued reading |

about" on her anecdotal note sheet, she turned to her journal that evening and used her anecdotal notes to jog her memory, writing: "Billy still has problems. I select several books he may be interested in. He says he really wants to read *The Mixed-Up Files,* but then he continues to fumble through it. I have to separate him from the group because he cannot help talking. The class is somewhat noisy because of all the groups working on their vocabulary goals—look words up and find out what they mean. Could this be the destructive piece in this whole plan? Those who are easily distracted, like Billy, and need quiet to read, aren't getting it?"

At the end of her first year of taking notes, Carey reflected that recording her observations systematically "has forced me to do it better. I learned that by looking at my notes, I can tap into things I really need to be doing for the kids, like checking with Billy's teacher, who thinks he should be reading at a lower grade level than is maybe right for him." She also realized that her words and ideas flow far more easily when she sits down at the computer at home periodically, and she has found that writing time to be essential: "Without all that writing, where do the thoughts go and how can they be transformed into ways to substantiate what happens in the classroom?"

Having a teaching journal handy can also be useful for recording those moments of insight in the classroom. Second-grade teacher Bitsy Parks noted in her teaching journal her realizations about a student who could easily slip through the cracks:

> It's writing time in Room 14. Michael doesn't hesitate to get out his journal, date a new page, and begin writing. He writes quickly—not too fast, but not too slow either. After each word he writes, he diligently lays down a finger to hold the white space, as if it will disappear without his finger hanging on to it. Michael occasionally looks up to check on the students around him. Although he doesn't try to manage them, he certainly doesn't want to be left out of knowing all that is going on at his table. Michael finishes with the other few who are always quick to get their thoughts on paper. He turns in a perfect amount of very neat writing. He stays on topic for the entire piece, and always includes an interesting detail or two. Each day it's the same—neat, semi-interesting, and at least a half page of writing. Michael's work is as tidy as his work space. Michael doesn't stand out as an overachiever or the opposite, and as a result, he is a student who could get lost.

Quickly writing about one student can give note taking immediate value for teacher-researchers. Bitsy immediately began to ask him to help in the classroom, made time to interview him about his processes, and met with his parents to share his growing self-confidence. At the end of the year, she worked to place him with a teacher who recognized his potential.

In your own classroom, you'll find little note-taking "tricks" that work for you. For example, teacher-researcher Lynn Dobash found a way to fold data collection into her teaching with style. Frustrated that the moments she wished to capture were sprinkled throughout the day, she found it wasn't practical to run to her desk and grab her teaching journal every time she wanted to write a note.

> To solve this problem, she began wearing a very fashionable necklace—a yellow sticky note pad with a pen attached. When a child said or did something she wished to capture, she simply jotted it down on a sticky note and continued on in her teaching. At the end of the day, she put each sticky note in her notebook. (Dana and Yendol-Hoppey 2009, 75)

Susan, Carey, Bitsy, and Lynn all continue to use their journals and teaching notebooks to observe and document the undercurrents in their classroom life. But although most of us recognize the importance of documenting what we notice, what we hear, and what sense we can make of it, it can be difficult to find the right vehicle for regular written reflection. We've talked to more than one teacher-researcher who resists starting yet another teaching journal because she's simply "journaled out," overdosed on journals as course requirements—journals with specific formatting whose pages were filled out of a sense of duty rather than used as a tool for genuine inquiry and reflection.

Yet when we use writing for our own purposes, and in the midst of our teaching lives, we can tailor the format we choose to our work style and preferences. You might create small books with just a few pages to slip into your pocket, like writer Kim Stafford; write daily reflections at your computer on a kind of "daybook," following the lifelong practice of writer and teacher Donald Murray; or try out Julie Cameron's recommendation of "morning pages," written by hand in her notebook, a pivotal tool in her creative life. It doesn't matter what time of day or what kind of recording devices you choose; what matters is finding what works for you.

In order for our tools to fit more comfortably into our hands, it's also very helpful to find ways to record events as they are happening. We can do this by fitting this into our current record-keeping strategies, as Susan MacKay did with her red binder of "kid-watching" notes. We can also create recording sheets that meet the particular demands of the questions we wish to answer.

First-grade teacher Nancy Csak decided to take a closer look at her storytelling time, and she created just such a tool:

> Armed with my questions, I set out to gather data using a recording sheet on a clipboard [see Figure 4.2]. I discovered some interesting things. I noticed that there were some children who consistently chose to pass. Happily, there didn't seem to be a pattern of children being willing to share with a group but not with me. Although it happened a couple of times, I noted that when they chose not to share with me, they were engaged with an activity they didn't appear to want to leave. I hope this means they are comfortable with me. In fact, there were a couple of instances where children did not share in the group but did share with me. I was also able to pinpoint a couple of students who seem to be rushing to tell everything they can. I have the feeling they are trying to say their piece before time runs out! Interesting. One of these students includes two topics each day, beginning her story with, "I have two things. . . ."
>
> As I recorded the number of turns in each exchange, it struck me that the number of turns is not as important as the quality or length of these turns. So I adapted my recording sheet to tap more information. I began noting either "short," "medium," or "long," indicating the perceived length of the entire story when it was completed. Although this is not very scientific, I did find that as I went back and sort of averaged these in conjunction with the number of turns, it gave me a rough idea of who talks a lot and who gives a short sentence or two without much elaboration. I want to expand on this and note which one of us talks more and what kind of language is used in the discourse.
>
> Also, as I listened, I realized that the topics of the questions discussed were not a part of my original set of questions but that this interested me a great deal. So I quickly added a column to my recording sheet and jotted down a brief description of the topic each child discussed each day. Looking back at the data I have so far, this is fascinating to me.

Figure 4.2
First Recording
Sheet

| Name | ① Total oppor. to tell | ② # of times shared with group | ③ # of times shared with me | ④ avg. # of turns | ⑤ Long, med or short turns | ⑥ Comments *Special attention |
|---|---|---|---|---|---|---|
| 1. Henry | 4 | 4 | 4 | 4.75 | Short/med. | Glad to see he's not just talk about Nintendo anymore |
| 2. Art | 3(ab) | 1 ←(different days)→ 1 | | 3 | short | *Often tardy/absent misses storytelling |
| 3. Graham | 4 | 3 | 4 | 4.5 | med. | turns themselves are often long w/out prompt |
| 4. John | 4 | 1 ← same day → 1 | | 4 | short | *this info confirms what I have noticed - often comments I don't have anything to write about. |
| 5. Jimmy | 4 | 4 | 4 | 16/4 | long | Loves to talk! Long turns. Sing-songy voice during storytelling |
| 6. Jake | 4 | 4 | 4 | 4.75 | Short/med. | Is more verbal in class then this data indicates |
| 7. Juliet | 3 (ab) | 3 | 2 | 7.5 | long. | Each turn is long, w/out much urging. She lights up at storytelling! |
| 8. Craig | 4 | 3 ← same days → 3 | | 3.3 | short | *Seems unsure about sharing - encourage more |
| 9. Lisa | 4 | 2 | 3. | 4.7 | short | Very shy. Although she has several turns, they are short. Lots of nods as responses |
| 10. Carmen | 4 | 4 | 3 | 8.3 | long | Seems to enjoy this! Passed when busy on white board |
| 11. Laura | 3 (ab) | 2 | 1 | 4 | short | *This surprises me. Laura + I have good rapport. I think? |
| 12. Janna | 4 | 3 ← same days → 3 | | 4.5 | long | Has lots to say, long, is often unconventional, difficult to follow |
| 13. Kara | 4 | 4 | 4 | 6.25 | med. | Very caught up in fami situ. Understandable |
| 14. Hannah | 4 | 4 | 4 | 7.5 | med/long | Enjoys this - covers a variety of topics |

As Nancy continued to collect data, her research questions changed. And so did her recording sheet (see her revised sheet in Figure 4.3). Although she continued to take notes on storytelling time each morning, she shifted the focus from the number of turns to the topic each child talked about:

As I began to look at these notes, another question came to mind. What was the time of the event relative to when the story was being told? In other words, did it happen long ago, just yesterday, that same day, or was the storytelling anticipating future events? I was curious about whether these young students would mostly tell about the concrete—something that had already happened—or were interested in looking ahead and perhaps speculating about what might happen in the future. I came up with a code to label the topics, based on clues the speaker gave, such as "A long

Figure 4.3
Revised
Recording Sheet

| Name | Oral topics | relative time | Written topics | relative time | Comments |
|---|---|---|---|---|---|
| Kathy | – Visiting Dad on weekend | Recent Past | ✱ Going to Dad's house + staying with a friend. | RP | Good variety of topics |
| | – Grandpa is moving | Future (?) | ✱ Grandpa got married again + is moving. | RP + future | |
| | – Got in trouble for not eating dinner | R.P. | – Her cat Charley is cute + sleeps with her. | Ongoing | |
| | – Being babysat by her sister | RP | – Tooth fell out at school. | RP | |
| | – Helping Mom in garden | RP | – "I wonder how you..." didn't finish | ? | ← This brought to mind other intriguing stories left unfinished. Did she run out of ideas, or was she being interrupted? |
| | – Baby sister | RP | – Name song | Environmental | |
| | – Going to the beach | Near Future | – Writing numbers | Environmental | |
| Emma | – Dressed up her cat! | RP | "I like school". | Ongoing | She has six notebooks. Is writing a lot! |
| | – Has a loose tooth | Ongoing | ✱ Shrew got into the house. | RP | Has several each a day. Seems to come back to it whenever poss. |
| | – Mom pulled her tooth | RP | – Sand dollar from Willie (classmate) describing it. | RP | |
| | – Cat is sick | Ongoing | ✱ Lost her tooth at recess + couldn't find it. | RP | Likes many things "really much"! U |
| | – Has another loose tooth | Ongoing | – Played with her cat described her. | RP-ongoing | Writes a lot about her cat. May need new topic ideas. |
| | – Family argument | RP | – Likes the Spice Girls + wants their CD. Looking forward to today. | Ongoing | |
| | – A shrew got into the house | RP | ✱ Cat again | " | |
| | – The cat caught a rat | RP | – Cat | " | |
| | – Missing tooth - spot is sore | Ongoing | – Cat | " | |
| Lisa | – Her cat sleeps with her | Ongoing | – Capital alphabet | Environmental | Lots of connection between oral & written topics. She is not very sure of where + I think she uses the storytelling to "try out" her topics before she is confident enough to write about it. For her, storytelling definitely supports writing. |
| | – Talked to Kamrie on the phone last night | RP | – "I like Stacie because..." | Ongoing | |
| | – Dancing with a friend | RP | – Easter egg hunt | RP | |
| | – Staying up late on weekend | RP | – Numbers 1–46 | Environmental | |
| | – Past vacation – Indian village + saw a mtn. – Mt. Hood | Long Past | – "My mom got sea-sick..." | RP. | |
| | – Playing with her cat + cat's habits | Ongoing | – Someone pushed her + she fell + bumped her tooth | RP | |
| | – A story Garrick told her in the gym – a kid with matches | Same day / RP. | – Dancing with her friend | RP | |
| | | | ✱ A boy with matches | Same day/ RP | |
| | | | – Playing with her friends. | Ongoing | |
| | | | ✱ Playing with her cat. | Ongoing | |

time ago," "Last night my mom," "Tomorrow we're going to," or "Someday
. . ." The labels I used were LP for long past; RP for recent past (I considered "recent" to be within the last few days—for instance, telling about the
weekend on a Monday); SD for same day; NF for near future; and DF for
distant future. I marked the relative time while the speaker was telling her
story, so that I would not forget when her words were over.

Nancy's process of revising and adapting her record-keeping forms as she
continued her research is a good one. As categories and findings begin to
emerge, you'll want to revisit your plans for written observations. There may
be other ways of indexing and coding your "in the midst" notes that can help
you analyze your data later.

# Interviews

Another important tool for the teacher-researcher is interviewing—asking questions to bring out the information we couldn't learn without getting inside our students' minds. Interviewing is not a new strategy for teachers but one that can be honed as they build on their conferencing skills, asking questions through a casual, conversational approach.

Middle school teacher Katie Doherty reports that she often begins her interviews with comments or questions such as, "I was so interested in what you shared with the class yesterday . . ." or "I didn't have a chance to ask you about this before, but can you tell me a little more about . . . " Then she continues to ask open-ended questions that follow up on her students' responses.

In reflecting on her questions, she notes, "The kids know I am going to ask them questions about what they are thinking or what they wrote about . . . the decisions they make about books they are reading and what's going on in their heads as they work. They know I don't know what they're going to say—and that I really want to find out!"

Katie's interviewing process is similar to that of Lori Widmer, a professional writer who blogs about her interviewing experiences and her writing process at *Words on the Page* (http://loriwidmer.blogspot.com/):

> Having conducted hundreds of interviews, I've found that the best interview strategy is to go into it with curiosity. This is a person [I'm talking to]. This person has great information, and by asking, I can learn something new or interesting. Creating rapport is easy—I treat my interview sources as the interesting people they are. . . . I never go into an interview without asking, "What would I really like to know about this?" (2008)

Artist and teacher-researcher Don Fels bluntly says that listening is the key skill in researching successfully:

> Part of your job as a researcher is to make sure the people you are talking to understand that you are genuinely interested and that it's not a trick. In my case, the most successful technique is to honestly say to students, "I'm interested in your story." People are flattered when you say, "I'm interested in what happened to you, or what you know about this," the fact that you're asking them for knowledge. . . . And that should flatter them; it's something they know they are giving to you. So it's easy to get people to talk; you have to listen. (Selwyn 2010, 220)

Many of the best interviews with students begin with an idea and then become improvisations based upon the students' responses. It's also important to give students the gift of time. Primary school teacher Nicole Heinlein noted that when her students say, "I don't know," they often are really saying, "I need more time to think about your question." She tries to reframe the question in a different way because the child may not have understood her question fully:

During my reading survey, I asked AJ, "What makes Kendra [his friend and next-door neighbor] a good reader?" AJ answered, "I don't know." He may have been thinking, "How would I know? Aren't you the teacher?" So instead of moving on to the next question, and just accepting "I don't know" as his final answer, I asked further, "When Kendra reads, how do you know she is doing a good job?" He thought about this new question and said, "She reads fast and doesn't mess up on words very much." His new answer was legitimate and let me know he understood the question better. As a teacher of many English learning students, I have to stop and think about what I am asking my students when I get an "I don't know" answer. Perhaps they do not understand the question. By stopping, rephrasing, and giving the child more time to think, the child should be able to give me a more thorough answer. AJ is not a dual language learner, but he is a good example of what happens when a child does not understand the question.

Third-grade teacher Bekah Raymond was intrigued by what she learned from her student interviews. Focusing on the answers from just one question gave her insights into her students' learning she would never have had otherwise.

My favorite was when I asked each of the students, "Do you ever write outside of class?" Each student said yes. They even seemed a bit shocked by the question, as if this were a given and that everyone should be writing outside of class. Noah said, "I write songs and poems at home. They are all bad [as in good] and I can't wait to have them sung someday." Makayla said, "I keep a journal of all that I am learning. I love to record what I keep in my brain. My brain is funny, and writing the funny stuff down is important." Stephanie said, "My favorite part of writing is home. I write Spanish. I know Mrs. Raymond can't read it, but she say it ok to write what she can't read so I do." Darius said, "I write at home all the time, so sometimes it is better than TV 'cause I can be in charge." Alexis said, "Writing at home is fun. I like to copy words from the cereal boxes and other things I can find. I like to write songs from the radio. There is so much to write in our world!"

Each of these responses showed me that my students are enjoying the process of writing. It also revealed to me that the styles of things they are writing at home differ from those pieces they are creating in class. It made me wonder how I could create a space for each of these different genres of writing to appear within the classroom. I was encouraged to hear that Stephanie is writing in her native language at home. Within the classroom she is very timid about her Spanish speaking and often does not participate with other Spanish-speaking students. I have pushed her to write in Spanish in the classroom because her language base in Spanish is so much larger than in English at this point in her life. So knowing that she transfers back and forth at home is a window into something I would not normally see, and it says to me that she is using writing as a tool to communicate, not just to turn in papers at school.

**HOW TO**

# Get Started with Interviews

Many of the best interviews start with existing protocols of questions. If you are new to interviewing students, you might want to begin by revising one of these protocols. For example, one of the most widely used interviews in literacy is the Burke Reading Inventory (Weaver 1994). Here are some of the questions in the inventory:

> Who is a good reader you know?
> What makes him or her a good reader?
> Do you think that she or he ever comes to something she or he doesn't know when she or he reads?
> If yes, what do you think she or he does?
> If no, suppose that she or he does come to something that she or he does not know. Imagine what they would do.
> If you knew that someone was having difficulty reading, how would you help that person?
> What would a teacher do to help that person?
> How did you learn to read? What did you or someone else do to help you learn?
> What would you like to do better as a reader?

These questions can easily be adapted to other disciplines. For example, if your research involves looking at students' scientific processes, you might ask questions like the following:

> Who is a good scientist you know?
> What makes that person a good scientist?
> How did you learn to do science? What did you or someone else do to help you learn in science?
> What would you like to do better as a scientist?

You can even adapt these questions to get at social behaviors. For example, if you are exploring the links between learning styles and social networks in the classroom, you might ask questions like the following:

> Who do you know who is helpful in our class?
> What makes that person a good helper?
> If you knew someone in class was having difficulty with a task, what would you do to help that person? What might someone else do to help?

Use the questions as a starting point for getting at the processes your students go through, and you'll begin to see new patterns between social networks in the classroom, individual personalities, and learning.

# Surveys and Inventories

Sometimes we want to find out what a large group of people think about a certain teaching practice or issue, and it simply isn't feasible to interview everyone one-on-one. Surveys and inventories can help tap information that would otherwise be inaccessible to us.

Early childhood teachers Tracy Crews and Nicole Sorley investigated their Family Literacy Program by using two kinds of parent surveys. One was distributed after each Family Literacy Night, and the other was tucked into a literacy bag they gave to families weekly. They found that parent inventories helped them understand how students and parents see the process and purpose of their classroom work:

> According to our final Family Literacy Program Survey, families saw a different side of their child's teachers as well. One family said, "I saw that Mrs. Crews truly cares for my child and his learning. She is very creative and has made us feel welcome in his program." Another family's response said, "I never knew my child knew so much. She never does these things at home for us! It has allowed me to see what my child is learning, how she is learning, and how much she knows!"

With the new cooperative relationships Tracy and Nicole established with families, they were able to provide specific family experiences that supported growing literacy.

See the Parent Literacy Form (Figure 4.4), Literacy Bag Survey (Figure 4.5), and Concluding Family Literacy Survey Form (Figure 4.6).

Susan Pidhurney, a kindergarten teacher who investigated the use of home-school journals, suggests that if you are planning to involve parents of your students in your classroom inquiry, it is helpful to think through these issues before you begin:

- Not all parents are comfortable responding in writing. Be aware of their difficulties and find another way to communicate.
- Be sure to write as simply and clearly as you can until you are sure of the literacy level of the parents. Some may not be able to read very well; some may be able to read manuscript writing but not cursive. Be sensitive.
- Keep entries as positive as possible.
- Keep writing even if the parents don't. . . . They will eventually get the hint.
- Don't let the home-school journal turn into a daily report card. You will soon tire of it and won't want to continue.
- Don't get discouraged by negative entries. Parents sometimes need to vent, and if they feel comfortable, they'll vent at you.
- Remember your intent: to increase and improve communication between home and school. If the parents are having too hard a time, find another way—maybe write on weekends only, for example.
- Keep a photocopy of the journal. A colleague had an extensive dialogue going when a journal got lost—forever.

Figure 4.4

## Parent Literacy Form

| Family Member's Name | Student Name | Teacher Name |
|---|---|---|
| | | |

Have you attended the parent meetings? _____

Have you volunteered in your child's classroom? _____

Do you read to your child? _____

How often do you read to your child? _____

Do you have a routine when you read to your child? _____

If you have a routine, please describe it. _____

_____

_____

_____

What types of reading do you do on a regular basis? (magazines, books, newspaper, etc.)

_____

_____

Does your child see you reading on a regular basis? _____

Do you make lists? (for example, grocery lists) _____

If you make lists, does your child see you when you write these lists? _____

How can we improve parent-teacher involvement? _____

_____

_____

Would you be willing to participate in a Family Literacy Program? _____

_____

Would you be willing to participate in a Family Literacy Night with your child?_____

_____

_____

Please list any questions you may have: _____

_____

_____

_____

_____

_____

Figure 4.5

---

## Literacy Bag Survey

Student Name: _____ Family Name: _____

Date: _____

Name of the activity bag: _____

_____

Did your child enjoy the activities in this bag? _____

_____

What activity did your child enjoy the most? _____

_____

_____

What activity did your child enjoy the least? _____

_____

_____

How many nights did your child work with this bag? _____

About how many minutes did your child stay involved with the activities? _____

On a scale of 0 to 5, (with 0 being "I never want this literacy bag again" to 5 being "I love the activities in this literacy bag and would revisit this bag again"), please rate this literacy bag.

    0              1              2              3              4              5

Questions or comments about this literacy bag:

Figure 4.6

---

**Concluding Family Literacy Survey Form**

Name: _____ Date: _____

1. What have you learned from the Family Literacy Program? (This includes the Family Literacy Nights and Literacy Programs.)

2. How has the Family Literacy Program affected your child?

3. What have you learned about your child's teacher?

4. Has this program increased or decreased communication between the school and home? Please give examples.

5. Has this program helped your family increase reading at home? If yes, please state how.

6. Has this program increased other literacy activities at home such as writing, drawing, pretend reading, and story retelling? If yes, please state how.

7. Have conversations increased with your child with the activities provided in the literacy bags? If yes, please say how.

8. How would you like to see the Family Literacy Program grow?

9. What themes would you like to see for Family Literacy Nights?

10. What themes would you like to see in the literacy bags?

Please list any further questions, comments, or complaints about the Family Literacy Program that you would like for us to know.

---

# Audio and Video Recording

An audio recorder can be an invaluable tool for the classroom researcher. It allows you to fit your research project into the nooks and crannies of time outside the school day. You can play back one-on-one conferences, classroom discussions, and small-group work sessions, and listen intently and repeatedly if necessary. You have verbatim quotations in your students' own words. Recording language also gives teachers a chance to re-hear the conversations in their classrooms and self-evaluate their own language choices. Recording devices have always been a staple tool for teacher-researchers, and with twenty-first-century technologies, the possibilities for capturing classroom events and language in a variety of teaching and learning activities has grown.

It's important to realize that recording can provide valuable data for your research study without requiring that every word be transcribed. There will be times when it makes sense to transcribe an entire recording; some class discussions or individual conferences beg to be analyzed, dissected, and presented to a larger audience verbatim. But much of the value of audio and video recordings is that they allow you to revisit your classroom, and your research issues, long after the actual event.

Linda Christensen regularly records small-group conferences in her high school classroom and then listens to the recordings as she commutes to and from school. Through reviewing the recordings outside her classroom, she can listen more intently to the types of conversations students have around literature. Rather than transcribing everything, she selects ones that are particularly good examples and shares those transcripts with her students so they have student-generated models of effective literature discussion strategies. She has the added bonus of discovering with her students what makes a good book discussion.

**HOW TO**

## Use Audio Recordings in Research

*Barbara Libby*

Recording and listening to students at work in my classroom can be an invaluable tool in research. The following uses are related to the research questions I had about myself and my students. Your questions may guide you in finding many other possibilities for taping to inform.

- Record yourself during direct instruction, group discussions, reading and writing conferences, and so on. Analyze these recordings for teacher/student talk ratios.
- You can use the same recordings to analyze your questioning levels and become more aware of opportunities for higher levels of questioning.

- Are there silent voices in your class? Listening to your recordings with a student checklist will make you aware of who speaks and who doesn't. You can also analyze your checklist for gender issues.
- Different places in the classroom can be used to record and check for a percentage of on-task versus off-task dialogue. This information might support use of the center or direct you to make changes. You will also think about the purpose of student dialogue, as I did.
- Model the kinds of questions you want students to ask each other during science workshop, literature circles, and writing share time, and then record these activities to monitor the influence of your modeling.

Heather Nihart was particularly interested in her own use of language in the classroom. She recorded her classroom through the day—especially during reading and writing conferences. Rather than transcribing everything, she played back the recordings initially, just to reflect on what she heard, and then focused on different segments that gave her insights for changing her teaching:

> I realized that much of my time was spent asking questions. Although I hoped my students were learning by answering those questions, I wasn't convinced they were. I began a closer examination of the questions I asked and my purpose for asking them. Most of my questions elicited very few words, and often an "I don't know." After analyzing one segment of the recording, I found I asked seven questions in three minutes. And when I listened to the questions I asked during conferences, I felt many of them were yes/no questions, leading questions, or surface questions.

Heather used the data to create a list of changes she would like to make in her language, as well as questions that worked (see Figure 4.7).

Andy Kulak works with older students at an urban high school. His research question is also concerned with the language he uses in the classroom—particularly to get his classes settled in and started on the day's lesson. He created a table organized by type of "choice words" (from Peter Johnston, 2004), such as *noticing and naming, identity, agency,* and so forth. Next to this column is a column for "Practice," which records the date and time and a brief note about the language excerpt. (See Figure 4.8.)

Andy writes about his research question:

> In a classroom of thirty-five tenth-grade learners buffeted from room to room throughout the day, I have come to put heavy weight on the moments just before and moments just after that ripping sound, that relic of the Industrial Revolution, that Pavlovian reminder of subservience, that *bell.* For my transcription analysis, I wanted to discover how I used language pre- and post-bell.

Figure 4.7  Heather's Question Categories

Questions I asked that I would like to eliminate or change, and *some possible changes*:
   Is this your best work? *(What did you do well in your writing?)*
   Have you added details? *(What will you add to your story?)*
   (When reading) Can you sound it out? *(What can you do when you get to a word you don't know?)*
   (When writing) Can you stretch it out? *(Can you tell me more about this part?)*
   (Asking about a word in the title of a book) Do you know that one? *(What parts of the title
      do you know?)*

Examples of when I told information instead of asking a question:
   Next time, remember to look at the words before choosing your book. *(Could have asked:
      What can you do next time when you are looking for a book?)*
   Change the vowel sound. *(Could have asked: What could you try?)*

I asked these questions and would like to ask more like them:
   What parts do you know in the title?
   What can you do when you get to a word you don't know?
   Does that make sense to you?
   Does that sound right to you?
   How did you figure that word out?
   Where is your story going? What are you going to write next?
   What's happened so far?
   What do you think will happen?

Figure 4.8  Andy's Table

| Choice Words, by: Peter H. Johnston | | |
|---|---|---|
| **Noticing & Naming** | | |
| Sounds like... | Theory | Practice |
| • "Did anyone notice...?"<br>• "Did anyone try...?" | preparing the field–helping students to realize what kinds of things might be noticed (13). | |
| • "I see you know how to spell the beginning of that word." | confirm what has been successful - attending to the "partially correct" (Clay) (13) - notice, and help students notice, what they are doing well - develops self-efficacy & agency (Eder) (14). | |
| • "Remember the first week when we had to really work at walking quietly? Now you guys do it automatically." | draw attention to their learning histories - helps to project learning futures (14). | |
| • "What kind of text is this?" | attention to classification - "naming and noticing make it possible to have focused discussions with less confusion" (15). | |
| • "You know what I heard you doing just now, Claude? Putting yourself in her place. You may not have realized it. You said, 'Will she ever shut up?' Which is what Zinny is thinking." | identifying cognitive strategies - making "the hidden mental skill of the individual into a future resource" (15). - also gives the student a chance to "claim competence." | |
| • "I want you to tell me how it [group discussion] went... What kinds of questions [were raised]?" | draw student attention to process | |

| Sounds like... | Theory | Practice |
|---|---|---|
| • "Write down a line you wished you had written." | turn attention to qualities of words - "I love that line!" expressing a clear, emotional response to language - emotional indicators are an important source of information (Repacholi)(16). | |
| • "What are you noticing?...Any other patterns or things that surprise you?" | assumes you are a "noticing" sort of person & a person who wishes to write valuable things..."these are invitations to construct particular identities" (17). "Children learn what they notice matters" - "Attentional following" (pay attention to what the learner in noticing v. "Attentional switching" getting the learner to attend to what the teacher deems important (18). | 11/1/10<br>1:05:05<br>1.6  "What?" |

**Identity**
Language helps us frame how we think of ourselves.

| | | |
|---|---|---|
| • "What a talented young poet you are." | | |
| • "That's not like you." | | |
| • "I wonder if, as a writer, you're ready for this." | | |
| • "I bet you're proud of yourself." | | |
| • "What are you doing as a writer today?" | | |

Andy's analysis showed that some of his most "choice words" were actually during those pre- and post-bell moments in the classroom. He reflects in his narrative about what he learned:

> Things begin to shift at line 21: a bell sounds. On the recording, my voice stiffens and deepens. The warmth that led to the dialogues before class has been replaced with a more austere delivery . . . [Looking at my chart], I can see opportunities for change, attending to individual needs during class time as effectively as I do before class. It is my hope that within the first couple of weeks in the next term, my classroom voice will have fewer dramatic shifts making my students' class-to-class transitions more seamless and productive for them.

When teachers do transcribe recordings, they often choose snippets of conversations to illustrate key points in their research. Bilingual teacher Michelle Schardt wanted to look at how her students learning English as a second language know how to use English words when they aren't thinking about language. She used the following transcription markers in her analysis of her conversation with Ruben as they looked at a picture book:

**Transcription Key**

| | |
|---|---|
| - | False start |
| . . . | Pause |
| ==== | Emphatic stress |
| CAPS | Very emphatic stress |
| /?/ | Unintelligible word |
| ( ) | Comment |

An excerpt from Michelle's transcript follows:

**M:** What is that bear doing?
**R:** Watching the . . . feather [a leaf] fall down.
**M:** Now what is he doing?
**R:** . . . Go hunting?
**M:** Hunting maybe? What does it look like here?
**R:** There's an old house. There's /?/.
**M:** Now what's happening?
**R:** Him's in the /?/.
**M:** What?
**R:** Him's inside the house.
**M:** What does he see?
**R:** Some plates [bowls]. See? A big plate and a big plate and a small plate.

Depending on what emerges in the conversation you are transcribing, you might want to use some other common transcription markers, such as these:

| [ ] | Overlapping speech |
|-----|--------------------|
| f | Forte (spoken loudly) |
| p | Pianissimo (spoken softly) |

Some teachers create their own markers that are tailored to the particular research they are conducting, as Anne Wallace did when she was focusing on the fluency of her preschool students' language. In this case, knowing the length of pauses would be helpful, so she noted in her transcription key the following differentiation:

| . . . | Pauses in speech for a half second |
|-------|-----------------------------------|
| . . . . | Pauses in speech for one second |

Digital video recording also has the potential to give teachers insights into untapped aspects of their classrooms. In research such as Andie Cunningham's about her students' work during her "movement workshops," video is a natural choice for data collection (Cunningham and Shagoury 2005). Other situations can be ripe for examination of the role of body language or facial expressions, or for a closer look at several things that are happening all at once that might go unnoticed in a busy classroom.

Head Start teacher Leslie Woodhouse wanted to take a closer look at circle time through the lens of her English language learner (ELL) students:

> I specifically examined two Vietnamese boys; these boys entered my classroom in September with no English skills whatsoever. Over the course of the first month and a half of school, I know they have acquired some basic survival English (like *bathroom, no,* and *stop!*) but I wanted to examine how my teaching does or doesn't connect with them. I know they tend to be very distracted during whole-group lessons, and I approached this inquiry in hopes of discovering what is successful for their learning, and where my communication is falling short. Among my questions were these: Are these boys engaged or misbehaving? When they're not engaged, are they understanding the directions and choosing not to follow them? And, Am I providing enough visual cues to communicate what I am teaching? For this analysis, it was necessary for me to video-record the circle time, since so much of their learning is based upon my visual cues and observations.

Leslie was stunned by how much she was able to learn from viewing this one segment of her teaching—through the eyes of her ELL students.

> I have been working with these boys for almost two months—and after viewing twenty-four minutes of lessons, I answered many of my questions. My most successful instruction for these two boys was through the use of (now) familiar songs and daily routines. . . . They also responded to the visual clues I presented, such as the picture card of "frightened" and the face vocabulary (nose, mouth, teeth, ears, hair) as I pointed to these parts

on my own head. Also, my expressions and affectations about being scared of the monster helped them enjoy the story with their classmates during the read-aloud. And, not surprisingly, the repetitive text allowed for their participation in the reading.

But the most eye-opening part of the analysis was in the science experiment. Although there was no point in the lesson when I saw either of the two boys deliberately misbehaving, my teaching assistant and I were often both frustrated by their distractedness. But the English-speaking children remained involved, which offers insight. I think it was too abstract a concept for Duy-An and Ryan, with nothing to anchor it to their home language. Duy-An had a higher skill set of *looking* like he was participating (such as copying his friends' actions and words), whereas Ryan made mischief; however, neither boy understood much about what was occurring in this part of the lesson. How frustrating that would be for me as a student! I don't think I had fully understood the need to anchor a skill, vocabulary, or observation in one's home language first, before fully understanding the presentation in English. In hindsight, I doubt they have ever used or applied the vocabulary of *sink, float,* or *heavy* in Vietnamese. The question I asked, Am I providing enough visual cues to communicate what I am teaching? didn't go deep enough. My visual cues were great for a story, or a matching game, but in scientific concepts, these pictures on a graph weren't enough to pose the question authentically. I would love to know what the exchange was when Duy-An pointed to the chart and said something to Ryan in Vietnamese. I also wish I could ask what was going through Duy-An's mind when he chose to put his name where he did on the chart. The fact that I will never know this information gives me a lot of insight about how teaching my ELL students falls short. In the future, I'll plan more time to have a translator present, or use questions posed by a translator the day before. The insights I gained from this video recording has already changed my research question—and will continue to affect my teaching!

It's important to decide the specific uses for the video you are planning to record. It is tempting to set up a video in a corner and simply record everything. The number of recordings pile up quickly, and it can take hours to review and make sense of the data. A complete transcription of a video recording—not only the audio portion but the many actions occurring simultaneously—can require several viewings.

We recommend that you use video for very specific purposes and with definite time limits around the activity you are recording. Here are some examples of ways teacher-researchers have used videos to good advantage:

- Second-grade teacher Nancy Winterbourne arranged to videotape a student giving a "tour of the classroom." This provided her with important data on how well this student understood the organization in her classroom as well as insights into the underlying social structure and where her students' perceptions and her own differed.

- In her English as a Second Language writing class, Virginia Shorey wanted to look closely at how her three Filipino students used Tagalog to help them write stories in English. The video of one twenty-minute writing conference among the three girls provided fascinating data about their reliance on one another and their use of "code-switching" that would have been impossible to capture on audio alone.
- Stacy Neary was investigating spelling strategies with early elementary students and videotaped the brief strategy lessons she conducted with small groups of students. Capturing these mini-lessons on video allowed her to look closely at her own teaching, at the effect of the lessons on students, and at the ways they discussed spelling with each other. Further, she found it valuable to share these five- to seven-minute tapes with her research group; the tapes were short and specific enough to serve as a useful focus for discussion and feedback.

You might also ask visitors to your classroom—aides or parent volunteers—to do some videotaping. Then, ask them what they recorded and why. Having your classroom recorded by someone else, with their comments about what they saw, can provide a needed new perspective on your students and your research topic.

# Documenting the Classroom with Photography

More teachers are turning to photographic documentation as a data-collection tool to help them understand their classrooms. Cameras can capture moments in a classroom that might otherwise go unremembered. As a tool that anyone can learn to use, photography can invite students to participate in our research with us. William Bintz found he was able to "see through different eyes" when he began to use photography as a research guide:

> I selected photography as a research guide for three reasons. First, it is a medium that is accessible to almost everyone. . . . Second, photography enables students to participate in the process of data collection and analysis. Specifically, it affords them the opportunity to assume a researcher stance by inviting them to explore what symbols at the school are personally significant, and discuss why these symbols mean so much to them. [Third] . . . I selected photography because it can be used as a "medium with a memory" . . . it has an open-ended potential where photographers can use themselves and their photographs as objects of inquiry. This potential was recognized by Diane Arbus (1972), an internationally renowned photographer, who stated: "One thing that struck me very early is that you don't put into a photograph what's going to come out. Or, vice-versa, what comes out is not what you put in." (1997, 34–35)

One way many teachers begin to collect data using digital pictures is as a complement to written observations. Photos can jog your memory of incidents in the classroom. Like other data-gathering tools, pictures can help you notice what's going on with fresh eyes and help you focus. This in turn helps you pinpoint more specifically where and how to gather future photos. You can also use digital pictures during student interviews as prompts for follow-up data gathering, helping your students remember their process as well.

## HOW TO

# Use Photography in Research: A Quick Guide

*Katrina Kane*

## Why?

This is a critical first step and will save you time and money. You need to determine the purpose for taking pictures before you begin. The purpose will drive everything that follows. Here are some examples:

- Data collection for a research brief
- Recording growth over time
- Materials for your portfolio
- Reflection tool to be used with students

## Who?

Once you have determined why you want to use photography as a tool in your classroom, ask whom you will need to photograph. This will depend on the purpose of the photographs and how they will be used later on. Some things to think about:

- Do you need to work with a whole class, a small group, or individuals?
- What permissions do you need from parents?

## What?

What do you need pictures of? Think about some of the following before you start taking pictures:

- Do you need photographs of students' work in progress or after it's completed?
- Will you photograph the project at the beginning, middle, and end to record growth over time?

## When?

When can you best capture what you are looking for? Try to seek a natural time rather than a contrived one. Some other things to consider:

- What time of day should you take the pictures?
- Will you need someone in the room to help so that you can focus your attention on your research?

### Where?

Where you shoot your pictures is very important. You need to think about your students and how different environments affect them:

- In your room
- In someone else's room
- Outside or inside

### Know Your Camera

Practice using its different features.

# Student Artifacts

Examples of student work can be one of the richest sources of data for teacher-researchers. It is tangible evidence of what kids are able to do and of the range of ways in which kids respond to different learning tasks.

Kelly Petrin's study of children's uses of the arts as part of their meaning-making process required her to have many samples of students' drawings and writings. She considered them an aspect of her field notes. For example, after a snowstorm, an unusual event in Portland, Oregon, she invited her pre-school students to tell stories about the snow using paper and crayons. This excerpt from her teaching journal shows how important the student samples themselves proved to be:

> And what stories they were! Trinity drew two figures that I initially thought might be snowmen, but she explained that they were drawings of herself and a friend in their "Christmas snow dresses." Her snowflakes were smaller and tumbled across the page. Like all good writers, she also noticed the details of this particular snowstorm and added them to her drawing. "I put this leaf falling, because while the snowflakes were coming down, some leaves that were still on the trees did, too!" Brilliant! (See Figure 4.9a.)

> Juan's picture of himself and a big snowman show two similar figures. But in between the two, he shows how he made the snowman, with several large circles that represent the snow rolling into big snowballs. (See Figure 4.9b.)

Figure 4.9a
Trinity's Story

Figure 4.9b
Juan's Story

Diamond's picture takes place after the snow stopped falling when the moon shone on the road and her yard. In her picture, she is outside, and her mother peers through a window, watching her. (See Figure 4.9c.)

Figure 4.9c
Diamond's Story

Figure 4.9d
Rachel's Story

They told their stories with detail and playfulness using their paper and crayons. They collaborated, too—Trinity teaching Rachel how to make an *I* so she could write out "I love you" (ILU). (See Figure 4.9d.)

Kelly made copies of each of these samples as part of the data she collected that day. Because she had previous artifacts of the children's work, she could place these particular drawings and sets of observations within a larger context. This points to an important aspect of collecting artifacts: Save everything! (Or as much as possible.) Though you may have a good idea of what specific sets of student work you need to save for a short-term study, it can help to have a folder of student work from throughout the year so that you can trace growth and notice differences.

It's helpful to let parents know early in the fall that you'll be keeping most of the students' work for the year and returning it the next summer. This gives you a chance to decide which pieces you will look at more closely and to make copies of those examples.

Other useful student artifacts include both drafts and final versions of their written work, lab reports, learning log entries, self-evaluations, and peer evaluations—essentially, any of the products that emerge from their classroom work. Most of us find, though, once we start gathering the rich harvest within our classrooms, we want to collect all of it. It reminds us of our memories as children gathering blueberries in August. The ripe fruit seemed to fall off into our hands. Each bush had so many delicious ripe berries, it was hard to pick them fast enough. As one branch was harvested, the one below emerged similarly laden.

Instead of slowing you down as a gatherer, this kind of plenty can simply serve to whet your appetite. It makes you eager and greedy to pick everything. At some point, you need to come up with a way to organize your student artifacts. You might store them alongside field notes, as Kelly Petrin does, or in separate folders. Some teachers now prefer to take quick snapshots with digital cameras, or even their smartphones, sending the photos directly to their e-mail accounts for storage and ready access. Use whatever system works best to help you find your way back to them. Just as with other data you collect, stacks of student work won't inform your research if they molder in piles and you never look at them again.

# Becoming Your Most Important Tool

When you become a teacher-researcher, you become your own most important tool. Your written notes, recordings, surveys, questionnaires, and interviews are good tools, but as Shirley Brice Heath reminds teacher-researchers, "You are the key instrument, and you must keep that instrument on all the time" (quoted in Power 1995, 27). This requires a special kind of mindfulness, a willingness to be wide awake to learning, which can provide you with a different presence in the classroom, one that can be a gift to you as well as to your students.

Teacher-researcher Ellie Gilbert personifies this stance. As a high school teacher creating a book club and writing workshop with nontraditional students, her research agenda informs her work with her students on a daily basis. In the following reflection, Gilbert writes about the wonder and the joy she experiences in this new role:

I love my friend—and fellow teacher-researcher—Katrina's directive to "notice things" this year in her classroom. I think about that a lot as I go through my day, interacting with kids. "Try to notice more," I tell myself. "What is actually happening in your class?" The more I notice, the more I write down. And the more I write down, the more I notice. Going through my handwritten notes, trying to decide what likes what, I see a pattern emerge. I notice a web of connections building. It is as though while I stepped away from my research to get a fresh cup of coffee, a spider has crawled onto my dining room table where I've spread out my pages of notes and has leapt from one pile of data to another, all the while spinning its silken thread until all the pages are draped in an orderly, logical web of connected events. Returning to the dining room with a fresh steaming mug of French roast, I suddenly see this beautiful pattern emerge, and as I move in for a closer look, I find smaller, tighter webs within the web: concentrations of connections. This "seeing" leads to more thinking, which leads to more questions.

I feel like, for the first time in my career, I am fully awake. I am teaching *my students*, not the English or social studies curriculum. I am more open—I share with students some of what I am seeing in my research. I talk to them about the things I am curious about and the kinds of questions I am asking in my research. By now they are used to me always having a notebook and pen in hand when we talk. They even slow down if we talk on the phone, because they know I'm jotting down what we're talking about. They see me as a practitioner of a craft, and not as a—I don't know—gatekeeper or time watcher, or "content announcer," as my colleague Xavier puts it.

This week we had a three-hour—that's right—THREE-HOUR-long book club meeting. We talked about our books, shared what we're writing, ate yummy snacks, and talked about their lives and the connections they are making to the books they choose to read. We also talked about my research and about our work together as a class. What I found so amazing was their willingness—eagerness, even—to talk about their book club experience. They wanted to talk about how much they appreciated the opportunity to read what they like and to share with others their thoughts and writing in, as one student put it, "like, a real way." The student continued, "I get to read to other kids what I'm writing and it's . . . it's what I'm actually thinking, you know? It's not, like, what the teacher tells me to write about." Another student chimed in, "Or think about." I, of course, immediately began scribbling this down and the kids laughed at me a little—our shared joke—and waited for me to finish. One girl even called book club her "sanctuary time." Yeah, I think we're doing something right here.

Ellie's experience demonstrates the paradox at the root of the researcher's role. Data collection is serious work that will take you to a new level of professionalism in your work. But you also need a healthy sense of fun in your inquiry. Allow yourself time to play with the different ways of collecting information, and enjoy the new views of yourself and your students as you begin.

William Stafford captures this sense of being attuned to the moment and finding pleasure in what can be learned through close observation and listening in his poem "You Reading This, Be Ready." We hope you take his advice to turn around in your own classroom. We suspect you'll find, as Ellie did, that collecting data is a gift you give yourself.

### You Reading This, Be Ready
William Stafford

*Starting here, what do you want to remember?*
*How sunlight creeps along a shining floor?*
*What scent of old wood hovers, what softened*
*sound from outside fills the air?*
*Will you ever bring a better gift for the world*
*than the breathing respect that you carry*
*wherever you go right now? Are you waiting*
*for time to show you some better thoughts?*
*When you turn around, starting here, lift this*
*new glimpse that you found; carry into evening*
*all that you want from this day. This interval you spent*
*reading or hearing this, keep it for life—*
*What can anyone give you greater than now,*
*starting here, right in this room, when you turn around?*

## RESEARCH WORKSHOP

## When to Write: Strategies to Find Time for Note Taking

*Brenda Miller Power*

For many teachers, taking notes is the key to their data collection. By observing your classroom closely, slowly compiling information about students and your curriculum over time, you build confidence in your research ability.

When you write will determine what you write and what you remember from day-to-day life in your classroom. As Kim Stafford writes, "Memory is made as a quilt is made. From the whole cloth of time, frayed scraps of sensation are pulled apart and pieced together in a pattern that has a name" (1997, 16).

From the "whole cloth" of everything that occurs in your classroom, you will eventually be piecing together the patterns that form your research findings—the story you will tell. Pick the time of day for note taking when it makes the most sense to gather the pieces of what you see, hear, and feel to tell that story. Determining when to take notes means you'll have to consider many factors: your personality as a teacher, the needs of your students, and the goals for your notes.

Regardless of what the story will be, there are two kinds of observational notes you can take: "in the midst" and "after the fact." It's helpful to test out each of these kinds of notes as you begin to get into a rhythm and routine of observations. You need to figure out when note taking makes the most sense in your classroom, fitting both your goals and the needs of the students.

## *"In the Midst" Notes*

"In the midst" notes are the observations you make while your students are at work. You might write "in the midst" while walking through the room, with your notepad in hand, jotting down what you see. The writing might be on sticky notes, address labels, or one side of a journal page.

If you're trying to find a time when it would make sense for you to take notes, consider those times when you want students to pay less attention to you and more attention to each other. Pat McLure takes notes during two components of the literacy program in her multiage primary classroom.

She writes notes, sitting on the back of the rug, when children read their writing in the author's chair to the whole class. When children glance at the back of the room, they are apt to see Pat writing. This teaches them to focus their attention on the writer in the chair, not on their teacher. Pat will still make comments and redirect the group if needed, but the note taking serves the dual purpose of being a tool for assessing the group and a means to focus the group on the writer and the writing, not on Pat.

The other time Pat takes notes is during student literature discussion groups. Pat is always present when these groups of four meet. Once again, because some of Pat's time is focused on note taking, children attend to each other and the books more than they do to their teacher.

Pat has another, more subtle goal in taking these notes during whole-class and small-group discussion periods. When she meets with parents for assessment conferences, many of her notes highlight how individual children are working within the class community. These notes reflect her value of placing individuals within communities rather than focusing on individual achievement.

Many teachers choose to do their "in the midst" notes with just the opposite purpose. They wander through the class, clipboard in hand, during individual conferences with students. This has almost become the standard for note taking during workshops, and I think it's one of the reasons teachers get frustrated with keeping anecdotal records and often stop doing it. When you're in a one-on-one conference with a student, it's distracting and time consuming to stop and take notes about what is happening. You establish a rhythm while moving among your students, and there is an intensity in those individual conferences that is rarely matched in any other part of the curriculum. You are trying to listen intently to one student and still continually survey what is happening in the rest of the room. Adding note taking to that delicate mix of close attention and rapid, repeated scanning of the room is just too much for most teachers. Taking notes in the midst of students working together discussing their writing or literature, with their attention focused on each other, is much more manageable.

## *"After the Fact" Notes*

"After the fact" notes are made when students aren't present. It might be in the quiet of your classroom early in the morning before students arrive. It might be at home, in the journal you keep on your nightstand to write in just before you fall asleep. It might be on address labels you write on while eating your lunch.

The benefits to writing "after the fact" are many. You can choose a quiet time, without the endless distractions that are always present when you're working with students. What bubbles up in your mind when you are alone, away from students, is likely to be the most important events that day in your classroom. The writing has more of a narrative flow—"after the fact" notes tend to be full sentences, whereas "in the midst" notes are brief, choppy words and phrases most of the time.

But there are also many drawbacks to writing "after the fact." Teachers are not often successful at preserving pockets of time for work that doesn't absolutely need to be done. If you rarely find time for a bathroom break in the morning, it's hard to believe you'll be able to carve out a consistent fifteen minutes of writing while your students are in morning recess.

I find it's best for me to take "after the fact" notes, and I do manage to keep to my routine even though I face the same distractions as any teacher. I meet with students for only three hours a week in each of my college classes, and there isn't a pocket of time in any of those hours where I would be comfortable taking notes. So I write for fifteen minutes after each class. I found that the only way I could develop this habit was to set some artificial rules and limits for myself.

I make myself remain in the classroom. This is important, because just being in the same physical space where I met with students sparks memories of events that occurred. I jot my notes on loose-leaf paper as I write responses to the in-class journals my students have written that day. It usually takes me no more than fifteen minutes to jot down my notes, and at most another fifteen minutes to finish responses to those in-class journals.

The good thing about staying in the classroom is that it strictly limits the time I write in my teaching log and respond to student logs. Another class always comes in within half an hour during the day, and after evening classes I'm eager to get home. When I'm sitting in the classroom, it's quiet and it's easy to reflect on my teaching, but I also feel the clock ticking.

Either "in the midst" or "after the fact" can be effective times for taking notes, depending upon how you work. And as you take notes, you'll find there are fewer boundaries between the two. As you sit in the back of the classroom, jotting down notes during whole-class writing discussions, it's likely you'll make a note or two about something that was said an hour earlier as you circulated during writing conferences.

Once you decide when you're going to write, find ways to preserve that time. This is no small feat for teachers. We want to capitalize on the teachable moments in our classroom, which means it's often hard to stick to routines. And unfortunately, others rarely see the teacher's time as her own. Administrators cavalierly schedule assemblies during writing time, featuring talking moose droning on about dental hygiene; colleagues stop in for a quick cup of coffee during the time they know your students are in music class; a parent can come in for a conference only during a time outside the designated conference period.

With that in mind, the following activities can help you establish some boundaries around the time you set for taking notes and observing students.

***Link when you take notes to your research.*** What times of the day make the most sense for you to take notes to answer your research question? List both potential times for note taking and how note taking during this time is linked to your research. Try to list at least a few potential times when you might take notes in your classroom.

| Research Question | Time for Notes |
| --- | --- |
| _____ | _____ |
| _____ | _____ |
| _____ | _____ |
| _____ | _____ |

***Experiment with "in the midst" and "after the fact" notes.*** Before you lock yourself into a routine of note taking, test out the different times of day you listed for making these notes. This may take a few days or a few weeks, but you'll want to explore which times of day and which kinds of notes work best for your needs.

As you test out different times for taking notes, don't worry much about what you write. Think instead of whether you are able to take notes consistently during these times. After at least a few days of trying to observe and write about students during different times, ask yourself, What period was most comfortable for me to take notes? What might get in the way of my taking notes consistently during this time?

***Initiate a ritual.*** Poet Georgia Heard writes, "Where I write, and the rituals I create for myself there, are crucial for keeping the writing spirit alive in me" (1989, 126). If you want to sustain the spirit of an active, questioning observer of your students, consider developing a few rituals that create a psychic space around the time you reserve for your note taking. It might be the habit of putting on your smock when it's time for your fifteen minutes of notes; it might be moving to your desk to pull out your treasured favorite pen reserved only for your notes (and returning it to that spot after the notes are finished); it might be sitting for a couple of minutes at the rug area in your classroom as students go about their work, thinking about what you'll write. My ritual of writing briefly after my students have left is so ingrained that I really can't leave the classroom until I've finished jotting down notes—my teaching feels incomplete without it.

Think about what rituals might work for you. Is there a hat or scarf you might put on to let students know you aren't to be disturbed as you're writing? Is there a sign you can post on your door during a planning period, to let colleagues know that only emergencies warrant an interruption?

Take a moment to list one or two rituals you could institute to encourage consistency in your note-taking routine.

***Let colleagues and students in on your work.*** If they know you value the time you put into your note taking, they will help you protect that time. Enlist as allies the people who might infringe upon your note-taking time, carefully explaining the purposes of your note taking. Once they understand why you need to protect this time, some students and colleagues will become protective of your note-taking routine. As you're beginning to establish the note-taking routine in your classroom, you'll also want to schedule at least a small number of class discussions explaining why you'll need time for notes and how they will be helpful to the classroom community.

***Save a small amount of time each week to look at all your notes from the week.*** Set aside just a half hour or so in the early weeks of your note taking to look over what you've written and to flesh it out. You can encourage yourself to do this by using project planner paper, which provides you with that extra margin for additional jottings. At least a small part of the time you schedule for your notes needs to be this reflection and cleanup time. If possible, schedule this time with a colleague, and talk together about gaps in your notes and how they might be filled.

## FEATURED TEACHER-RESEARCHER

# Middle School Readers' Mid-Year Surveys

*Katie Doherty*

As a reading teacher, I start each school year by trying to find out as much as I can about the relationship my students have with books and reading. The ever-popular reading survey is a quick and easy way to do that. I have been using reading surveys for the past three of the five years I have been teaching and have always found them to be helpful. I like to give one in the fall and one at the end of the school year. It's an interesting comparison and a helpful measure of what my students have learned about their own reading processes over the year.

This year I used Nancie Atwell's September Reading Survey (2007). I liked the format; the questions addressed a wide range of reading issues from exposure at home to strategies the student uses. I gave the survey to my students within the first week of school and away they went, pencils furiously writing in the information that I hope to find useful. At the start of the school year with sixth graders, however, many of the answers are thin and give very little information other than telling me my students lack the language needed to talk about the reading process and books. These surveys help me see which students have a firm grasp on reading, choosing books, and using strategies and which ones need to tighten their grip a bit. They help me find a place to start.

And now, several months later, we are officially halfway done with this school year. Second-quarter grades have been posted and report cards have been sent. It is like clockwork that at this point in the school year I start to have a mid-year crisis of sorts. I freak out. I think about how much time has gone by and how much more my kids need to learn. I start to think of all the instructional time I have wasted and really start to wonder, Have my students learned anything at all this year? This year, as I was contemplating what has been taught, and where to take my reading instruction, what I was really wondering is what my students have gained so far this year. Are they more competent readers? Do they know what strategies to use when they get stuck? Are they taking anything away from the lessons I teach? And most important, do they enjoy reading more? I was feeling unsure. I thought back to the September reading survey; at the start of the year, very few of my students could name strategies they used as a reader. By the same token, very few could list several books or authors they loved. I decided to give my students another survey. This survey would be similar to the one that I gave them five months earlier, with the purpose being to see what had been learned with regard to the reading process. It would tell me what they had learned so far and, with a comparison to the September reading survey, if they were growing as readers. I wanted to know what my kids were taking away from our seventy minutes of reading class every other day. I wanted to know where to go from here. What lessons needed to be retaught? What were my kids still lacking as readers and lovers of books?

I sat down and wrote up a reading survey that was designed around specific things taught this year as well as the students' personal thoughts about books and the reading process. I revised the survey form (Figure 4.10).

Figure 4.10
Mid-Year Reading Survey

Mid-Year Reading Survey          NAME: _____
Please complete the survey questions honestly and completely.  Thanks!

1. How many books would you say you have read and completed so far since school started? _____

2. How many of these books did you choose for yourself? _____

3. What are the three (3) BEST books you have read this year?

4. What are your favorite genres (realistic fiction, mystery, Fantasy etc) at this time and WHY?

5. Who are your favorite authors you've read this year? WHY?

6. What are some strategies you use when you are CHOOSING a new book to read?

7. What are some reading strategies you use to help you comprehend (understand) the book or text you are reading?

8. Think about reading a book; how do you feel about reading?

9. What are some things that you do if you get stuck or confused while you are reading?

10. What are the three (3) things that you do BEST as a reader?

11. As a reader, what would you like to do better?

12. How do you feel about yourself as a reader?

13. What is the title and who is the author of the book you are reading right now?

14. What are your thoughts about this book?

Adapted from Nancie Atwell, *The Reading Zone* (Scholastic, 2006)

When I handed the survey out to my kids, I was expecting to hear the usual whiney groans of "We did this already, Miss Doherty." But to my surprise, as I was explaining the assignment and the purpose of the mid-year reading survey and the similarities and differences to the September reading survey, what I heard was an almost eager, "Oh, yeah! I remember that!" "Oh, this one's different!" "How long do we get to work on it?" It was as if my sixth graders were excited to write about their thoughts on reading and books. I think they were excited that their knowledge was so important to me.

## *Learning from the Surveys*

This time, their responses were much more fruitful than early in the fall. Many more of my students were able to name authors they liked, whereas in September some couldn't think of anyone. Many students were able to list reading strategies they thought they were getting good at using and WHY the strategies helped them as readers. Some students came up to me and asked, "Do I have to put just three of my favorite books? What if I have more than that?" Looking over the shoulders of my students and reading their mid-year responses was encouraging. It was validating to see that they are learning and growing as readers of books. They are becoming more proficient at talking about books and reading and what they do as readers.

I can't say that every single one of my students wrote an amazing in-depth response that showed they are thoughtful, purposeful readers. Like every class I have those kids who do think deeply and who are truly insightful and understand how and why they read. Then there are those kids for whom it doesn't come as naturally. These kids know they are using strategies when they read and choose books, they are starting to understand and use the language they have for discussing their strategies, and they keep trying. And then there are those kids who seem to need a lot more time to understand the concepts. The kids who are still having trouble choosing books to read and who struggle to like and understand reading and why it's important. But even these children are trying to understand. They are learning how to learn. Like James, for instance, who came up to me while he was completing his survey and asked, "What strategies?" I reminded James that we talk a lot about reading strategies during class and he said, "I know, but I can't remember their names . . . Oh! Can I go look at the chart we made?" He pointed to a chart with three sections: Activating Schema, Making Connections, and Visualizing. Beneath each section were statements written in the words of my students explaining each strategy and why or how it is useful to them.

Of course I let James look at the chart. The reading survey is not a test. It is a way to access the knowledge inside the heads of my students. And even though James doesn't know the strategy names off the top of his head, and even if he can't verbalize why or how they are useful, he does know how to access that information, and he does know that it is an important part of our learning as a class. For me, heading into the second half of this school year, that is an important place for me to start with James. The rest of the surveys, as well as my observations while my students were completing them, hold a plethora of validating, encouraging, and, most important, useful information to guide and strengthen my teaching.

## Reference

Atwell, Nancie. 2007. *The Reading Zone: How to Help Kids Become Skilled, Passionate, Habitual, Critical Readers.* New York: Scholastic.

---

## FEATURED TEACHER-RESEARCHER

## Focusing on Student Talk

*Sherry Young*

The main focus of my research has been on student talk. I am interested in learning how boys and girls use language differently. I also want to know how these differences play a role in students' ability to express their ideas and opinions. My goal has been to find new strategies to help all students find their voice by learning more about the ways they interact in whole-group and small-group situations.

I designed an interview on talk and administered it individually to all my students (see Figure 4.11). I enjoyed the personal contact with them and appreciated the seriousness and honesty with which they gave their answers. It was interesting how differently students interpreted the same question. At other times I noticed how their answers sounded like what they thought their teacher wanted to hear. I heard my voice in their replies.

In two of the interview questions, students indicated strongly that they had heard teacher directions about how to participate in classroom talk. One of these questions was, When you are at school and you want to share something you've learned, what do you do? Two-thirds of the students replied, "Raise your hand." I had had a hunch this might happen, so I asked a follow-up question calling for another way to share. Girls had fewer strategies for what they would do, whereas boys had several ways to get their ideas heard. Two of the nine girls had no response at all.

The second question that generated responses that sounded like my voice was, How do you know when someone is listening to you? This time, sixteen students, or more than two-thirds of the class, said, "When the person is looking at you." This is a strategy I have taught them to use to check whether their audience is ready.

Another set of questions asked about their feelings about speaking or participating in class discussions. More than three-quarters of the students said they felt good about participating in class discussions. Many students said they "liked it" or they "wanted to" contribute, but others hinged their participation on being part of the group. For example, one student said, "It's important. It's part of the community. I feel like I'm part of something important." One girl said, "I feel happy because I can help people." Several

Figure 4.11
Interview

22 students
9 G   13 B

Grade 3          Talk Interview
Name: S. Young                    Date: March  97

1) When you are at school and you want to share something
you've learned what do you do?    Why?
Raise hand = 14      Ask teacher  4          Other  4
   5G   9B              2 G   2B                2G  2B

2) What is another way you share what you know?

* 3) During a class discussion, how do you feel about
participating?
   Good  17          Depends  5         No   0
    7G   10B            2 G   3B

* 4) How do you feel if someone disagrees with what you say?
   O.K.  9        Bad  6        Mad  2      Other  5
   5G 4B          2G 3B          2B        2G  3B

5) What would a teacher do to help a person share their
ideas?

X 6) When you talk to your classmates, do you prefer a small
group, talking to a partner, or a whole class discussion?
Why?  Small  5      Partner  8      Whole  6      Other  3
      3G 2B          4G  4B          1G  5B        2B  1G

X 7) Do you prefer a group of all boys, (or all girls), or a
mixed group of boys and girls?
   Boys            Girls              Mixed  17      Other  1
    2               2                  6 G   11B

8) How do you know when someone is listening to you?
   Looking  at  you  16              Other  6
      7G    9B                        2G  4B

9) What would you like to do better as a speaker?

10) Do you think you are a good speaker?
      Yes  12          No  4          Sometimes  6
       5G  7B           1G  3B          3G  3B

X 7.b     Classmates 9      Grownups 6    Either  7
           4 G    5B          2G  4B       3 G  4B

boys said participating was an important part of learning. One boy said, "It helps me out. Helps me learn!" Another boy said, "If you don't participate, you might not learn something you are supposed to." Students viewed talk as an important part of our class, and most of them seemed to have positive feelings about it. More than half the students considered themselves good speakers.

Another section of the interview dealt with student preferences concerning the groups in which they work. One-third of the students liked working with a partner because it was easier to talk or they trusted their partner to be respectful. Seven of the nine girls preferred working with partners or in small groups. Only one girl liked whole-group learning better, and five of the boys preferred this grouping.

When I asked if they preferred working in a group of the same sex or a mixed group, students were overwhelming in their support for mixed groups. Only two girls and two boys thought they might like to work in groups of the same sex. Students thought it wouldn't be fair to leave out the other sex: "They would want to be part of the group." Many students thought that the mix of boys and girls brought more ideas and more variety to the group. "Different kinds of people, different ideas!" "Boys know stuff girls don't! Girls know stuff boys don't!"

Another question I asked about groups was whether students preferred talking to their classmates or to grown-ups. I asked this question because in an earlier interview about students' home journals, some of them had said that they didn't like talking about books with their parents. During the talk interview, I had the feeling students strongly preferred to talk with their classmates rather than grown-ups, but the final tallies did not show this. Only nine students said they preferred talking to their classmates, and six students said they preferred talking to adults. Seven students said they liked to talk to either classmates or grown-ups. Students thought parents or teachers could help the most when they had a problem.

While I was interviewing my students about talk, I began a new class procedure to observe the talk in our classroom. During our daily morning meeting, I appointed a student observer. The observer's job was to take notes about what he or she saw and heard during this time. I also used sticky notes to record my own comments or observations. Before we left the group, we shared our observations with the rest of the class.

I also had students run small groups while I observed. I did not participate as a talker, only as a watcher. On two occasions I was able to observe while another adult led the group in lessons on art and a discussion of paintings. I contrasted the work of the small group with that of the whole group. I recorded whether boys or girls did the talking, in addition to as much of the conversation as possible.

## FEATURED TEACHER-RESEARCHER

## Assessment: Inside and Outside Views

*Andrea Smith*

Every day children try to remind teachers about an important promise they made when they began their teaching careers:

*Pay attention to what matters.*

Children's wisdom is a gift that grounds me in practicality. Paying attention to what children say and do allows me to uncover what my students need next as learners, and helps me make sense of my work as a teacher. Observations are practical assessments that teachers know how to use to improve instruction.

Recent events tested my view of assessment tools used to capture students' growth and learning. I finished publishing my report cards, and our school "went live" using a new, online grade-book tool that parents and students view from their home computers. After the blur of report cards and the launch of this public grade book, I felt a mixture of confidence and jitters about a communication tool that caused more questions than answers for me as a teacher.

I am happy to share my assessment documentation with parents, but here is my nagging worry: How will a spreadsheet with letter grades or symbols fully explain the growth of my third and fourth graders to others? How will comments added to these spreadsheets capture the living elements of children's learning?

One day during a productive writing workshop, I realized that parents deserved the same conference information I gain when I talk with students. They needed to see their children at work discussing their growth as learners. Witnessing the work and words of children is powerful, so why not add this information to our online grade book? Rather than keeping my conferences as a private "teacher-student moment," I knew the raw film footage of writers at work could reveal many insights about my students, their learning, and our community. I wanted to use video clips in addition to grades to bring our online grade book to life.

I will be honest: I am not the best at using a video camera. I am learning how to ignore the camera and just conduct a conference without sounding staged. Thank goodness kids pull teachers through learning experiences! I've included several conference clips and described the kinds of comments I can now add to my online grade book to support parents' understanding of their children's learning. If you'd like to view these short video clips online, you can see them at www.choiceliteracy.com/public/1156.cfm.

Here are sample reflections I wrote to put the videos from the children in context.

## *Reflecting on Jordan's Work*

Jordan's planning and purpose for his literary nonfiction project seemed evident as he chatted about his gerbil story. Looking back on the past six months together, our lessons about having a vision, a purpose, and a plan for writing seemed evident in Jordan's prewriting work and confidence as he discussed how he moved ahead with this challenging project. Literary nonfiction is not an easy genre for third-grade writers, but Jordan knew how he could maximize his prewriting work by creating his story outline. This tool would then allow him to embed facts within his story as he told the adventure of a child acquiring a new pet.

What do I know about Jordan's progress from this two-minute discussion? When Jordan came to my classroom in September, he wrote like a tornado. He had nine unfinished projects by the end of the first two weeks of school, projects that reflected a writer with strong spelling skills, language abilities, and mastery of conventions. At our first conference, he piled crumpled, dog-eared loose-leaf pages in a chaotic mound in front of me and beamed. "Look how much I've written." He was shocked as we read the stories, because I asked the same questions over and over:

"What is the purpose of this piece?"
"What were you trying to tell the reader?"

I saw writing that resembled a backyard the day after a windstorm; I discovered ideas, words, and possibilities scattered all over, waiting for a purpose. Six months later as I review and write comments about this quick interview, I can describe a writer who harnessed his creative ideas, strong language skills, and desire to share his writing with others. Jordan's grades and report-card comments show a child achieving grade-level standards; this video interview reveals how a confident writer who believes his ideas are worth sharing goes about the writing process. His parents need to know this about him.

Next I chatted with another third grader about how he uses our class wiki to help him as a writer.

## *Reflecting on James's Work*

James arrived in third grade a very skilled, creative, and isolated writer. He wrote only for himself, and did not see the value of feedback or revision. When I initiated the practice of having writing partners to help children consider their writing from different points of view, James seemed frustrated by the arrangement. "I already edited my piece—it's fine," he would often mumble, trying to politely mask his frustration. The idea of improving his work seemed like a waste of his writing time. He was always ready to move on to his next project.

When I introduced my students to our class wiki, things changed for writers like James. As students drafted and revised on our wiki, I presented a series of mini-lessons showing how our writing-buddy feedback could be expanded with the wiki discussion tool. Using our wiki and my classroom smart board, a student would share his or her current writing project. We called them our "mentor-text students." On Day 1, the student shared his or her project and our mini-lessons focused on giving useful and productive feedback. Rather than leaving our lesson with discussion ideas in his or her head or as scribbled notes in a writer's notebook, the mentor-text student left with class feedback stored as a friendly e-mail message on his or her wiki page, using the wiki's powerful discussion elements. On Day 2, the class would view the same mentor-text student's revised work, and then, using the history element of the wiki, we could read the text before and after class feedback. Using the discussion tool and history elements, we could see how feedback influenced and, ideally, improved a writer's work.

This was a defining moment for James and for me. Because he was a highly capable student, I always assumed that James understood what revision meant for the writer, and how it supported the writing process. I was wrong. Watching James's reaction to the power of feedback was startling. He watched other writers take someone else's feedback or revision ideas and personalize it to fit their purpose and writing needs. He discovered that revision was not the sign of a failed piece, but just the beginning of making stronger connections with his audience.

James is a reborn writer. He loves the power of digital writing not only for the speed of word processing, but for the social connections created by our class wiki. The discussion elements united his thinking and his inner journey as a writer with the social network of an audience and a learning community. James's defining moment came during a conference two weeks after introducing our wiki and the discussion tools. "I really like the wiki. It is helping me with my writing, but . . ." He paused and I waited, eager to hear his opinion. "You really should have introduced this to us sooner. I really needed this way of writing." I agreed.

What did I learn about James? At the beginning of the year, I discovered that although James met all the standards and had skills beyond what a child his age was expected to master, he lacked the social connections needed by a responsive writer. It is not enough to use conventions and craft different forms of writing. Writers need to know that people are reading and thinking about their words, caring enough to help them make a piece even better. This is a powerful moment in a writer's development. No matter how hard we work alone, we need the support of others as we write. Not only does it improve our craft, but it leads us to the purposeful sharing of our ideas and questions. No standard will ever match the powerful social connections shared by a writing community.

Finally, I met with two writing partners to see how their conversation about drafting story leads was helping them move ahead as writers.

## *Reflecting on Partner Work*

Both girls arrived in third grade as eager students with very little confidence about their writing. Some days, after a student would share his or her work in progress during a mini-lesson to showcase my teaching point, these two girls would use the mentor text as a template and their own work would mirror the shared piece. On other days the girls would churn and spin, stalling until I met with them and cheered them on to select an idea and write. Getting words on a page seemed daunting to them unless I coached them to leap "off the riverbank" and plunge into the "river" of the writing process, as I often joke with my kids. (My kayaking experiences give me plenty of analogies for the classroom!)

What did the video clip reveal to me about the growth of these two writers? How did these writers gain the confidence to share independent ideas, listen to feedback, and then have the nerve to apply the feedback to revise their leads? Many opportunities influence writers in a workshop classroom. Let's be honest: my instruction played a very small part. I read about kayaking and listen to the experts, but the best learning comes when I am faced with a moving kayak and a really tough set of rocks. The bigger shift came for these growing writers as they navigated the writing process with their writing partner. Sitting face-to-face with someone and asking, "How can I make this piece better?" is a big leap off the riverbank. Bigger shifts happen when a writer is asked to help a peer make sense of his or her work. Less confident writers bloom when they realize they are members of a writing team. A writing partner provides the same relationship that partners share in a two-person kayak: you work out a plan and you stay afloat, and if you get stuck, it's up to you and your partner to move the kayak or flip over. Children grow by leaps and bounds when they navigate the tough parts of writing. They grow even more when both writers "flip over," thrash around in a mess of rocks, finally manage to find the sky again, *and* get down the river. The happiest kayakers are often the wettest, just as our growing writers are the ones who toughed it out and found the words or the way around writing challenges.

## *Final Assessment*

What did my students teach me through their videotaped conferences? I will continue to use writing rubrics, conferences, face-to-face conversations, weekly family newsletters, and trimester reports as tools to inform parents about their children's learning experiences and progress. In addition to these tested communication tools, my students and their parents will now track our learning using the online grade book and our recorded conferences. How will my instruction improve as a result of these assessments?

I need to take ownership and guide the shared element of assessment if I want parents to understand the true value and meaning of assessment in the lives of children. Parents need to see a workshop classroom from the inside to fully understand the resources teachers use to monitor student growth. It is not acceptable for me to be complacent, worried, or negative about a partial assessment tool such as an online grade book. It is no different from being stuck or rolled on a tough part of a moving river, and it is up to me to manage how student learning and assessment tools are shared. Telling parents about learning is not enough; showing parents how kids are navigating the world is powerful.

Kids are smart, and they remind us to pay attention to what matters. Watching them learn reminds us that our classrooms are about the journey and the accomplishments. This is a lesson I am happy to revisit and share every day as I work and learn side-by-side with my students.

# 5

# What Likes What?
# Data Analysis

*The joy of seeing connections and patterns is a physiological thing,
documented by neuroscience. The brain loves to make connections and
patterns out of things. And particularly, it loves to make them more than it
loves to have somebody else show it, and that's where I think we miss the
boat sometimes as teachers; we forget that the real thrill is in the discovery.*

—JAN MAHER

Remembering the joy of discovery is one of the hidden gifts of teacher
research, a chance to delight in (and be inspired by) patterns as they
emerge. As Ellie Gilbert noted in Chapter 4 (see page 119), "The more I
notice, the more I write down. And the more I write down, the more I notice.
Going through my handwritten notes, trying to decide what likes what, I . . .
suddenly see this beautiful pattern emerge, and as I move in for a closer look,
I find smaller, tighter webs within the web: concentrations of connections."

## Finding Patterns in Data

In the novel *Cold Mountain*, by Charles Frazier, Ada apprentices herself to
another woman, Ruby, to learn everything she can about working and living
in the world around her. She is amazed at how much Ruby knows—how she
can answer almost any question with quiet calm. Ada finally asks her where
all her knowledge comes from:

> How did you come to know such things? Ada had asked. Ruby said she
> had learned what little she knew in the usual way. A lot of it was grand-
> mother knowledge, got from wandering around the settlement and talking
> to any old woman who would talk back, watching them work and asking
> questions. Some came from helping Sally Swanger, who knew, Ruby
> claimed, a great many quiet things such as the names of all plants down to

the plainest weed. Partly, though, she claimed she had just puzzled out in
her own mind how the world's logic works. It was mostly a matter of
being attentive. You commence by trying to see what likes what, Ruby said.
Which Ada interpreted to mean, Observe and understand the workings of
affinity in nature. (1997, 107)

The categories Ruby uses to define where her knowledge comes from are
all helpful in thinking about data analysis. The "grandmother knowledge" is
the stuff you've always known at some intuitive level. Don't discount it as a
researcher; draw upon it. For teacher-researchers, it's all right to ignore some
of the traditional research edicts such as, "If you didn't write it down, it didn't
happen." You can draw on all of your experiences and observations of kids,
throughout your history as a teacher, to analyze the data in your current
project.

Once you become comfortable trusting some of your hunches in data
analysis, you need your own "Sally Swanger"—someone you trust as an interested friend who is willing to pore over your data and findings with you,
unafraid to challenge what doesn't make sense. In Chapter 8, we show how
teachers find research partners and build communities. Although it's possible
to collect data quietly on your own for months of a study, it's essential to have
someone willing to listen to your first ideas about findings, looking over your
shoulder at the same data set as you show the path of your thinking.

But the biggest part of data analysis involves Ruby's last piece of advice:
learning to see "what likes what." These are the patterns in your work, the pieces
of data that fit unexpectedly next to each other, leading to flashes of insight. It's
an organic process, one of learning to be comfortable with what works for you
in analyzing data and what doesn't. This was the experience of Ann Hurd as she
found herself uneasy through much of the early stage of her research:

> The research has produced a variety of reactions in me. I experienced anx-
> iety as I tried to develop a topic. More anxiety as I was advised to trust
> what bubbled up as I taped. More anxiety as there appeared to be nothing
> and deadlines loomed. Yet each time I looked at the transcripts, I began to
> see what I hadn't seen before. To do this, though, I had to work with
> handwritten words and not computer-processed words. I had to lay out
> my pages of type where I could see them all at once, mark them, and gen-
> erally make a mess. From there I could create order.

Finding the patterns within your data, viewing each bit of information as
part of a larger puzzle you must put together, is the task that will take most
of your time during data analysis.

# "Appearance Versus Reality"

Looking closely at our data can give us a reality check on what's really going
on in terms of our students and their learning. When we get discouraged, it

can be useful to revisit students' work and note their growth and progress. High school teacher Emily Gromko was researching "What happens when my tenth-grade language arts students set semester-long reading goals?" (See Chapter 3, page 79 for Emily's complete research design.) She writes about her experience in her essay called "April's Appearance Versus Reality":

> I had been feeling a little melancholy earlier this week, as it seemed the students hadn't been progressing as they potentially could be with their reading and writing. Part of my unease related to their reading and goals. I updated their reading goals and noticed again how many students wanted to "read one good book . . ." over five months. This exposes how little they read, or perhaps how little they feel they read "good books." Maybe they don't connect the group texts we read to being good. I wonder if they consider only the books they choose to read "good." Did they think *Of Mice and Men* was good? Their thoughts, commentary, and disbelief about plot and character seem to say they did. Will they think *Persepolis* is a good book? One question my research is leading me to is what defines a good book for them. I want to include this question in an end-of-the-semester evaluation of their reading.
>
> After meeting with students over the last month and reading their reading journals, I did a recent note-card check-in about their goals, and feel a little uplifted and less tense about their progress after examining and charting their comments. (See charts, Figures 5.1a and 5.1b.) I notice that more than 50 percent of the students in each class think they are well on their way to meeting their goal by June. In fact, in my second-period class, 78 percent of them think they are well on their way to meeting their goal. A few have already met their goals and reset them. Very few—far fewer than I thought once I charted it—are not moving toward their goals. The reality of their progress is much different from what it appears to be in the classroom. Overwhelmingly, students are thinking about their goals and working toward them.
>
> A sampling:
> - Jordan, whose goal is to read different genres, writes, "on track, just started another book."
> - Nichelle, whose goal is to finish a book, writes, "close, just need to be a little more motivated."
> - Raymond, whose goal is to read a series of five books, writes, "have finished 3 out of 5."
> - Ricky, whose goal is to read 20 books, writes he's "at book 17, should have had a harder goal."
> - Marquise, whose goal is to read a book all the way through writes, "62% there."
> - Matt, whose goal is to read 3 books, writes, "met goal and reset goal to read 2 sci-fi books."
> - Stanley, whose goal is to read two books, "feels far away from meeting it."
> - Matthew, whose goal is to read two books and become a faster reader, writes that he "kind of forgot about it."

Figure 5.1a

| Seventh Period | Second-Semester Reading Goals | | 4/2011 |
|---|---|---|---|
| **Quantity** | **Time** | **Attitude** | **Choosing Books ("Find a Book I Like")** |
| Maria—5 | Steven— 2 x week★ | Michael—✪ enjoy it more | Forrest✪ |
| Calum—3★ and better reader | | Shakyla—✓ get back into it | José★ |
| Stanley—2✓ and faster | | Isabella— read more w/open mind at home | Antoine✓ |
| Erika—2✓ | | | Jessie✪ |
| Matthew—2✓ and faster | | | Sean |
| Tavin—Series★ | | | Alex★ |
| Juan—1★ and improve reading comp. | | | |
| Barby—at least 1★ | | | |
| Laif—finish book★ | | | |
| Jerryd— >1 book | | | |
| Matt S.—2 sci-fi ✪ | | | |
| 11 | 1 | 3 | 6 **21** |

12/21 have met or are on track to meet (57%); 5/21 need more support to meet (24%)
✪ = Met
★ = Working toward goal
✓ = Not on track

Figure 5.1b

| Second Period Quantity | "Find a Good Book" | Types of Reading | Different Genres |
|---|---|---|---|
| **Second Period** Quantity | **Second-Semester Reading Goals** "Find a Good Book" | Types of Reading | **4/2011** Different Genres |
| Jason—2✓ | Andrey★ | Eric★ Read more | Jordan★ |
| Ricky—20★ from a series | Emma★ | Alberto★ More that "pull me in" | |
| Kayla—8★ from 5 | Jovi—5 to enjoy✪ | | |
| Brandon—4★ from 3 | | | |
| Raymond—5★ | | | |
| Brenda—2 | | | |
| Nichelle—1★ | | | |
| Jaquan—1✓ | | | |
| Frank—1★ | | | |
| Jared—1 | | | |
| Tera—1★ | | | |
| Brandon D.—1★ | | | |
| Derek—1★ | | | |
| Kevin— >1★ | | | |
| Abraham—2✓ | | | |
| Marquise—1★ | | | |
| Julian—1★ | | | |
| 17 | 3 | 2 | 1          **23** |

✪ = Met  
★ = Working toward goal  
✓ = Not on track  

18/23 (78%) = Met or on track to meet  
4/23 (17%) = Need more support to get on track

- Michael, whose goal is to shift his attitude about reading, writes that he "no longer think[s] of it as a chore."
- José, whose goal is to find a book he likes, writes, "I have found an interesting book and I am currently done. Finding a book to like and enjoy was hard."

Looking over their comments and thinking about conversations I've had with them, and the writing they've done in their reading folders, I have evidence of the students working toward their reading goals. Maybe it feels like a chore for some, but meeting a goal feels good for anyone. I hope it's motivating them.

My next steps are to check in with students who need more support—Abraham, Jaquan, Jason, Matthew, Stanley, Shakyla, Antoine—to see how I can help them. I want to continue to encourage students these last months and craft a thoughtful, thorough self-evaluation so I have feedback about the goal setting. And I want to put a big "I met my goal!" sign on the wall and start writing their names on it. That tangible evidence will help energize and celebrate students' efforts, and will serve to remind them to keep working toward their goals.

When Emily shared her progress with her teacher-research support group (the League of Teacher Researchers), she noted what a surprise the data was. "Things were going *much* better than I thought! It's such a reminder of why actually keeping track is so important. It was such a reality check."

Second-grade teacher Sarah Christenson also found a difference between her global perceptions of her students' progress and what her data revealed. She photocopied pages from their take-home writing journals from early September and mid-April to look at how their writing had changed. "For the ones who actually return their journals on a daily basis, I was, more often than not, pleasantly surprised." She notes:

Jake is beginning to make progress with the amount of writing he is doing each night. There are . . . more words, more words are spelled correctly, more lowercase letters are used than uppercase. [See Figure 5.2.]

Hunter is writing nearly the same amount each night since the beginning of the year. His handwriting is getting better and overall his writing is becoming more developed. [See Figure 5.3.]

I can read Ryan's writing!!!!! Ryan is writing more, capitals and lowercase letters are used almost correctly, as well as punctuation. [See Figure 5.4.]

Like Emily, Sarah was encouraged when she looked closely at what the data revealed. And looking at the difference in a student's writing samples over six months is an easy way to get that important reality check on what's really going on with student growth and progress.

One important bit of advice is not to wait until you've collected all your data to analyze it. Those "reality checks" often set in motion your next steps. It's an ongoing process—and can be daunting as the piles of data grow.

Figure 5.2
Jake's Data

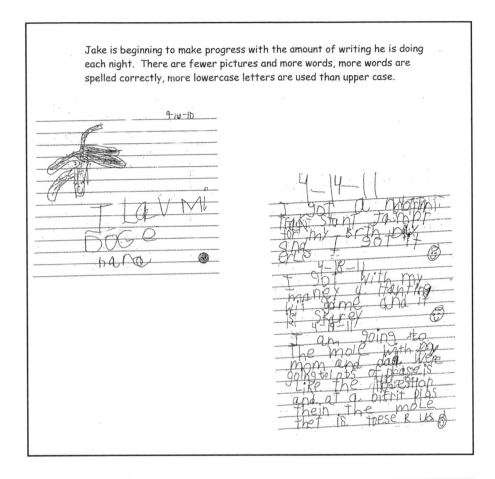

Jake is beginning to make progress with the amount of writing he is doing each night. There are fewer pictures and more words, more words are spelled correctly, more lowercase letters are used than upper case.

Figure 5.3
Hunter's Data

Hunter is writing nearly the same amount each night since the beginning of the year. His handwriting is getting better and overall his writing is becoming more developed.

Figure 5.4
Ryan's Data

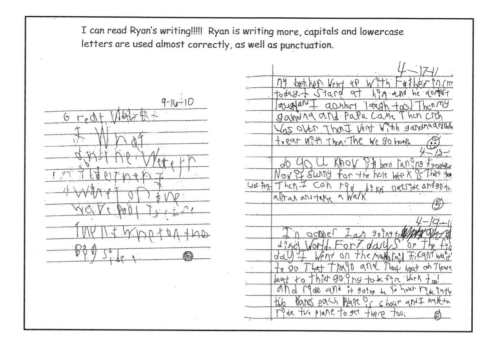

As researcher Dana Cox writes, "Data is a burden in that you've got so much of it. It's very much like taking twenty pounds of mashed potato and shoving it through a straw." Like Cox, we may shake our heads in despair at that mountain of "mashed potato" and the enormous task of funneling it through a straw. Paradoxically, we quickly see many gaps in our notes, interviews, and artifacts, and regret all the information that wasn't collected. There is often a rush of insecurity at this point in the research process. It's one thing to write faithfully in a teaching journal for months or conduct a slew of interviews with kids; it's quite another to say with confidence what all the Big Truths are, culled from the information you've gathered.

The murkiness of data analysis is what scares any researcher. If it doesn't spook you at least a little, you're not opening yourself up enough to the new learning that can come during analysis. If the analysis seems very easy, you've probably found only what you already knew before the project began.

Analyzing your data thoroughly comes with a fair degree of uncertainty. Human relations are complex, so any analysis of what goes on in a classroom teeming with kids will end up with some unknowns and ambiguities. Good research analyses raise more questions than they answer. If you are a neat and orderly teacher, you have to be willing to wrestle with a little more messiness in your life as you analyze your data. Susan Ohanian writes about this need for disorder:

> Only the territorialists to the right and left of us seem to know Truth.
> They are like Louise, a character in Josephine Humphrey's *Fireman's Fair*,
> who finds her pleasure in the "maintenance of daily order in the real
> world. She kept her shoes in the original boxes." Too much of what travels

under the name of research is concerned with keeping the shoes in the
original boxes. For classroom research to be significant, the teacher needs
to take the risk of getting those shoes out of the boxes. She needs to ask
herself a lot of hard questions and in the end learn to accept the ambiguity
of the answers. (1993, 33)

Although it's hard for anyone to "get the shoes out of the boxes" and tolerate
unanswered questions, we'd argue that teachers are better equipped for this
task than many university researchers and administrators. You need to accept
change, uncertainty, and complexity to survive as a teacher for any length of
time. Whether you realize it or not, you probably developed long ago the
ability to see events in your classroom as far more complicated than they
would appear to an outside observer.

Data analysis over the past two decades for teacher-researchers has
changed from a few limited options, defined by university researchers, to a
range of creative strategies developed by teacher-researchers who find that
traditional analysis methods didn't make sense in their studies.

---

**Common Analysis Terms and Methods**

*Audit check*—A check or confirmation of your findings by someone
outside the research process. This can be done at any point in the
process.

*Member check*—A check or confirmation of your findings by
someone involved in the research process. This is often done
after an initial analysis of interviews or other data sets and
asking a few informants if the data rings true. It can also be done
after a write-up to make sure participants think their quotes and
examples are in context. This can be done at any point in the
research process.

*Case study*—A detailed, in-depth examination of a person or people
from a specific group.

*Confirmability*—Often used in place of the term *objectivity* by qualitative researchers; refers to the ability of others to reach similar
conclusions with the same data set.

*Constant comparison*—A data-analysis method developed by Glaser
and Strauss (1967) to "enable prediction and explanation of
behavior"; involves deriving categories from data over time, and
then using the categories to build theory.

*Crystallization*—A method of analysis that includes creative forms of
representation to tap deeper thinking. The method, as detailed
by Laurel Richardson (1994), uses crystals as a metaphor to
describe the data-analysis process.

*Grounded theory*—A research method in which the theory is developed from the data rather than the other way around. The
method is based on concepts and categories rather than in
working from hypotheses.

*Sociogram*—A picture of a social network.

*Thick description*—A sufficient amount of detail in describing the research setting and techniques to allow others to make needed comparisons to research completed in other settings.

*Transferability*—Often used by qualitative researchers in place of the concept of "external validity"; relies on thick description of relevant research to allow outsiders to determine if findings could be transferred to other settings.

*Triangulation*—The use of multiple and different sources, methods, investigators, or theories (at least three) to confirm findings.

*Working hypothesis*—Often substituted for the concept of "generalization" in qualitative research, because hypotheses will change as data continue to be analyzed in research.

# Choosing a Data-Analysis Method

## *Narratives*

In their collaborative teacher-research project in Georgia, Betty Bisplinghoff, JoBeth Allen, and Barbara Michalove spent a year collecting data around issues of using home-school journals in Betty's first-grade classroom and with Barbara's second-grade students. They developed codes for their data based upon the constant comparison analysis method, a respected and well-known method of data analysis for qualitative researchers:

> We studied home-school journals, written family stories, oral stories, and other artifacts. JoBeth had been studying grounded theory and suggested we use the fine-grained coding of the constant comparison method. We spent several days reading about the methodology, coding four sets of transcripts together, and generating an extensive code list. We agreed to code the other sets on our own and meet weekly to compare our analyses.
>
> We were all unhappy with the process. Betty came to the next meeting with a new plan. We agreed that we were losing the children, their families, and the real stories by reducing these rich exchanges to codes. Betty suggested, and we immediately adopted, a plan to read all the data about one child/family unit independently, write a one- to three-page narrative interpretation, and come together weekly to read and compare our analytic narratives. Studying a well-established methodology led to the creation of a new approach, a methodology that was responsive to this particular study, its participants, and its goals. (Bisplinghoff and Allen 1998, 65)

The Georgia research team respected different ways of analyzing data and read widely to find different models. But in the end they didn't discount their feelings of discomfort when a method wasn't working for them, and they were quick to discard it.

## *Codes*

What one teacher-researcher discards, another pulls from the trash heap, revises, and uses. Lee Anne Larsen and Sherry Young are primary teachers in Maine who decided to undertake a research project studying the effects of home-school journals on their relationships with students. Unlike the Georgia researchers, they found developing codes early in the process essential for their analysis of data: a code sheet for analyzing the responses children and parents gave in the home-school journals.

Research still seems like a linear process to most of us—finding a research question, collecting data, and then analyzing what is found. Lee Anne and Sherry found they could organize and understand their data best by beginning with preliminary codes for the data, based upon what other researchers had found in a similar study. Figures 5.5–5.7 show their blank code sheet, a filled-in code sheet, and a summary of the response.

Figure 5.5
Blank Code Sheet

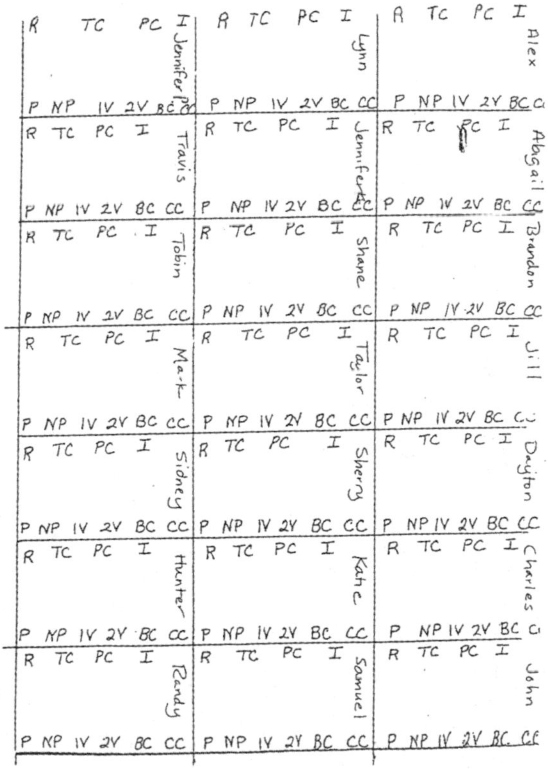


**Codes Explanation**

Top of entry
R = Retelling Only
TC = Theme Connection
PC = Personal Connection
I = Illustration

Bottom of entry
P = Parent Participation
NP = No Parent Participation
1V = 1 Voice Response
2V = 2 Voice Response
BC = Book Connection
CC = Child Connection

Figure 5.6
Filled-in Code
Sheet

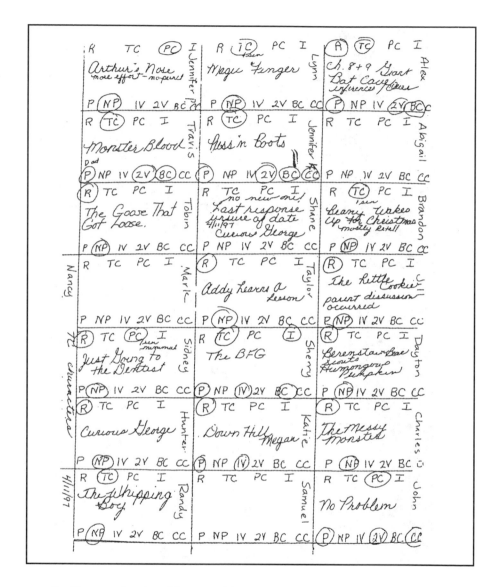

Coding can begin with something as simple as plus and minus marks on the page. This was the case for Debbie Glazier, a Title I reading teacher who was doing a case study of Andy:

One day, in the middle of October, I was rereading my notes from the previous few weeks. I have set up my journal to write on only the left side of the page: the right side is for comments. I picked up my pen and started making plus (+) signs next to all the times Andy was "with" us; reading a book, writing in his response journal, listening to a read-aloud, or speaking in an appropriate classroom situation (asking or responding to questions, etc.). I put a minus (-) sign next to all the times he did not appear to be "tuned in."

Figure 5.7
Summary of
Responses

Reading Journal Response Information

| Name | Week of 3/2/07 | Week of 3/27/07 | Week of 4/10/07 | Week of 4/11/07 | Week of 4/24/07 | Week of 5/1/07 to 5/5/07 |
|---|---|---|---|---|---|---|
| Retelling Only | ‖‖‖ ‖‖‖ | ‖‖ ‖‖ | ‖‖ ‖‖‖ | ‖‖‖ ‖‖‖ | ‖‖ ‖‖ | ‖‖ ‖‖ |
| Personal Connection | ‖‖ ‖‖‖ | ‖‖-‖ | ‖‖‖ ‖ | ‖‖ | ‖‖‖ | ‖‖‖ |
| - Feelings | ‖‖‖ | ‖‖‖ | ‖ | ‖ | ‖ | |
| - Opinion | ‖‖‖ | ‖‖‖ baby book | ‖‖‖ | ‖‖ | ‖‖‖ | |
| - Past Exper. | ‖ | | | ‖ | | ‖ |
| · Asked quest. | | | | | | |
| | | | | | | |
| Text Connection | ‖‖‖ | ‖‖‖ ‖ | ‖‖‖ ‖‖ | ‖‖‖ ‖‖‖ | ‖‖‖ | ‖‖‖ |
| - Character | ‖ | ‖‖ | ‖‖‖ | ‖‖‖ ‖ | ‖ | ‖ |
| - Setting | | | ‖ | | | |
| - Plot | ‖‖ | | ‖ | | ‖‖‖ | |
| - Theme | | | | | | |
| - Moral/Lesson | ‖ | genre ST | | | ‖ | ‖ |
| - Another Book | | ‖ | | | | ‖ |
| - Author Style | | ‖ | | ‖ | | |
| - Genre | ‖‖ | | ‖‖ | | ‖ | |
| - Prediction | | | | ‖ | | |
| - Asked Quest. | | ‖‖‖ | | | | ane. quest |
| - New Learning | | | | | | |
| | | | | | | |
| Illustration | | ‖ | | | | |
| - Personal | | ‖ | | | | |
| - Text | | | | | | |

Reading through these new additions to my journal, I began to add words and phrases, noticing if Andy was focusing his attention on another student, or on an object on his desk. Next to the pluses, I noted what specifically drew him into an activity: a tape recorder, a student reading her story in the author's chair, a picture book read-aloud with plenty of humor.

It was a turning point for me in my classroom-based research. I wrote in my journal on September 6, "It's going to be important for us to get Andy to read and write for longer periods of time." That was the initial period when I was recording how many seconds or minutes he actually stayed with an activity. That particular day, he stayed less than two minutes with a book he had chosen to read.

I'm still using clock time to emphasize the length of time he is able to sustain an activity, but my emphasis now is on the positive happenings in Andy's responses. Because of the daily journal entries with their quick pluses and minuses right next to the description of activities, I feel I have a fast and easy way of retrieving the day's high points. What enables Andy to be successful today drives tomorrow's decision making for teaching.

For Debbie, codes were a way to link her classroom research to teaching in powerful and more immediate ways.

## HOW TO

# Cook Your Notes

Anthropologists refer to two types of field notes—"raw" and "cooked." Raw notes are just what you've written, as quickly as possible, without any analysis. Cooked notes are the analysis of these raw materials.

One simple scheme for cooking involves codes developed originally by the famed anthropologist Levi-Strauss (adapted by Corsaro 1981). We recommend the use of three of these codes:

PN     personal notes
MN     methodological notes
TN     theoretical notes

Personal notes include any information relevant to your mood or that of the class. Events such as an argument before school with a colleague, or a child vomiting in class ten minutes before you began note taking, will affect the notes you take, and it's good to include these to jog your memory later about why the notes for that day might be unusual. Methodological notes include any questions or statements about how you're doing your work. They might be statements such as, "I should put a tape recorder by the science center to get those interactions" or "Maybe students should keep logs of questions asked during literature discussions."

Theoretical notes include any hunches about patterns or why events are occurring as they are. A theoretical note might be as formal as "I think Tadd's behavior after time in special education supports Kohn's notions about the danger of external reward systems." But most are less formal—they are those "aha" moments that are essential to good teaching. These might include statements such as, "Perhaps Jason's frustration in science is caused by the fact that he has been absent so much in the past two weeks. The group seems unwilling to bring him up-to-date on the project."

Cooking notes can also be as simple as adding questions to them, to extend and expand your thinking about what you are seeing. The Latin root of the word *theory* means "to see or behold." Cooking with questions in mind extends your sight about what patterns are emerging. Questions to consider while cooking your notes might include, Why did I think this was important to write down? How does this connect with what I saw earlier in the day, week, year? Based upon what I'm seeing, what action should I take to change the curriculum or my research project?

These questions can easily be abbreviated in your notes. For example, thinking about the importance of what you're noting becomes *I?* as an inserted code. Issues of curricular change become *C?* as a code. Potential additions to assessment narratives become *A?* as a code. What you're trying to do is develop a mind-set that constantly questions as you write your notes—that is what cooking is all about for researchers.

Codes for notes can be developed at almost any point in the research process. Some projects lend themselves to early coding; others require a large chunk of data to be analyzed before the codes can emerge.

When deciding upon codes for your work, start with these principles:

- As a general rule, develop no fewer than three codes and no more than six. Regardless of your research project, if you have too few codes, you are probably thinking of the categories and patterns in your data too broadly. And if you have too many codes, you will struggle to keep track of them.
- Don't be afraid to change, shift, or abandon specific codes that are no longer useful. A code that makes sense early in a project may not be useful by the end. Also, if you get too rigid about using certain codes, you might miss important new codes that would serve better.
- Try to represent the patterns emerging from your codes visually. This is a good test to see if your codes are really helping you understand your classroom. If there isn't some way to move from the codes to a visual representation of what the codes are showing you (for example, a pie chart of different kinds of responses in math workshop or a bar graph of who responds when during whole-group writing discussions), then you will probably struggle to move from your codes to findings later in the research.

## HOW TO

### Analyze Audio Recordings Without Doing Full Transcriptions

- Listen to recordings, and note what strikes you. This can be done during the odd moments of the day—while you are commuting, doing yardwork, fixing supper.
- Flag only the comments of a case-study informant.
- Have students listen to the recordings and analyze what is going on. If you choose this technique, you might want to frame the activity with a

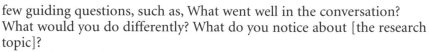

few guiding questions, such as, What went well in the conversation? What would you do differently? What do you notice about [the research topic]?

- Note only topic changes.
- Note only who controls the conversation.

All these techniques take far less time than full transcriptions, and in the end, they may give you all the information you need for your particular study.

## *Memos*

It can often help to look through your data and choose one of your findings to write up in a brief narrative, a memo to share with other teacher-researchers. This helps you focus your thoughts and begin to write up your data along the way. One teacher-research group conducting case studies of English language learners (ELLs) in their classrooms relied on these memos—which they called one-pagers—as the conversation starters for each monthly gathering.

"Abdia Aden is fresh from the Bantu region of Somalia," Samae wrote in her monthly "one-pager."

"She's 15, has a delightful smile, and without sharing words, I can tell she has a sweet heart. Every day she has the same T-shirt on with her favorite soccer player, El Hadji Diouf, and wraps her head in a red scarf. I can't imagine what must be going on in her head. This America that she has come to live in is as different from her home village as tint white is to shade black."

Melody, another member of Samae's group, explains the concept of memos in their coauthored article "New Teacher Researcher Conversations: Understanding English Language Learners and Ourselves":

> Our "one-pagers" are brief memos that we write for each of our teacher-researcher meetings. The memos are narratives about the themes we see emerging, the questions we have about our study, or even first-draft ramblings from our teaching journals. We make copies for everyone and read them aloud and discuss each one as a way to frame our research conversations. We also read excerpts to illustrate our classroom discoveries when we share our work with teachers and teacher educators. (Bro et al. 2006, 9)

In the actual writing of these memos, teachers often have insights into their research. For example, Melody wrote in one memo about her struggle to understand Carlos, a student in her high school art class:

> He has now been here for about three months, and I have noticed several language characteristics about him. His native language is not Spanish, as I had assumed, but rather an indigenous Honduran language, which in its written form looks like a combination of Asian characters and Egyptian hieroglyphs. He seems to be verbally fluent in Spanish, but is very reluc-

tant to write in Spanish. Also, even three months in, I rarely hear him even try to communicate in English and have never seen him write anything in English at this point. Maybe learning and using language is like learning to walk: it percolates in the brain and body, and then all of a sudden you are just doing it.

With Carlos it is always a struggle to convey content concepts, even when I use my limited Spanish and have students do complete translations for me. I wonder if Carlos, in his timidity with language use, is equating all learning with his struggle to learn English. His mantra seems to be *"No me puedo"* (I can't do it). Every day it is a challenge to get him on task, and even then I usually have to nudge him back to work several more times within the period. He works best when I am sitting working on his art-work with him, and when I am not, he needs reassurance with each next step or color change. He is unfortunately treating art like math, as if there is only one right answer and I hold the golden key to it. Of the three assignments he has done, two of them have been traced rather than drawn from his own imagination, and the third is a design that I created while trying to show him an example of how he could do it.

*In reading this I understand my challenge with Carlos more clearly.* I become complicit in his "No me puedo" mentality when I give him the answers, which I do regularly out of frustration in wanting him to stay on task. I need to quit giving him the "answers" and start challenging him to think for himself and experiment more artistically. Maybe if he becomes bolder in his artistic expression, he will become bolder with his language learning and use.

In writing her memo, Melody came to an important insight about her own "complicity" in Carlos's passive stance toward learning in her class-room. The writing—and discussion of her memo with her teacher-research support group—helped her frame next steps with Carlos, as well as with other students in her classroom. (For more information on writing memos, see the Research Workshop in Chapter 7, "Seeing What Is Not Seen," Suggestion 3.)

## *Crystallization*

"Crystallization" is an intriguing approach in qualitative research that has emerged in recent years as a kind of three-dimensional data-analysis strategy that welcomes the new lens that artistic thinking can bring to research, whether it is storytelling, painting, poetry writing, metaphor, or photography (Ellingson 2009; Janesick 1998; Richardson 1994). It expands the field of data collection and analysis. Crystallization makes room for those creative leaps in thinking that teacher-researchers need to help ground their work.

The term *crystallization* was coined by Laurel Richardson as a method of analysis that includes creative forms of representation in order to tap deeper thinking. The method, as detailed by Richardson, uses crystals as a metaphor to describe the data-analysis process:

> [Crystallization] combines symmetry and substance with an infinite
> variety of shapes, substances, transmutations, multidimensionalities, and
> angles of approach. . . . Crystallization provides us with a deepened, com-
> plex, thoroughly partial understanding of the topic. Paradoxically, we
> know more and doubt what we know. (Richardson 1994, 522)

Other researchers since Richardson have built on her original work.
Valerie Janesick (1998) has used this method extensively in her work with
researchers, with the idea that the researcher uses other disciplines to help
understand findings. By including different genres such as storytelling,
poetry, artistic expression, visual thinking, live performance, and so on, we
have more and more angles of vision on a particular topic of research question (Ellingson 2009).

Crystallization offers the possibility of representing ways to produce
knowledge about a particular phenomenon through generating a deepened,
complex interpretation.

For example, Jessie Early (2010) was working with a group of new
teachers. She was seeking to understand what is central to them in their
teaching. Rather than discuss or journal about "what is central in my
teaching," she asked them for two stories.

First, "Tell me about a time this year when you felt like you were born to
teach."

A woman Early refers to as "Joanie" told the following story: "It was just
really simple: we were all sitting on the floor, and I finished reading a book to
the kids, and I said, 'OK, turn to one or two people near you and start talking
about your questions.' You know they're all sitting there talking—and I was
walking through them, kind of just sitting down and listening to some of
their questions and seeing everybody chatting with each other. That was
really—things like that are: ok, this is good."

"And on the other hand," Jessie said, "Tell us a story about a time when
you were in the classroom and you wished you'd never been born."

Joanie: (laughter) "Yeah, those happen, too. Let me think. In my last-
period class of the day, one time, I went through a whole lesson and explained
something and gave them time to work on it, and right away someone raised
her hand and said, 'Um, I don't understand. What were we supposed to do
here?' I had to explain again. And then another kid raised his hand—pretty
soon, there are 10 kids coming up to me and saying, 'I don't understand.
What do we do?' And then I just knew, Gosh . . . I didn't do this right, this isn't
ok, I don't know what else to say. I just felt kind of frustrated and bad about
myself—because I obviously didn't do a very good job communicating.
Maybe it's a bad lesson. And I thought, 'What do I do now?'"

So, with these two stories in mind, Jessie asked Joanie another question
to take the conversation a little deeper: "Do you see any relationship between
those two stories?"

"I guess I was just thinking what I see in my experience when I felt really
good about it, it was that I was so excited to see that they were independent
learners. . . . And I think that when it is frustrating is when they don't take the

ball and run with it. It's when they really need me to almost do it for them. I guess that would be the big thing. The best parts about teaching for me, the best days, are when the kids are really creating the lesson and they're really taking the learning themselves."

So, what Jessie discovered is central to Joanie's philosophy is a belief in children being able to be independent learners. When Joanie told these two stories and compared the beliefs they represented, she engaged in a different kind of introspection, an analysis using "crystallization."

Middle school teacher Carra Barratt found crystallization useful in uncovering a new perspective in her research on how audience affects her student writers. At her teacher-research support group meeting, one of the teachers brought a collection of pictures cut from old calendars: black-and-white as well as color photographs and art reproductions, from abstract art to still-life bowls of fruit to close-up images of people in a variety of settings. Each teacher-researcher chose an image and used it as a metaphor to describe their findings in a ten-minute quick-write. Carra chose a picture of a costume ball with revelers celebrating on a balcony:

> My picture is of some excited characters at a masquerade ball, celebrating and waving from a balcony exploding with streamers and confetti. Some wear masks, and others are elaborately dressed. All are projecting an attitude of carefree excitement and jubilant celebration. Perhaps these characters could symbolize my student writers in their most creative mode, putting on the spectacle for some unseen audience, shadowed by the starry night? My question is: how does audience affect the process and product of student writers? There are certainly different masks we wear as writers, different voices we "try on." What costume and what mask is needed for each different audience?

When Carra shared her writing with the group, she talked about her plans to use the mask-and-costume metaphor to explore with her students the ways in which they change their writing for different audiences.

Teacher-researchers are finding many benefits to integrating the notion of crystallization into their teacher research. The creativity and conversation are invigorating—and it's also a way to intentionally bring our own teacher voices into our work. Using narrative, story, personal images, and poetry bring the reality of our teaching and living experiences to our audiences.

## *Graphing*

"I sat down to examine my data and decided, being the visual person I am, to graph my students' growth—or lack thereof. By doing this, I can see patterns in doing or not doing their homework, as well as how they have done from assessment to assessment," writes Sarah Christenson. (See Sarah's Research Design on pages 81–86.)

A graph summarizes data in a concise and pictorial form. There's something about a graph that allows researchers to see patterns they might otherwise overlook. This can be especially useful for some forms of data, which was the case for Sarah:

> I decided not to graph the survey information, as I couldn't really figure out how to map it out, but I went ahead and did reading and writing. For reading, I graphed the percentage of time they spent on homework for each trimester and their DRA [Developmental Reading Assessment] levels. In writing, I also graphed the percentage of time they spent on homework. I added together each student's scores for ideas and content, conventions, and organization on the writing samples from each trimester and graphed that.
>
> Here's some data:
>
> Lisa rarely reads or writes at home, and that has been consistent all year. Her reading has improved immensely, while her writing is still lagging behind where it should be. [See Figure 5.8a.]

Figure 5.8a
Lisa's Data

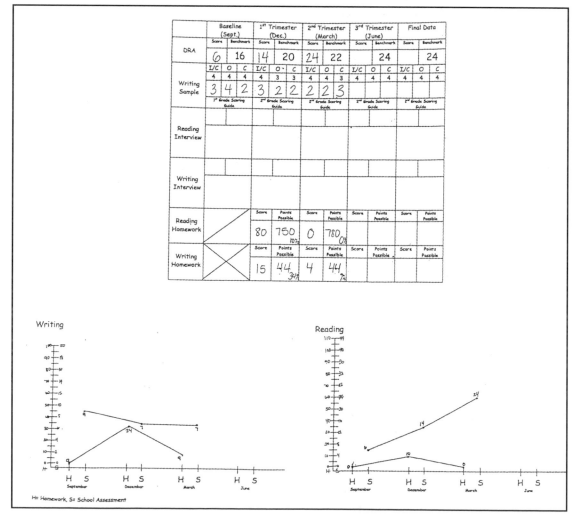

H= Homework, S= School Assessment

Juan does his homework on a regular basis, and his reading and writing scores have improved since the beginning of the year. Homework definitely hasn't caused him to regress, but there is no way for me to tell if doing his homework has directly affected his progress. [See Figure 5.8b.]

Alexis reads and writes every night, which is reflected in her formal assessments. She is reading and writing well above grade level. [See Figure 5.8c.]

What does all this mean? This is the question I find myself asking constantly throughout this process. It is really difficult for me to say there is a direct correlation between the amount of homework a child does at home and their overall success in reading and writing. There are too many outside factors in the classroom and at home that can affect a student's success. However, I do believe that homework doesn't negatively affect a student.

As teachers, we know that any one-on-one time with a student, whether they acquire new knowledge or practice a skill, directly affects their overall growth and, more times than not, pushes them higher academically. It is because of this that I am going to frame my homework assignments next year as "enrichment opportunities" instead of typical

Figure 5.8b
Juan's Data

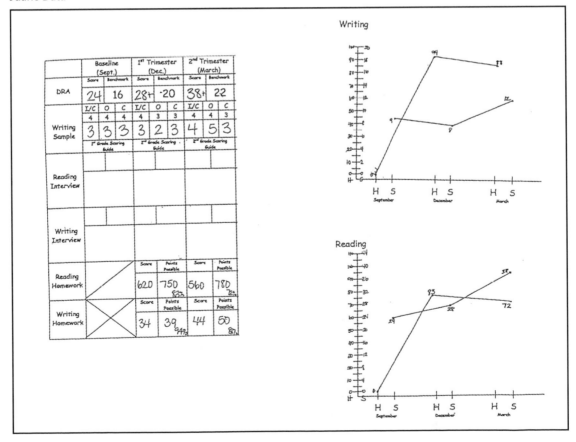

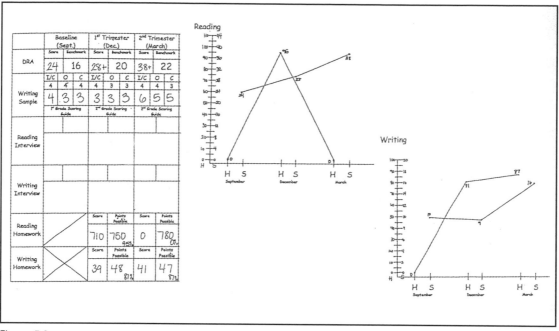

Figure 5.8c
Alexis's Data

homework. Parents who don't like homework will not be obligated to do it, and those who do want it will have it. I also think that if I share my results from the research this year with my future parents and emphasize the growth that is possible for each of their children, they will be more likely to follow through with their children at home.

Sarah's data analysis led to a deeper understanding of her theory about what is going on with the students in her classroom. The benefit of the findings that emerge from her data is the generation and articulation of a personal theory of how things work or how they might be changed to enhance classroom practice. Next year, her parents and colleagues will have the benefit of her rich findings in the specific context of their school. And the data is visually represented in her graphs to share with all the stakeholders.

## Sociograms

Sociograms are a useful source of information for analyzing the social networks in your classroom. What you need first is a question for individual interviews with your students that requires them to answer with the names of their classmates. For example, If you could eat lunch with anyone, who would you sit next to? Who do you know who is a good writer in this class? If you could read a book with anyone in the class, whom would it be? Ideally, the question should have some link to your research topic, even if the link is weak.

With younger students (grades pre–K through two), you or a colleague will need to interview each child separately, in a space slightly removed from the rest of the class. These interviews should be done very quickly—lasting no more than a minute per student. Resist the urge to ask "why" when a student gives a surprising response—those open-ended questions are useful for other aspects of your research, but not with sociograms. With older students, you can pass out slips of paper and have the whole class write their responses immediately to your question; this takes less than five minutes of class time.

As you're interviewing or after you collect the slips from the students, you'll need to do a tally sheet. To do the tally sheet, list the name of the person interviewed and the names of classmates she or he lists as first, second, and third choices. For example, if you were interviewing Theresa, the tally sheet might look like this:

**Theresa**
1. Jennifer [her first choice]
2. Kelly [her second choice]
3. Melissa [her third choice]

This would continue for the whole class:

**Harry**
1. Jim
2. Joe
3. Kelly

and so on.

Once you've completed the tally sheet, make a whole-class chart with names of students on horizontal and vertical margins. Children get three points if they are the first choice of another student, two points if they are the second choice, and one point if they are the third choice. Add the number of points for each child to get a sense of who has the most social power in the class and who has the least. (With a positive question, students with the most points are those who have the most social power in the class, and those with the fewest have the least.) Many times, it's helpful to ask two questions—one from a positive social perspective, the other from a negative social perspective: Who would you want to sit with at lunch? Who would you not want to sit with at lunch?

When you have the negative data, you can differentiate between children who aren't noticed by classmates and those who are disliked or avoided. For example, a student who has few points for each question is for some reason not visible to classmates. But a student who has low points for the first question and high points for the second is behaving in a way that has a negative effect on their social status. If you have the time, you might want to chart your findings for the question. But many teachers save time by adding up only the tally points.

Sociograms never stand alone as a data source. The results need to be triangulated with other data sources to provide truly valid findings. But if you're stymied in trying to understand links between the social networks in your classroom and the learning going on, sociograms can provide terrific quick looks at complex social relationships.

Some teacher-researchers avoid sociograms because they are concerned about hurt feelings if students share choices with each other. We have not found this to be an issue with many teachers who have used sociograms, but we respect that concern.

These examples of data-analysis methods are diverse, but they all show evidence of working from the same basic principles:

1. Find something to count. For many novice researchers, it is easier to see patterns first through numbers than through language. Many teacher-researchers find it useful to count the number of instances in different code categories and then to chart them in some way to begin to visualize their findings.
2. Look for models from others, but feel free to adapt them. Betty Bisplinghoff, JoBeth Allen, and Barbara Michalove were eager to try a tried-and-true system for categorizing their data but felt free to abandon it when it didn't work for them. Lee Anne Larsen and Sherry Young used specific codes developed by others but tailored them to their own particular studies.
3. Find and follow the story of your research. The best lesson from these researchers may be that the codes, analysis systems, and procedures are all a means to one end: finding the narrative thread of the research. As you develop and use any system of analysis, ask yourself, Is this getting me closer to the story of my students and teaching, or is it distancing me from it? If you don't find the system is revealing new truths, but instead feels cumbersome and artificial, then it probably isn't the right analysis procedure for you.

# Welcome the Unexpected

Perhaps the most important advice we can give you about data analysis is never to allow yourself to become too comfortable with your findings. As you sort through and weigh different possibilities, there will be some part of what you are seeing or not seeing in your research that niggles at you. It can be a sense that something is not quite true, or accurate, or honest in how you are representing what you've learned. Pay attention to those feelings of discomfort, because often they provide clues to the major breakthroughs in understanding possible through your research.

The great Native American leader Seneca said, "It is not because things are difficult that we do not dare. It is because we do not dare that things are difficult." Data analysis is the point in research that calls for true daring. The magic in the best research studies comes from teachers who are willing to explore the unexpected places their inquiry leads. Like Ellie, Melody, and

Emily, they explore what isn't working as they try to analyze their data. Like JoBeth, Barbara, and Betty, they are able to recognize a discomfort in their process, not as a deficiency in their skills but as a mismatch between the analysis method they have chosen and their needs as researchers. Take Don Graves's advice: "Listen to yourself and what you see in the shadows and sense just around the corner of thought" (1994, 39). A willingness to chuck old methods and categories, try new ones, and consider unorthodox possibilities can make data analysis less of a chore and more of an adventure.

## RESEARCH WORKSHOP

## Language Patterns: Reflecting with Transcripts and Wordle

*Heather Rader*

When a colleague shared the word-cloud generator at www.wordle.net with me, I was intrigued. I pasted quotes, poems, lyrics, and bios into the generator, and found an entirely new way of looking at words. Wordle increases the size of words according to how frequently they appear. For example, in a carol with a great deal of repetition such as "We Wish You a Merry Christmas," the lyrics "Now bring us some figgy pudding" would be three times larger than "a cup of good cheer." Inputting a transcript from a presentation of mine, I laughed when the word *so* was larger than most other words. It's true. I am a *so*-er. It's my equivalent of *ummm* . . . and serves to help me transition and think of what I'm going to say next. With transmitting language to text in mind, I was curious about what would happen if I pasted in transcripts from the teachers I was working with. What would Wordle reveal?

## *Magnification*

I decided to analyze transcripts from two writing lessons: one from a beginning teacher, and another from a more experienced teacher. (Student names were changed, though not the repetition.) Even more synchronous was the fact that both the writing lessons were at the same grade level.

Take a moment and consider the two samples (Figures 5.9a and 5.9b). Which one came from the early-career teacher? What assumptions lead you to your selection? What does the word cloud make you think about in your own journey as an educator?

What was magnified for me in the first sample (Figure 5.9a) is the reactive management language (for example, *waiting*). Most of the repeated words were commands or students' names. *Maribeth? Maribeth?* The few content words that appear are less specific.

In the second sample (Figure 5.9b), I see evidence of proactive management and language of the discipline of writing: *details, exaggeration, strong verbs, drafts,* and *revise.*

Figure 5.9a
Wordle Sample 1

Figure 5.9b
Wordle Sample 2

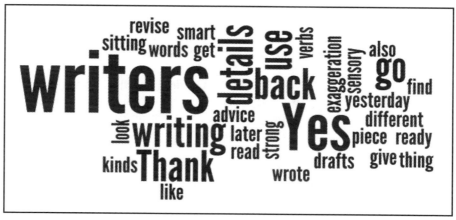

The first sample is from an early-career teacher and the second is from a more experienced teacher. However, there are many teachers all along the experience continuum that could represent Samples 1 and 2. Were your assumptions correct?

What we can see from the word cloud is that one teacher's language is focused tightly on content and using specific vocabulary, and the other teacher's language is focused on corrective management. If what we say in the classroom and what we repeat is what gets reinforced, what did the students in each of these lessons learn? If we included only student language, what other patterns might we find?

## Transcripts from Coaching Conversations

As I became interested in looking at my language as a teacher during my coteaching and demonstration lessons, I also started to think about my language as an instructional coach. Recently as part of the work in my coaching Professional Learning Community group, I took my Flip camera out. I pointed it at myself during a conversation I had with a first-year teacher about conferences. The next day I sat with my laptop while the Flip video played, transcribing my questions and the gist of her answers.

I reflected on how I had brought seven resources on the topic of conferring in my coaching binder that I might share with the teacher. In my first year of coaching, I would have handed all the resources over to the teacher at the start or end of the conference. But now I know to use my questioning to distill what might be truly useful to her.

For example I asked, "How much do you want the kids to be leading?"

She explained that she would be leading the conference, and students would chime in about their work. The article that I'd brought on student-led conferences would not be of interest to this teacher.

I probed for how much she was going to do proactively with the kids to set them up for success with questions such as, "Are you going to practice before students share their work? Or will it be in the moment?"

More than halfway through the conference I asked, "When you think about conferences, what are you most nervous about?" The conversation shifted. She shared that she was nervous about not being able to anticipate parent concerns. Being on the spot with an inquiring parent can make any new teacher anxious. I pulled a parent questionnaire out of my binder that I used when I was teaching to survey parent concerns before conferences. This was a timely and valuable resource for her. Through our conversation, she had discovered within herself why she wanted the resource and how she would use it.

Figure 5.10
Pronoun Use Wordle

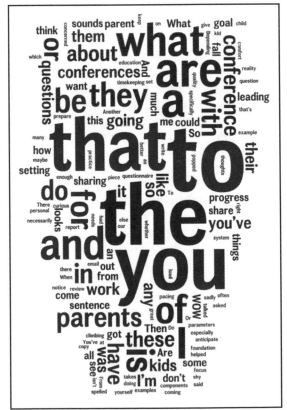

## *Pronoun Preferences*

After reading an excerpt from Laura Lipton and Bruce Wellman's book *Mentoring Matters: A Practical Guide to Learning-Focused Relationships* on the different stances of coaching, collaborating, and consulting, I was interested to see how my pronoun use Wordled out in the conference transcript. As a consultant, I'd say *I*, as a collaborator I'd use *we*, and as a coach I'd use *you*.

With the "common words included" box checked, the Wordle in Figure 5.10 showed me the language of my questioning:

I mostly stayed in my coaching stance, using *you* a majority of the time. I went into the consulting stance of *I* when I shared anecdotes that were related to the first-year teacher's questions and concerns.

As a busy educator, I don't take time to Wordle myself very often. But when I do, I always take away new learning about myself, as well as ideas for how to improve my teaching and coaching. Try it for yourself. What "Wordles up" for you? Here are some questions to help you start linking language, Wordle, and data analysis:

- Which words are repeated most often in your word clouds?
- What might Wordle tell you about your instruction?
- What might Wordle help you understand about student talk?
- Which pronouns do you use most in your teaching coaching?
- After Wordling, what new things have you learned?

## RESEARCH WORKSHOP

## The Draw a Reader Test: Informal Assessment Supporting Teacher Inquiry

*Suzy Kaback*

My department was trying to fill a position in science education, and we were interviewing a candidate who had worked extensively with inner-city youth to support their interest in and confidence about science. The job candidate presented a fascinating PowerPoint presentation showing photographs of the summer workshops she facilitated in which girls and boys from economically disadvantaged homes gathered for six weeks in the summer to explore science.

To measure the effect of the summer program on children's perceptions of what it meant to be a scientist, the facilitators asked students to take the Draw a Scientist Test (DAST) at the beginning and the end of their summer experience. The DAST was designed "as an open-ended projective test to detect children's perceptions of scientists" (Nuno 1998) by asking them to draw a picture of a scientist doing science. Other researchers used Chambers's (1983) data to develop a checklist of children's stereotypes about scientists. (For example, Scientists are men in lab coats with crazy white hair presiding over bubbling flasks.) Using this checklist, researchers have explored the connection between students' perceptions of what it means to "do science" and how their beliefs are affected by age, sex, geographic location, and instructional approaches.

The uses of the DAST to explore possible influences on students' images of scientists suggested the potential for a modified version, what I called the Draw a Reader Test (DART), to explore children's beliefs about what it means to be a reader. When I floated this idea to a group of third-grade teachers with whom I work, they were intrigued. Their district, in accordance with Reading First guidelines, had recently purchased a basal reading series for students in grades K–5, and teachers were expected to fully implement the program after a weeklong summer training. Many of the teachers in my study group were concerned that the Harcourt program was focused too much on the quantitative gains students made in reading rather than encouraging them to enjoy reading for its qualitative pleasures. Two teachers had just read Nancie Atwell's *The Reading Zone* (2007) and saw the basal reading program as the complete antithesis of her reading workshop approach. Targeting the disconnect between teachers' beliefs about effective reading instruction and the reading curriculum mandated by their school, I suggested that we try the DART with third graders to see what we discovered.

With the help of preservice teachers working in a professional development partnership at the local school, we devoted five thirty-minute sessions to collecting DART data. Third graders were asked to "draw a picture of a reader reading" on one side of a piece of paper. On the other side, we asked them to write a brief explanation of their drawings, and to add their name, age, and sex. In total, we collected and analyzed drawings and explanations from sixty-two students in four third-grade classrooms. Here is a copy of the template we used:

---

Draw a picture of a reader reading below:




Age:                    Are you a boy or a girl?

Tell us about your drawing. Why do you think your picture represents what readers do?

---

## Data and Expectations

Before diving into an analysis of the DART, my study group talked about what we expected to find. We imagined we would see pictures of students at desks, hovering dutifully over textbook-like tomes, perhaps filling out worksheets. One teacher said she expected to see drawings of readers with *no* books in front of them; instead, "readers" would be writing answers to the all-too-frequent chapter assessments. Another teacher anticipated seeing the classic school scene with a teacher at the front of the room, writing on the blackboard, with students watching her work. Again, no real reading in sight.

We reached consensus in our prediction that the DART, as an assessment tool, would reveal students' limited descriptions of "doing" reading, thus confirming teachers' beliefs that using a basal series undermined reading instruction. Defying our certainty about what we expected to find, the emerging patterns in our DART data surprised us. Rather than pictures of students bent over basal readers at their school desks, the majority of third graders in our sample drew readers outside of school, relaxing in their bedrooms, outdoors, or in libraries. One student drew a picture of a boy reading while riding on a skateboard that was headed directly toward a tank filled with sharks. On the back of his drawing, he wrote, "Sometimes when you read, you don't pay attention to where you're going!" Of the sixty-two drawings we examined, only six showed people reading in school. (One was a picture of a student in the library looking up a word in the dictionary, and another showed a student with a thought bubble over her head that said, "I wonder what I can talk about in book group today?" The other four drawings showed readers in small discussion groups tucked in the corners of their classroom.)

We were particularly surprised by the lack of a school context in students' DART drawings. We had predicted that having a teacher ask students to complete the DART during class time would automatically bias kids' selection of setting. Our examination of the data suggested that the context of the assessment was not an influence. We puzzled over this "out of school" pattern for a while, until one teacher said, "I get it! They have two different definitions of what reading is. There's school reading and real reading. Most kids drew pictures of *real* reading—on their beds at home, leaning against a tree in the park, snuggled next to Mom on the couch. They don't think what they do in school is 'real' reading; it's something completely different." My study group liked this interpretation and began strategizing about ways we could follow up the DART to dig deeper into students' perceptions of what reading is—and isn't.

## Next Steps

As our study group inquiry continues, high on our list of next steps are the following ideas:

1.  Develop a think-aloud protocol to test our theory about students' definitions of real reading versus school reading. After completing the DART, some probing questions might include, Why did you choose this setting for your illustration? or How did you decide where to put the reader in your picture? If the setting of the original picture was out of school, we might ask, If you had decided to draw your reader in school, what would the setting look like? What would your reader be reading?
2.  With subsequent classes of students, have one group complete the DART in class and another group complete it at home. As one teacher pointed out, "With two contexts, we can look at whether *where* you do the DART influences how you characterize a reader."
3.  Try the DART with younger students and older students to compare and contrast emerging patterns.

4.　Finally, we feel obligated to ask the "so what?" question. As an inquiry tool, what does the DART yield that might help us support our students' reading development? What can we learn from students' drawings that could influence the direction of our instruction?

No one likes this "so what?" question because we are all intrigued by the unusual approach ("*Finally*," one teacher commented, "a way for students to share their thinking that doesn't involve writing paragraphs of self-reflection") and by the initial results. But as reflective practitioners, we are duty-bound to identify relevance.

The answers to "so what?" are still surfacing. One study group member wondered, "What if we just present the data and our idea about school reading versus real reading at a faculty meeting, then open it up for discussion? At least this would move the conversation about using the basal reader forward." Another teacher said, "If looking at these data helps reassure me that what we're being asked to do with the basal reader isn't overshadowing other parts of my reading instruction—like SSR [sustained silent reading], discussion groups, read-aloud, and home reading—then I can live with the decision to bring this program to our school. The DART doesn't have to be any more rigorous than that."

From my perspective, the DART is valuable for several reasons. First, the decision to use it was spurred by teachers' discomfort with teaching practices that didn't square with their professional beliefs about reading instruction. Identifying that tension and finding a way to explore it in a systematic way is the heart of teacher research, a process I believe is the best way to support what Hord (1997) calls "professional learning."

Second, the DART has the potential to broaden our definition of reading by soliciting students' perceptions of what it means to be a reader. People use reading for many purposes; our newest readers are just beginning to see the potential of reading in multiple contexts for multiple reasons. By asking young students to draw pictures of readers reading, we are given a window into the many ways reading is "working" in their lives. With this information, we see what they already know, and we identify the places that still need to be revealed through our instruction. Carol Ann Tomlinson reminds us of this in an article called "Learning to Love Assessment":

> Informative assessment isn't an end in itself. . . . The greatest power of assessment information lies in its capacity to help me see how to be a better teacher. If I know what students are and are not grasping at a given moment in a sequence of study, I know how to plan our time better. I know when to reteach, when to move ahead, and when to explain or demonstrate something in another way. Informative assessment is not an end in itself, but the beginning of better instruction. (2007–2008, 9)

Finally, the Draw a Reader Test accomplishes many of the objectives of the Draw a Scientist Test. The DAST was designed to explore students' perceptions of scientists before and after a high-quality experience in the teaching

and learning of science. Researchers were able to use the DAST data to identify gaps in students' understanding of what it meant to do science and then
to address those gaps through instruction. A post-DAST gave researchers
more information about the effect of the intervention on students' perceptions of what it meant to do science.

## Changes Over Time

The science educator I referred to earlier in this article showed before-and-
after illustrations from the children who participated in her summer science
program. The differences were astonishing. Illustrations before the summer
science enrichment were filled with those Einstein look-alikes installed in
classic science laboratories complete with Bunsen burners and hen-scratched
blackboards. When compared with their predecessors, it was impossible to
tell that the drawings after the summer session had been done by the same
children. Illustrations depicted scientists of both sexes, multiple ages, and
many nationalities. One picture showed a woman knee deep in the Red Sea
studying marine life. Another showed a young African American boy on top
of Mt. Everest laden with meteorological equipment. My favorite was a team
of anthropologists huddled around the remains of the Ice Man, the world's
oldest natural mummy, with the word *Eureka!* floating in a thought bubble
above one scientist's head.

Teachers who use the DART may tap into similar richness when analyzing students' perceptions of reading, before and after teaching. They might
identify impoverished conceptions of reading, or definitions that cross the
boundaries of academic instruction. In either case, I would encourage
teachers to think about the influence of their instruction on students' perceptions of what reading is. In our initial inquiry, as we sifted through more than
fifty illustrations of readers reading in comfortable locations with, we can
assume, self-selected texts, I pointed out that these images suggested students
were paying attention to authentic encounters with books and using these
experiences to explain their understandings of what it meant to "do reading."

Cream rises to the top. Again, I turn to Tomlinson's ten understandings
about informative assessment to frame my argument about the value of tools
like the DART:

> Informative assessment isn't always formal. [It] could occur any time I
> went in search of information about a student. In fact, it could occur
> when I was not actively searching but was merely conscious of what was
> happening around me . . . I began to sense that virtually all student prod-
> ucts and interactions can serve as informative assessment because I, as a
> teacher, have the power to use them that way. (9)

The DART was attractive to teachers in my study group because they
were "conscious about what was happening around them" and they were
uncomfortable with that consciousness. Looking more closely at the influence of a scripted reading program on students' definitions of what it meant

to "do reading" was exactly the kind of inquiry these teachers needed to do to gather evidence about their misgivings. Like Tomlinson, they used the DART to explore their questions because they *had the power to do so*. The world offers many opportunities to connect the power of teaching to learning opportunities for students. The potential of inquiry through informal assessment is one way teachers use their power to transform teaching and learning.

## References

Atwell, Nancie. 2007. *The Reading Zone.* New York: Scholastic.

Chambers, David. 1983. "Stereotypic Images of the Scientist: The Draw-A-Scientist Test." *Science Education* 67 (2): 255–265.

Hord, Shirley. 1997. "Professional Learning Communities: What Are They and Why Are They Important?" *Issues About Change* 6 (1).

Nuño, Judith. 1998. "Draw a Scientist: Middle School and High School Students' Conceptions About Scientists." University of Southern California  Rossier School of Education. www.jdenuno.com/Resume%20Web/DAST.htm.

Tomlinson, Carol Ann. 2007-2008. "Learning to Love Assessment." *Educational Leadership* 65 (4): 8–13.

## FEATURED TEACHER-RESEARCHER

## "180-Degree Turn? Or Close to It?"

*Audrey Alexander*

My initial research question in September was, What is the effect on fourth graders who are at least two years below grade level in reading when they are in a reading workshop where students are given the opportunity to choose their own reading material(s) during independent reading time?

While doing this research for the past seven months, I have learned more about myself, teaching reading, and my students than I ever would have imagined. Of course, I still have day-to-day struggles, but remembering where my students were in October, I realize how far we have all come.

Do students' perceptions of their reading skills change when they choose their reading materials? Yes, they all view themselves as readers.

Will students be more apt to read on their own after being taught from a reading workshop? They bring in books they have checked out from either the public or school library to read in my room.

How do district-mandated monthly reading scores change? I haven't seen as much growth as I would like to, but through my daily conferences, I know how much their reading has improved.

How do other staff members' perceptions of students in special education change? Teachers are asking me for book ideas for our students, and sometimes even buying specific books for them. I hear a lot fewer negative comments about my fourth graders in the staff room now.

What is the effect on fourth graders? Positive! Just yesterday, I asked the students to grab a sticky note and write down two of their favorite books they have read this year. I, foolishly, thought this would be a difficult task because just in January when I asked them, they all struggled to write anything down. Not anymore! The students kept asking me for two, three, even four sticky notes so that they could write down all their favorite authors and books. I could not stop smiling; this is what I had wanted and desired from my research. I wanted students to feel comfortable with reading and know some favorite good-fit books and authors they enjoyed.

Their stamina has increased from barely three minutes to almost an entire thirty minutes (with a quick water break to get out the wiggles). I used to have students moaning when it came time for me to say, "Happy reading." Now I have students asking me if I can pick up certain books for them at the library. I hear them talking about books in the hallway down to my classroom. They are sharing books and partner reading. They feel comfortable telling me and each other predictions and connections they have with books and characters.

In our journals, the students used to struggle with writing two sentences about their reading. Now I have students turning the page and writing two full pages! They are doing amazingly well; Lance even wrote this as his summary:

"Little Critter wanted to build a snowman. But the pieces were missing! So Little Critter found the pieces. Then it was time for lunch. Then the dog ate the soup. Finally Little Critter had to make the soup again."

My two nonreaders at the beginning of the year have blossomed into confident readers who hate the words "Please put your bookmark in your book and find a seat at the table." I no longer feel the need to sit right next to them the entire reading time. They are independent readers who use comprehension strategies regularly to understand the stories.

Marie and Marco have started reading chapter books! Marie is dying for the Green Princess book to come in from the library, because, she says, "Ms. Alexander, you know I have been waiting for this for a *long* time!"

I feel I am ready to begin small strategy groups again; now that the students are independent enough, I know they can read for at least twenty-five minutes by themselves. I also want to begin a book group and discussion on Fridays where students have structured conversations with each other about books.

Are we where I expected to be in April? I don't really know, and I'm okay with that. I still believe we have room for improvements, and I look forward to seeing where these wonderful confident readers are in June. (See Audrey Alexander's Research Plan in Chapter 3, page 59.)

## FEATURED TEACHER-RESEARCHER

# "Simple Truths"

*Ellie Gilbert*

> *The trouble about man is twofold. He cannot learn truths which are too complicated; he forgets truths which are too simple.*
>
> —REBECCA WEST

I hadn't intended to use video in my research; it had seemed too cumbersome, too invasive—superfluous, even. What would there be to capture on film? I don't have a traditional classroom. In fact, the only time I actually see my students in person is when they come in to my office for our monthly book club. Five teenagers, sitting around a table eating snacks and talking about books: not exactly riveting material. I'd used video in the past to observe my classroom behaviors, seeking answers to questions such as, Do I call on boys more than girls? Does everyone get a chance to talk? Is there anyone not participating? But let's face it, it's pretty hard to hide when there are just six of us sitting around a table. Besides, my research question this year was about reading—not exactly the sort of thing you can capture on video. Imagine my surprise, then, when video entered the picture and changed *everything*.

It was my student Ian who started it all. We were just wrapping up a book club session when Ian asked me how my research was going and what I had learned so far. I was excited by his question, because just the night before I'd typed up the conclusions that I *thought* my research had led me to: namely, that having an in-person book club had led to increased student interest in writing, which led to the creation of a weekly in-person writing workshop. Thankfully, before I could gush about the conclusions I'd come to, one of my students suggested instead that I interview *them* about what *they* thought my data had led me to. As I reached for my notebook to jot down their responses, I mumbled a lament about not having anything to record their answers with, and one of my students showed me how to use a program on my laptop to record video. Eureka!

I began each student interview by asking my essential research question: "What happens when we have an in-person book club at an online school?" Ian was my first interview. He responded, "I think that fun happens. You know, back . . . before I started doing this, I never read any books. . . . This book club helped me regain the love of reading that I had somewhere inside me." Marnae was up next. She said, "Book club is not one of those really big things where there's going to be a bunch of people and then you'll feel overwhelmed. It makes me feel more comfortable to speak openly on my thoughts and opinions when there are only half a dozen people in the room. I feel like I can be myself." Kealohi echoed Marnae's thoughts, saying, "When we are talking about a book, if something comes up, we have an in-depth discussion about it. It's comfortable to talk deeper about stuff that comes up when you're not in front of a whole bunch of people."

I am embarrassed to admit that I was initially quick to brush off these responses. Yes, of course teenagers would like the social aspect of it, but what about the meatier academic links? I tried to avoid asking them leading questions about the book club leading to writing class, but by the third interview temptation overtook me and I slipped in a question about writing workshop. Why couldn't my students see this obvious connection? It was, of course, me who couldn't see. It wasn't until I reviewed the footage of my students interviewing me that I realized that I'd gotten it all wrong. The answer was there, plain as day. I'd even said as much in my own interview. A student asked me, "What do you like about book club?" I responded, "I've made no secret of the fact that book club is my favorite part of my experience at this school. I look forward to book club. It's the highlight of my month. Just like each of you said in your interviews, I feel like I can be myself here at book club. . . . I feel like I've gotten to know you through the books you've chosen to read." I'd been so intent on finding what I thought was the academic answer—the quantifiable, justifiable answer—that I'd completely ignored the truth: What happens when you have an in-person book club at an online high school? Fun, connection, reading, and learning happen. Book club has become the heart and soul of our online school and the core of our learning community.

In the end, without the video footage, my eyes would not have been opened to the truth. It's a funny thing, truth. As teacher-researchers, we seek the answers to our questions, trying to ferret them out from their hiding places under the couch, failing to notice that they've been there all along, sipping tea on the davenport and patiently waiting for us to notice them.

# 6 Citing a Tea Bag: When Researchers Read

*In her first home each book had a light around it,*
*The voices of distant countries*
*flooded in through open windows,*
*entering her soup and her mirror.*

—NAOMI SHIHAB NYE

What we read as we do research determines in part what we see in our classrooms and who we are as researchers. As teacher-researchers we are showing through our practice that we can change the old images that "a review of the literature" sometimes conjures up: paging through dry, dusty tomes, squinting to decipher tiny print on microfiche, and so on. Instead, reading can be one of the joys of the research process—the stories we read of other researchers, writers, and teachers inform our inquiry, broaden our perspectives, and connect us to a wider network of writers and ideas. We are open to a world of new possibilities when we begin to "read like a researcher."

When we first began to do research, we asked a veteran researcher how to balance writing up our research narratives with citations from our readings of other researchers. She said dismissively, "Just write your own research—don't worry about citing anyone. Then when you're done, you can sprinkle a few references like croutons across the writing." We were pretty young and naive at the time, but even then we found her response a bit cynical.

We suspect her advice is followed by too many education researchers. Often research studies in any discipline cite the same small core of researchers in the same ways. It's the same old croutons in even the tastiest research studies.

Many teacher-research studies contain few, if any, research citations. Teachers sometimes have an aversion to reading education research, and with good reason. Let's face it: the prose of most education researchers would never be mistaken for Hemingway (or even Nicholas Sparks). No wonder much teacher research is lightly referenced, citing only a few well-known and well-worn research studies.

But that's our loss as teachers and researchers. Many published research studies are compelling reads, able within a few pages to transform a researcher's sense of her own findings. And some of the most transformative reading for teacher-researchers takes place beyond the realm of traditional research writing. Teacher research challenges many traditional conceptions of the research process, and nowhere is the challenge needed more than in considering how we read other research, how we cite who influences our work, and how we connect our research to texts beyond research journals and books.

One of the reasons teacher-researchers often have few citations is because the process of learning from others during research (both in written texts and beyond) is not linear. We learn from a chance comment by a colleague down the hall, from another researcher still in the midst of his study—and we're unsure how to cite this tentative and new knowledge. It doesn't fit the traditional concept of how research knowledge builds, neatly and cleanly, from the work of others. Anne Wilson Schaef (1992) is writing about knowledge in general, but she could easily be discussing research learning: "All too frequently, our culture's prophets, philosophers and critics forget the levels of truth they have passed through and try to impose the distillation of a more advanced level on us" (159).

Teacher-researchers itch to show that undistilled, raw process of reading and learning from others, orally and in print. But because this reading, like our research, may be unorthodox, it often doesn't appear through citations in teacher-research studies.

In her provocative analysis of Lucy Sprague Mitchell's influence on current teachers, Yetta Goodman exhorts teacher-researchers to think hard about who and how we cite those who influence our work (Wilde 1996). Lucy Sprague Mitchell was a teacher-researcher working early in the twentieth century. She founded the Bank Street School in New York and was a tremendous influence on John Dewey's work and on education reform at the time. But because her work was rarely cited, it is only recently that historians have begun to unearth her profound influence in fostering reflective inquiry. In contrast, Dewey is one of the most heavily cited figures from the same period, and so his value in the evolution of current theories of learning is unquestioned.

Goodman challenges us to find ways to cite other teachers who influence our work, even if those citations fall under the category of "personal communication" or "unpublished studies." Part of the emerging tradition of teacher research is the sense that knowledge in this research community is shared, cited, and distributed in different ways. We need to avoid the limits of sharing only those insights available from traditional print resources.

Once you become immersed in your research, you'll begin to see links to your studies in almost everything you read: other research studies, novels, plays, billboards. It's a process similar to what writers go through when they are working on a story, as Eudora Welty wrote:

> Once you're into a story everything seems to apply—what you overhear on a city bus is exactly what your character would say on the page you're writing. Wherever you go, you meet part of your story. I guess you're tuned in for it, and the right things are sort of magnetized. (Shaughnessy 1993, 189)

A teacher-researcher we were working with called us one morning with an important question about her research. After weeks of reading through dozens of studies related to her own, she'd finally found the quote she needed to summarize a section: "I was making some herb tea this morning, and the box had a series of sayings about relationships on it. One of them is perfect!" she exclaimed. "So how do you cite a tea bag, anyway?" Here was someone highly tuned to her research story, ready and eager to find her citations in unexpected places.

This willingness to link research to reading, regardless of genre, can lead to creative leaps in thinking and writing. When you read the work of veteran teacher-researchers, it's often peppered with quotes and connections from a range of literature.

Mountain-biking enthusiast Andie Cunningham found a quote that shifted the focus of her teacher research. It was from Marla Streb's (2011) account of why getting lost is part of the journey of being a biker:

> I love being lost. I love going on bike rides, not knowing where I am, and having the challenge of trying to find my way home. I have no idea what life is, and it's really fun to ask questions. You have to keep wondering, "What is it, what's it all about?" As soon as you stop asking questions, or if you stop feeling lost, it gets boring. (15)

The connection between being lost and finding new questions was a powerful one for Andie. She viewed her interviews and her own teaching notebook through a new lens, and began her study linking healing and literature in classrooms.

Sharon Frye, in her interview with Maureen Barbieri, author of *Sounds from the Heart* (1995), noted that she always finds great books to read from what Maureen cites in her research. She went on to ask, "What books have you been reading lately?" and received a whole new batch of books she couldn't wait to get her hands on:

> **Maureen Barbieri:** As far as girls, there's a book of poems called *Dreams of Glory: Poems Starring Girls*. They're all different poets, but the compiler is Isabel Joshlin Glaser. It's pretty good, it's not as good as the title. Some nice things in here—girls doing sports, very positive girl images. There's never enough time! I'm trying to read ESOL [English for Speakers of Other Languages] books, and teacher research books. There's a book called *Poemcrazy*, one word. The writer is Susan Wooldridge, and it's fabulous. I'm very interested in poetry, so I read a lot of it.

**SF:** Who's your favorite poet?

**MB:** That's easy: Naomi Shihab Nye. My very strong favorite. I love Pablo Neruda and Mary Oliver, but Naomi's poems just really get me. (Frye 1997, 55)

Maureen's research is full of theoretical connections to others; poets such as Naomi Shihab Nye and Pablo Neruda give her ideas and images that provide poetic allusions in her eloquent and beautifully written classrooms accounts.

What a contrast Maureen is to the mythical researcher who dutifully plows through a minimal number of research studies and sprinkles a few references in her writing. Maureen merges her personal reading passions with her professional interests. In doing so, she inspires other researchers to expand their reading repertoire.

# Reading Before Breakfast

Who are the writers you turn to for your morning reading? Kay Ryan (1998) writes, "The books I regularly pick up in the morning, for the few minutes or half-hour before I set about my own writing, are not casual interests. I go to these writers because they contain the original ichor. They are the potent Drink Me" (14).

Our "Drink Me" fellowship includes Marge Piercy, Karen Gallas, Saul Alinsky, William Stafford, Anne Tyler, Linda Pastan, Deborah Tannen, and Julia Alvarez. These authors' works jostled next to each other in our book bags at a recent teacher-research retreat, getting us going and sustaining our thinking and writing, and not just before breakfast but throughout the day. Some draw us closer into our work, some help us find new ways of approaching it, and others give our minds the needed space so that we can return to our data renewed and refreshed.

If you've been pushing your own "potent" authors aside, it's time to welcome them back, making time for reading as part of your research agenda. We think you'll find that when you're thinking about something in the back of your head all the time (like your evolving research question), you'll make connections to really different material because you don't know how it will strike you. Don't be afraid to reread old favorites with fresh eyes. Which professional books or authors matter most to you? What books do you read for pleasure that might inspire your research? Betty Bisplinghoff writes about the effect of reading for pleasure on her research:

> When I read for pleasure, I find myself almost unconsciously making associations with issues of research. For instance, while reading *The House on Mango Street* (1989), by Sandra Cisneros, I longed for the skill and art to describe the scenes and scenarios of classroom experiences with such beauty and clarity. I think how remarkable it would be to read research that was so totally engaging and purposefully appealing to all the senses. (1995, 107)

A rereading of these favorite authors, with your own current research in the back of your mind, might prove the best starting place for discovering new writers and researchers to cite in your work. What is it about these books that drew you in the past and that might continue to help you frame new connec- tions? As you turn to books from your reading history that have been a source of inspiration to you in the past, you might begin to notice who your reading mentors turn to. Kay Ryan (1998) writes about the effect this has on her:

> Quotes by my favorite writers offer a double joy. First, there is the attrac- tiveness of what is quoted; and second, there is the pleasurable sensation of endless doors opening, author through author, all the way back to the first word. It is much bigger in here. (14)

You can also open those doors, author through author, by noting whom the folks you are reading cite as well as quote within the text. Reading the ref- erences and bibliographies can turn up interesting new possibilities, espe- cially when you see them repeated by more than one of the writers whose work you admire.

You can build your reading community in a similar way by listing some of the teachers you admire who are struggling with the same issues you are. We often encourage teachers to imagine some of their favorite researchers and favorite people from all walks of life attending a dinner party to discuss the teacher's research question. We've had teacher-researchers envisioning conversations about community between Parker Palmer and Jerry Garcia, or discussions of diversity between Helen Keller and Lady Gaga. When you imagine what people with different interests would consider in discussing your research question, you cut through accepted notions of what the critical issues are. These fanciful conversations can lead to all kinds of new possibil- ities for literature reviews.

In her "fantasy dinner," Suzy Kaback took this concept to its playful extreme, inviting nine mentors (living and dead) "to sit at my table, eat fine food, and discuss my latest question about teaching reading" (1997, 112). She found that the imaginative dialogue she created as her mentors "talked" to each other about her research question helped her differentiate more clearly the shades of difference in their reading theory and brought her own theory and practice into sharper focus. The whimsical touches in her dialogue make it an enjoyable as well as informative read. For example, when Lev Vygotsky notes that her shrimp bisque is as good as his grandmother's borscht, Suzy modestly replies, "That's high praise, especially from a guy who's not actually alive" (122). The evening ends with her modern husband doing the dishes while she retreats to her office to write up what she has learned from the dinner party in her teaching journal.

High school teacher Susan Tetrick's question centered on adolescents finding voice in their writing in her imagined dinner party. She created invi- tations to send to each guest (Figure 6.1).

Her invitation reads, "You are invited to a summer evening under the stars, where we'll savor good food, wine and conversation. Celebrate the end

Figure 6.1
Susan's Dinner
Party Invitation

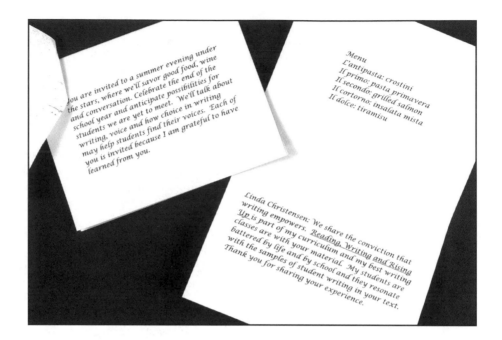

You are invited to a summer evening under the stars, where we'll savor good food, wine and conversation. Celebrate the end of the school year and anticipate possibilities for students we are yet to meet. We'll talk about writing, voice and how choice in writing may help students find their voices. Each of you is invited because I am grateful to have learned from you.

Menu
L'antipasta: crostini
Il primo: pasta primavera
Il secondo: grilled salmon
Il cortorno: insalata mista
Il dolce: tiramisu

Linda Christensen: We share the conviction that writing empowers. *Reading, Writing and Rising Up* is part of my curriculum and my best writing classes are with your material. My students are battered by life and by school and they resonate with the samples of student writing in your text. Thank you for sharing your experience.

of the school year and anticipate possibilities for students we are yet to meet. We'll talk about writing, voice and how choice in writing may help students find their voices. Each of you is invited because I am grateful to have learned from you." She invited Linda Christensen, Barbara Kingsolver, Anne Lamott, and fellow teacher Wendy Doss.

After completing her dinner party invitations, Saundra Hardy reflected, "I really enjoyed the dinner party invitations. It really made me think deeply about my research question. . . . I had to consider my question and what I am *really* wondering about. It also gave me the opportunity to think about the inspirations in my life, as well as teacher-researchers and other academics."

For more information on this exercise, see the Research Workshop on page 178.

An equally enjoyable task—though one that is limited to the living!—is to write letters to teacher-researchers whom you admire, enlisting their ideas and book recommendations as a way to build your reading community. Teachers we know have been inspired by the work of Kelly Gallagher, Debbie Miller, Tom Romano, and others, and have picked up their pens to tell them so.

# Expand Your Horizons

We encourage you to wander through the library stacks, picking up journals in disciplines you wouldn't ordinarily connect to your research endeavor, perhaps in disciplines you never knew existed. We discovered the *Journal of Mental Imagery* on a library stroll like this. This journal makes for fascinating reading; it reports on the study of mental images—everything from daydreaming to drug hallucinations to the annual issue on the mental images we form when we read and write.

Another benefit of expanding your reading horizons in this way is that you are exposed to a field of new terminology and fresh metaphors. Look for those metaphors in your new reading, challenging yourself to ask not what it is but what it is like.

You may also find new terminology and metaphors in the writings of familiar authors you've never actually read before. That's right—we're talking about reading primary sources. Don't always rely on secondary interpretations of a well-known theorist's work. If you are studying social interactions around learning, for example, it's important to hear Vygotsky in his own words and make sense of what you believe he is exploring. You may be surprised to discover you see a different angle in his work that speaks especially to your research and that another reader might not notice.

The Internet is invaluable in your research quest. Besides the obvious benefits of increasing your professional connections through virtual communities such as mailing lists and news groups, you have access to a wealth of information previously out of your reach. And much of this information is available at little or no cost. Here are just a few of our favorites:

TeacherResearcherNet, www.teacherresearch.net/
National Writing Project (Teacher Research Section), www.nwp.org/cs/
public/print/resource_topic/teacher_research_inquiry
Teacher Action Research, http://gse.gmu.edu/research/tr/

# Read, Read, Read . . . and Then Write

Perhaps the most important reason to read like a researcher is that it will make you want to write. You'll see ways to connect your work to others', possibilities for new contributions from your own research. You'll quake at the thought of trying to write as well as your favorite poet, or piecing together a narrative as beautiful as your favorite novelist's, or presenting findings as elegantly as your favorite teacher-researcher. Yet you'll still have the urge to put pen to page, as Donald Murray (1990a) warned:

> Watch out. As you live and read there will probably come a time—especially if you don't believe such a time could come for you—when you will be invited to write or commanded to write or when you will simply have the itch to write. Then write. When you are in terminal middle age or beyond you may not be able to dance as you once intended or twist and turn toward the goal line as you once believed you could, but it is never too late to write—and all that reading you have done is stored away, waiting to be called upon as your words move across the page. (345)

We love that image of carrying all the researchers we've read with us as we research. Once you begin to see the possibility of adding a new voice from anywhere—a research journal, a blog, a tea bag—to your writing, you'll read almost anything in a deeper way, knowing that it could be part of your dance of words across the page someday.

## RESEARCH WORKSHOP

## You're Invited

*Kimberly Hill Campbell*

What do Dr. Benjamin Spock, J. D. Salinger, Deanna Troi, Howard Gardner, Paolo Freire, and Kermit the Frog have in common? They are all "invitees" listed by my graduate students in a research methods class. As my students worked to bring different perspectives into framing their research questions, I wanted them to think about individuals and wider communities that might inform their research designs and plans in new ways. So, I asked them to create a dinner party guest list of folks who would be helpful to them in pursuing their research questions.

The instructions for the assignment were simple:

1. Invite a minimum of six guests.
2. The guests can be anyone: dead, alive, even fictional.
3. For each guest, state your reason for inclusion and what you think or hope each would contribute.
4. Be as creative as you like.

Wow! The invitations were marvelous. As each person described his or her invitees, I was struck by how rich and varied the teachers' experiences were, as were their invitations. One woman commented, "I think I would be intimidated to attend my own dinner party—so many great minds in one room." Meril's guests included a respected deaf teacher; a college chum; a mentor; Lawrence Van Der Post, the author of "the two best books I've ever read"; Anne, a friend whose American Sign Language interpreting ability "listens past the words and signs and conveys the concepts—the spirit as opposed to the letter"; and counselor Deanna Troi from *Star Trek: The Next Generation*: "Her primary reception (and expression) of communication does not deal in realms of cultural biases, standards, or linguistic parameters. Her communication lies at the very expression/definition of life. . . . Also, she has agreed to bring a replicator, so that everyone may eat whatever they desire." The final guest on the list was Winnie the Pooh, for his "simple, straightforward nature." God was also a consideration, but rejected because "I've never been able to get him/her in on a group discussion. God is good for one-on-one." Meril's hope was that the invitees would convene to discuss how she, as a teacher of the deaf, could enable her students to communicate, to explore the "concept of communication" itself. What does it mean to communicate?

Others predicted there would be fireworks at their parties—lots of heated, emotional discussion, lots of intense personalities. One woman had even designed a party that included an invitation to her father, her big brother, J. D. Salinger, and an old boyfriend whom she described as "the guy who broke my heart." Her research question focused on the question of disciplining children, and each of these guests would have something to contribute. Her father could talk about his "eager use of public discipline." Her brother was described as the "primary victim" who could shed some light on how he was affected. J. D. Salinger, it was hoped, would add "any tips he could spare." He was also included because of her "admiration for his writing."

Another student requested that each of her invited guests bring "their biases" and "some artwork that you have done in the past, or create something new. You can draw, paint, sculpt, etc. Be creative and have fun with this." Her research question was, How does art reflect gender in grades K–12? She included in her guest list Mary Cassatt, an artist who went "against her father's wishes and became a professional artist in a time period when women's paintings were accepted as hobby only." It was hoped that Mary could "shed some light on the pressures society places on children and what they can do to break unhealthy norms while discovering themselves."

Several teachers included menus in their dinner party invitations; one even enclosed a seating chart. Kristin's "Acting Out Amphibians" party seemed to combine the best of all worlds in what she describes as "a dinner party experience that is mind opening and only for the open-minded. Be prepared to act." It was to be hosted at the Monterey Bay Aquarium. The menu consisted of Brie, cheddar, and Swiss cheeses with crackers, homemade clam chowder, crab legs, squash, Ben and Jerry's Chocolate Chip Cookie Dough ice cream, peach melba, wine, beer, and water. Each hand-drawn invitation listed the name of the invitee and a brief description of his or her qualifications. On the reverse side was a detailed explanation of why this person had been invited and "what he or she would add." She provided this example:

**Connie Mayer**
- Author of "Action Researcher: The Story of a Partnership," which is Chapter 6 of *Changing Schools from Within*
- Teacher of the deaf
- Signer

On the reverse side of the card Kristin wrote, "Why? Because she is a teacher of the deaf, and obviously a good one. She is innovative and loves children. Also she studies language acquisition of deaf children, which is the topic of discussion.

"Connie would add a wealth of knowledge to the party. I think she could provide lots of support and advice regarding acquisition and understanding of vocabulary for deaf children. Plus, I want to know her better and thank her for publishing teacher research about deaf kids."

Kristin's plan was for each guest to be given the name of an amphibian, which they would then act out. This reinforced her research question, which looked at how deaf kids best mastered vocabulary. It also reflected her strong science background and her delightful, fun-loving approach to learning. Her guest list reflected a central objective for doing the assignment: to discover other researchers who can support and inform your work.

During our discussions of the invitations and dinner plans, we added to each other's knowledge bases and provided names of folks who might be future experts to consult in our teaching. This workshop brought a sense of playfulness, creativity, and imagination into our research plans. While we were sharing and laughing, we were building our community—as teachers, learners, and researchers—in powerful ways. I was truly awestruck by the power of the imagination, of a community of learners, of spirited and lively discussions, voiced and voiceless, that were stimulated by the wonderings of teacher-researchers and enhanced by good food. I think we're on to something here.

## FEATURED TEACHER-RESEARCHER

# Writing a Literature Review: Joining a Conversation in Progress

*Jessica Singer Early*

*As a high school English teacher, Jessica Singer Early conducted and published research from her classroom (Singer,* Stirring Up Justice, *2006). Now as a professor at Arizona State University, she teaches graduate students, many of whom are conducting research in their own classrooms. Passionate about helping teacher voices enter the educational conversation through their writing, she provides students with accessible approaches to reading research others have done— and writing thoughtful literature reviews. Her essay unpacks the process, and provides a great resource for teacher-researcher support groups and individual researchers, as well as graduate seminars.*

Maria, one of my graduate students, expressed concern about writing a literature review for the first time. "I don't feel like I know enough yet to review research. This feels like something you do once you're an expert in your field, not when you're just starting out." In many ways, Maria's fears are completely justified. It is challenging to show your knowledge and expertise in an arena you are just beginning to learn. Although the teachers I work with almost always arrive in the program as strong writers, they undoubtedly experience a huge learning curve when asked to try writing in new and complex genres such as the literature review, master's thesis, dissertation, research article, and grant or fellowship proposal. I try to provide graduate students with opportunities to practice the kinds of writing they may need in their careers. The literature review is an academic genre in which they might write, as either stand-alone essays or key sections of research articles, fellowships, grants, or conference proposals. Whenever possible, I use seminars as a place to demystify these writing forms.

I structure my seminars as writing and reading workshops (Atwell 1987), and at the beginning of each class, I teach a mini-lesson on an important writing skill or strategy. I then provide time and structure for students to practice these new skills, read and discuss mentor texts, conduct searches of relevant research, confer about work in progress with peers or myself, or revise and polish some aspect of their work. The time I set aside for them to learn these writing skills is an important step in their professional learning curve.

## Preparing to Write the Literature Review

When talking about writing a literature review, we start by discussing why this kind of writing is useful. We think about *areas* or *lines* of research as conversations that have been taking place for a long time. In the social sciences, a line of research is formed in much the same way a cathedral is built, one brick at a time, with different builders or contributors adding to the structure and foundation. One of the main purposes of a literature review is to understand what a conversation has been about in a specific area of research, gaps that have taken place in the conversation, how the conversation has led to important findings, and places where the conversation needs to change or grow. Although writing a literature review can, at times, seem like a complex and overwhelming task, making sense of a body of research can also be empowering. The process of reviewing, summarizing, organizing, and commenting on a body of research is what will allow students to join an existing research conversation and, eventually, add to it in important and lasting ways.

Long before writers begin writing reviews, researchers need to gain access to a whole body of research conducted over a period of time in article, chapter, or book form. As a way to support our research and reading, we go to the library and ask the research librarian to give a presentation on conducting searches of research using ERIC, the Education Research Information Center. This is the database most commonly used in the field of education. Some have prior experience using ERIC, but many find it useful to have an expert librarian give them a "refresher" with tips geared toward conducting searches of lines of research. The librarian provides ideas for using "key words" to find research articles under a specific topic, or he or she will often give students a list of the major journals in the discipline. Librarians are also willing to give a tour of the part of the library where users may find hard copies of the educational research journals. Nowadays, students—and teacher-researchers in general—may go through their graduate studies and research processes without ever stepping foot in the library because they have online access to the texts they need. However, teachers have told me year after year that taking time to find, thumb through, and read copies of the research journals has helped them gain a sense of the research territory and to see where research conversations are taking place in print.

I also encourage the teachers I work with to spend time every week reading online journals connected to their areas of interest as a way to stay up-to-date with the continuing research conversation. Now that the majority of journals are available online through college and university libraries, students have easy access to hundreds of journal articles and have the opportunity to pick and choose what works for their own reviews more quickly than when thumbing through journals in the stacks. I also recommend the *Review of Educational Research,* which is a journal made up entirely of current literature reviews in education. This is a wonderful venue for researchers to find examples of well-crafted literature reviews with a wide range of topics and writing styles.

Finally, to provide a general overview of the genre expectations associated with the literature review, we read *Telling a Research Story: Writing a Literature Review,* by Christine Feak and John Swales (2009). This handbook uses a concrete and pragmatic style to describe some of the structure, style, and language expectations for this genre. For instance, it lays out examples of the different kinds of literature reviews, such as (1) Narrative—telling what has been found in the area of research and implications for the body of research, (2) Interpretive—looking at the literature from a particular point of reference, and (3) Meta-analysis—a statistical review of the literature that looks at research on a topic. Teacher-researchers often use this book as a guide and reference throughout their writing process.

## Using Mentor Texts to Study the Literature Review as a Genre

One of the best ways to learn to write in a new genre is to read great examples. Over the years, I have collected examples of well-written literature reviews that demonstrate writing strategies I find compelling or enviable. There are some writers who are exceptional in their flow of ideas and others who have a natural voice. I share examples of the literature reviews I admire and we read them together, not for the content but for the writing "moves." I want students to look at the "moves" the authors are making in the literature reviews as a way to make sense of the genre. What I appreciate about a good literature review is that the author finds a way to take something complex, such as a collection of research studies, and condenses them into a few succinct lines or paragraphs. Steve Graham is one of my favorite academic writers who has published a number of literature reviews on teaching writing to adolescents (2007, 2008). He has a way of taking complicated thinking and writing and articulating it so that someone with only moderate amounts of knowledge in the field will understand. This is a skill, and it is something that can be acquired with time and practice.

When we meet, we usually read two samples of literature reviews with a specific task or guiding question. This is a way to highlight one of the strategies covered in a mini-lesson or to help pick out the "moves" an author makes so students may eventually learn to try these strategies on their own. For example, I share copies of Arthena Ball's (2009) literature review on teaching writing in culturally diverse classrooms and ask them to notice how she takes the reader on a tour of this line of research. She describes the major contributions in this area based on history or chronology. After covering the scope of the research, she takes a turn in the essay to push researchers to think about new avenues for supporting multiethnic writers. When we read this review, I suggest the following guiding task to help them notice the way Ball organizes her piece: "Find examples of specific headings, phrases, and transitions that help organize the piece and work to guide the reader on a tour of the research area." Examples of other weekly tasks or guiding questions we use while reading mentor literature reviews include the following:

1. How does the argument unfold?
2. How does the author present two or more schools of thought arguing with each other?
3. How does the author use model phrases or templates for sentences that serve as different transitions or functions? (For example, "Having moved over time from _____ to _____ the next logical move in the literature was to _____.")
4. How does the author evaluate what he or she is reading, not just list it? (For example, "Here is a study that adds to the body of work because . . ." or "This study is flawed because . . .")

## Making Sense of a Lot of Information

After we have read mentor texts and identified key features of the literature review genre, we are ready to begin a search for studies in their line of work. However, this search is not a simple process, and it is easy to spin out of control. Meredith is in the process of writing a literature review chapter and shared what she thought was most challenging about writing in this genre. "It's difficult to determine when 'enough is enough' in a literature review. When you're immersing yourself in the literature, it can be hard to make sense of which studies are most pertinent to your own work and which are only loosely related." It's difficult to corral ideas and keep a clear focus. A big question is how much detail to go into: which studies should be talked about in depth, which to describe just briefly, and which can be combined in a serial citation.

As we wade through what can feel like a sea of material, there are strategies to help focus the reading and research.

First, it's useful to identify classic or seminal studies that have been cited repeatedly over a period of time. If the seminal studies seem to be places where the research conversation began or where the line of research shifted in an important way, include them in the reviews. Or, if there are studies that are really similar to the kind of study you are doing, present them in more detail. I suggest reviewing studies that have taken place within the past five to ten years so that literature reviews are up-to-date.

There are also strategies for making sense of a great deal of material. Sharing my own process has proved helpful. For example, I often create a spreadsheet for all the studies and then go through and code them in the same way I would use grounded theory—organizing them first based on general theme, findings, or topic.

Next, I do a second reading of the research articles to begin summarizing important works. As a way of structuring this close reading and summary work, I create a table or cover sheet for each of the important studies I want to include in the review. In this table or cover sheet, I fill in details about the following categories and questions:

1. What issue or question is the author trying to address?
2. What type of research design was implemented?
3. How many participants were in the study?
4. What did the participants do?
5. What was the intervention or research move?
6. What are the findings?
7. What are the implications for that finding for what you want to do?

Although coding, categorizing, and summarizing the body of research can be one of the most time-consuming aspects of the literature review process, it is a great way to take part in the close reading that is necessary to truly learn about a body of research. Completing this step lends confidence about writing the literature review, because you can't help but feel knowledgeable about your area of research.

## Organization and Flow of Ideas

Once you've read, coded, and summarized your collection of research studies, you are ready to begin drafting reviews. At this stage, I focus on the flow of information in a literature review and how the writer should take the reader seamlessly through a body of work. A common problem I find is that beginning researchers jump from big idea to big idea without clear transitions. I share examples of well-organized literature reviews, such as George Hillocks's (2008) review of the literature on high school composition. Hillocks organizes his piece using broad headings and then, within each one, includes subheadings. His use and choice of headings are what allow him to move the reader from broad ideas or general findings to very specific ones.

## Mentoring and Supporting Teachers as Writers

As we move from drafting to polishing our literature reviews, we share the work in peer conferences to receive revision feedback from fellow students. One of the teachers, Mary, told me this was the single-most helpful step in the whole process of writing her literature review.

> I loved having the opportunity to read another graduate student's literature review. This allowed me to see that I was not way off track in my own writing and, even more importantly, it gave me a clear picture of what was expected. I could read her review with more distance than I could read my own and this helped me think about my own writing in new ways.

In the end, the most important thing beginning researchers need is guidance. They need support even though they may not always express it. Sometimes we expect teachers to just "know" how to write a literature review without actually teaching them what this genre looks like, how it functions, who it is written for, and how to meet the audience's needs. The more writing support teachers—and all beginning researchers— receive, the more prepared they will be for their writing as researchers.

## References

Atwell, Nancie. 1987. *In the Middle: Writing, Reading, and Learning with Adolescents.* Portsmouth, NH: Heinemann.

Ball, Arthena. 2009. "Teaching Writing in Culturally Diverse Classrooms." In Christine Feak and John Swales, *Telling a Research Story: Writing a Literature Review.* Ann Arbor, MI: University of Michigan Press.

Graham, Steven. 2008. "Research on Writing Development, Practice, Instruction, and Development." *Reading and Writing: An Interdisciplinary Journal* 21 (1 and 2): 172–183 and 210–221.

Graham, Steven, and Jill Fitzgerald, eds. 2008. *Handbook of Writing Research.* New York: Guilford.

Graham, Steven, Charles A. MacArthur, and Jill Fitzgerald. 2008. *Best Practices in Writing Instruction: Solving Problems in the Teaching of Literacy.* New York: Guilford.

Graham, Steven, and Diane Perin. 2007a. "A Meta-analysis of Writing Instruction for Adolescent Students." *Journal of Educational Psychology* 99: 445.

———. 2007b. "What We Know, What We Still Need to Know: Teaching Adolescents to Write." *Scientific Studies of Reading* 11 (4): 313-335.

Hillocks, George, Jr. 2008. "Writing in Secondary Schools." In *Handbook of Research on Writing: History, Society, School, and Text*, ed. Charles Bazerman. Mahwah, NJ: Lawrence Erlbaum.

## RESEARCH WORKSHOP

## "What's the Most Beautiful Thing You Know About . . . ?"

*Melanie Quinn and Ruth Shagoury*

We've been meeting each week this spring with a group of pre-K through grade twelve teachers, all of us exploring literacy teaching in our classrooms around our teacher-research questions. We've all been looking closely at one student in our class whom we are intrigued by or wondering about. To look at each student through fresh and positive eyes, we read aloud the book *What's the Most Beautiful Thing You Know About Horses?* (1998) by Richard Van Camp.

Van Camp is a member of the Dogrib nation of the Northwest Territories of Canada and an emerging voice in the Native American literary movement. He wrote this children's book in order to understand horses, since his people are not horse people and he's always been curious to learn more about them. The format is simple: he asks different people, "What's the most beautiful thing you know about horses?" He receives responses such as, "The most beautiful thing about horses is that they always find their way home" and "I love their breath. You can feel their breath move through their chest. They stare at you as they breathe. Their soul comes right out."

After we read the book aloud and shared the vivid and colorful illustrations, we asked everyone to write, "What's the most beautiful thing you know about . . . your student?"

Following a ten-minute quick-write, we shared our writing with partners and then with the whole group. As we discussed our discoveries, we found different ways to approach how we might work with our students.

Sandy wrote that the most beautiful thing about Jack is "when he is excited about something, his face lights up as if it is the best idea he has ever been part of. He is, at the same time, joyous and serious, determined and open, elated and hardworking." Sandy plans to try to tap into this energy more intentionally.

Erika decided, "The most beautiful thing I know about Skye is her smile and the quirky, flirty way she said, 'Maybe I will.' When she gives me hints of confidence like this, I'm going to believe her and pursue it."

Rob wrote about his case study's "quiet determination to succeed that [he] could not see at first." This realization in turn sparked Rob's determination "to stick with him and share in his vision of success."

It's important to see—and re-see—our students. What we can recognize as "the most beautiful thing we know about them" can lead us to see new possibilities in our work together.

Springtime is a wonderful season to turn to these possibilities, remembering that during this long winter, just under the ground (and snow!) were plants ready to shoot up and blossom. We're planning to expand into other ways to use Van Camp's terrific book as a nudge for our study groups and work with colleagues with similar questions:

What's the most beautiful thing you know about your teaching mentor?
What's the most beautiful thing you know about teaching reading?
What's the most beautiful thing you know about conferring with students?

# 7

# Honest Labor:
# Writing Up Research

*All the good stories are out there waiting to be told in a fresh, wild way.*
—ANNE LAMOTT

Teaching and writing are labor, and only those involved in birthing research projects in chaotic classrooms can understand fully what the experience is like. We remember some years ago talking to a man whose wife had just spent twenty-six hours in labor giving birth to their first child. We were clucking about how hard that must have been for the woman. He brushed aside our concerns, saying, "Hey, it's not that bad. It's not like she was in labor all the time. I mean, you have a pain, but then you get a break for five or ten minutes. Heck, you can practically take a nap or read a magazine during those breaks."

We write and teach, but we don't work full time as teachers in K–12 schools, so we're giving advice from the outside, and we risk being as clueless as that spouse. The view from the outside doesn't acknowledge what the teaching process is like for those on the inside in the midst of busy classrooms. Teachers are often told that weekends are the perfect time to revise the drafts they've been working on in the classroom. We might just as easily tell them to read a magazine or grab a nap in the author's chair in class during those moments when they aren't actually teaching their students throughout the day.

We do know a couple of teachers who write beautiful essays and books in the midst of their teaching day; they grab moments here and there between lessons and workshops. But this certainly isn't the norm. Writing, like labor, is a slow, hard process for most teacher-researchers. It requires a fair amount of time outside the classroom—quiet, unstructured time to let your thoughts percolate.

Teacher-researchers have a response for the experts who say writing can easily be integrated into the teaching day: it's much harder than you think. Teachers are in labor all day long, and no matter how nice the person is who holds your hand, the experience can be understood and described only by

**187**

those who go through it. The rhythm of any good teaching day includes rapid and steady bursts of insight, delight, and unease about students' learning and our role in it.

Writing and teaching take such different energies that many argue that it isn't necessary for teachers to write up their research. Just the process of collecting the data and trying to analyze it will bring them new learning and understanding. Adding the layer of writing to the findings and bringing them to a larger audience is a step many teacher-researchers don't want or need. And yet . . . we've had our own professional lives transformed by a few great teacher-research studies. We bet you, too, can identify books that marked your own emergence as a confident teacher—books such as *In the Middle* by Nancie Atwell (1987), *Teacher* by Sylvia Ashton-Warner (1963), *Reading with Meaning* by Debbie Miller (2002), *Reading Reasons* by Kelly Gallagher (2003), and *The Book Whisperer* by Donalyn Miller (2009).

We see quiet, persistent changes in our teaching over the years, changes that would not have happened without our having read the detailed accounts by other teachers about the learning in their classrooms. Even more transformative for us are the bits and pieces of writing done by teachers in the midst of research, like the snippets included in this book. This text is peppered with the writing of teacher-researchers, writing we wouldn't have had access to if they hadn't done the labor of writing about their research.

If we're honest enough to acknowledge that writing up research is difficult, we hope you trust us enough to consider the possibilities anyway. We need more voices from teachers on the Web, in journals and in books, more accounts of how complicated and exciting learning can be when teachers look closely and aren't afraid to write about what they are seeing. The practical advice that follows is culled from the experiences of teacher-researchers who have managed to write and publish their work; they tell us that no other experience has brought them more professional growth.

# Getting Started

When we wrote the first edition of this book almost fifteen years ago, it was a different world for teacher-writers. E-mail was starting to become part of our daily lives, but the World Wide Web was rightly nicknamed the World Wide Wait. We had hints of what possibilities there were, but it would take so long for any Web sites with images on them to load that few people had the patience for surfing. There was no Google, there were no blogs, and the 800-pound gorilla among browsers was Netscape.

What a different world it is today: technology has opened up myriad new options for teacher-researchers to write up their work. Our own writing lives have been transformed by the Web, with most of our daily writing now devoted to online venues. Ruth and her daughter, Meghan Rose, publish their writing at their site Lit for Kids (http://litforkids.wordpress.com/); Brenda writes feature articles as part of her weekly e-newsletter *The Big Fresh* (www.choiceliteracy.com).

If you're a teacher-researcher, there is no better way to get started writing up your work than participating on the Web. You can start anonymously by commenting on writing you like from other teachers who blog, or by contributing to education Web sites. Even if your role involves far more lurking than commenting, you'll learn a lot about the norms for posting, responding, and being a good citizen on the Web by considering which teacher-authors are most relevant to you.

We've spent years now writing about our learning on the Web for others, as well as coaching other teachers as they begin to write up their research in Web venues. Here are some tips for getting started with writing up your research on the Web:

1.  *Find a writing partner.* It's not surprising how many teacher blogs and Web sites that endure for years are written by teams. A Year of Reading (http://readingyear.blogspot.com/) is coauthored by Mary Lee Hahn and Franki Sibberson; Two Writing Teachers (http://twowritingteachers.wordpress.com/) is written by Ruth Ayres and Stacey Shubitz. Life always intervenes over the long haul with big writing projects, and a partner is invaluable for sharing the load when one or the other collaborator has to tend to home or school crises.

2.  *Stick to a routine.* As Paul Silvia explains in *How to Write a Lot* (2007), "The secret is the regularity, not the number of days or the number of hours. . . . *Finding time* is a destructive way of thinking about writing. Never say this again. Instead of *finding time* to write, *allot* time to write" (83). Ruth and Meghan have posted a minimum of two entries a week on their blog for years; Brenda sends out her newsletter every week. Having weekly and daily deadlines is essential for building the habit of writing. Monthly deadlines are tougher to stick to, if only because there is too much time between them.

3.  *Be a good citizen on the Web.* Cheer on the teachers you enjoy by commenting on their posts and linking to them. If you don't know where to start in finding those kindred spirits, the Kidlitosphere (www.kidlitosphere.org/) is a great place to start.

4.  *Don't vent.* For every teacher like Natalie Munroe (Goanos 2011), the Pennsylvania teacher who became a dubious folk hero for raging against her "rat-like" students, there are dozens who are suspended for unprofessional writing on the Web. It's tempting in challenging times to let loose, but that's what journals with locks on them are for.

5.  *Capture moments.* The "slice of life" writing you do from your classroom is perfect for the short formats that work best on the Web. These quick pieces will not only resonate with colleagues, but will be the catalyst for long pieces and keep your writing centered on concrete, showing-not-telling writing about your students.

6.  *Be patient.* It takes months or even years to build an audience, and that's not even the primary purpose of writing on the Web for many teacher-researchers. The discipline of writing regularly is what will build your skills, as well as generate a wealth of raw material to work with later when you write up your work as a longer article or even a book.

If you write regularly in any kind of Web forum, you'll soon find the lessons about how you are changing as a writer spilling over into your classroom in unexpected ways. Karen Terlecky, a fifth-grade teacher who blogs with her colleague Bill Prosser, explains:

> How often do we have the student who just does not know what to write next or what book to read next? I empathize with those students now. I now know that when it is time to launch a new piece, with either a blank piece of paper or a blank computer screen in front of them, students are taking a risk that might feel monumental to them.
>
> I share my own uncertainties about what to write next with my students. I explain that I've learned to keep a notebook full of possible topics to write about, so that if I get a good idea I don't forget it. I let them know that there is risk involved, and sometimes out of risk, comes our best learning and writing. I might share with them the volume of blog posts I've written, and that not every piece is excellent, but the sheer volume that I write helps me become a better writer. My students see me as a writer through the blog, and that is a wonderful model for them. (2010)

# Getting Organized for More Extensive Writing Projects

If you've reached the point where you're ready to write up your findings in a journal article, thesis, or book, the first thing you'll need to do is organize what you have to work with—the raw materials you've collected over the past months or years. Gather all this stuff, lay it out, and look it over. Your materials might include writing and reading logs by the kids, your notes or teaching journal, printouts from your blog, kids' projects, data-analysis code sheets or charts, or photographs.

As you go through everything you've saved, look for the breakthrough moments, the instances when you discovered something about your kids and yourself. Begin to compile lists of those key incidents or events. Flag them in your notes; pull them off the transcripts. You need gallons and gallons of sap to make a cup of maple syrup: you need to look over all the raw stuff you have before you can distill it into the story of your classroom.

Technology is great for flagging, cataloging, and logging information, but sometimes there is no replacement for seeing everything across a larger canvas. We've often commandeered the living room from family members to lay out reams of notes, photos, and video clips with teachers who are starting to draft conference proposals, books, or articles. Writer Annie Dillard (1989) explains this process well, in *The Writing Life*:

> How appalled I was to discover that, in order to write so much as a sonnet, you need a warehouse. You can easily get so confused writing a

thirty-page chapter that in order to make an outline for the second draft, you have to rent a hall. I have often "written" with the mechanical aid of a twenty-foot conference table. You lay your pages along the table's edge and pace out the work. You walk along the rows; you weed bits, move bits, and dig out bits, bent over the rows with full hands like a gardener. (46)

Once you pull out some of those breakthrough moments, you need to start writing. When you're drafting, it's probably not going to be a linear movement from page one to page two, from section one to section two. It's usually best to write about some of those moments of insight from your classroom in small chunks and as vividly as possible. What were students wearing? Saying? The smallest details will be critical for making those moments come to life. If you get stumped in trying to re-create a scene, give yourself prompts: "I saw . . . ," "I heard . . . ," "I felt . . . "

Many times it's the seemingly insignificant details that can make the scene come to life. Bonnie Friedman (1993) writes about the importance of details:

> You may paint a soul only by painting a knuckle. You may convey terror or longing or regret or exhilaration only by giving us the color of someone's hair and exactly what she ate for lunch, and red high heels, and an attaché case's handle stained dark by the oils of a human hand, and a skinny buck-toothed girl singing "Yes We Have No Bananas" on a black-and-white TV, and olives, and three o'clock, and the Scotch-taped hem of a Bergdorf Goodman dress, and venetian blinds, and a woman's eyes fixed for many minutes on a scarred tabletop, and a tin spoon ringing against the side of a mug. There are no shortcuts. (87)

Photos and videos are a wonderful way to get ideas for freewriting about the classroom. Use some of your photos as writing prompts, and you'll be surprised at the memories that are sparked because you've got a full-color reminder of an event right before your eyes.

Once you've got some pieces of the story—strong, clear writing on critical incidents in your classroom—you can begin to see how these will fit together to tell a larger story. It's helpful to remember that we *are* writing the stories. Author and writing teacher Roger Rosenblatt (2011) stresses that everything we write is essentially a story:

> Stories are central to life. They're everywhere: in medicine, a patient tells a doctor the story of his ailment, how he felt on this day or that, and the doctor tells the patient the story of the therapy, how he will feel this day and that, until, one hopes, the story will have a happy ending. (18)

These powerful stories from your classroom, whatever meaning is taken from them, are the glue that will hold all your data and analysis together, making the reader want to get to the end of your piece to see how it all turns out.

# Learning from Distant Writing Teachers

The best writing coaches are often "distant teachers"—the authors of your favorite books and blogs on teaching and learning who relate the stories of their classrooms. Terri Austin, author of *Changing the View* (1995), credits her ability to write her classroom research to learning from a "distant teacher" whom she had never met:

> In terms of style, I have to say that I learned to write by reading Nancie Atwell's *In the Middle*. I taught myself how to write like that, not that I'm anywhere near her ability, but that book probably is the most influential book for me because it came right at the time I became a teacher-researcher and when I was struggling not only to be a researcher, but to be a writer. It flowed like a story. I still have her original book in its original pink cover. . . . I have it marked out—this is how she introduced this, this is how she explained her record keeping, this is how she wove in the stories of her students. I taught myself how to write with this book. (1998, personal communication)

We encourage you to reread your favorite books by teachers—not as an educator, but as a writer. Look at the leads to chapters. How do the authors draw you in? How do they lay out information on the page to make it inviting? How do they balance classroom incidents and anecdotes with practical advice? What kinds of materials do they put into their appendixes? Once you start reading like a writer, your favorite books will seem brand new and full of practical tips to improve your own drafts.

# Why Your Writing Matters

You won't be far into the process before you'll wonder if you really have something worth saying. As you lay out your raw materials, you're going to see big gaps in what you need. And as you begin to write up those moments of insight, you'll get discouraged about your writing ability. Know that all teachers who end up writing wonderful articles and books feel this way early in the process. Your first drafts, even if they look good to other readers, will seem pretty awful to you. Everyone writes terrible first drafts. That's the beginning step in writing up your research. Writer Anne Lamott (1994) describes why it's important to hold your nose and keep writing:

> All good writers write shitty first drafts. This is how they end up with good second drafts and terrific third drafts. People tend to look at successful writers, writers who are getting their books published and maybe even doing well financially, and think that they sit down at their desks every morning feeling like a million dollars, feeling great about who they are and how much talent they have and what a great story they have to

tell; that they take in a few deep breaths, push back their sleeves, roll their necks a few times to get all the cricks out, and dive in, typing fully formed passages as fast as a court reporter. But this is just the fantasy of the unini-tiated. I know some very great writers, writers you love who write beauti-fully and have made a great deal of money, and not one of them sits down routinely feeling wildly enthusiastic and confident. Not one of them writes elegant first drafts. All right, one of them does, but we do not like her very much. (21–22)

Even if your work doesn't get published in a traditional book or journal format, we hope the process of writing it up brings you to a new under-standing of your classroom. That's why teachers write—not to transform the field, or to be famous, or to get a book published. We write to understand our classrooms, our students, ourselves. Wrestling with words on the page, we finally understand why our research and teaching matters, and what we need to carry away from one year into the next. We see ourselves and our class-rooms anew, in ways not possible without the intense reflection that writing demands.

Abandon any pressure you feel to write something great or something that's just perfect for a certain journal or book publisher. Many of the most widely read teacher-authors today publish only on the Web, and that avenue is open to anyone. Write first to learn more about your classroom through the writing. If you have that as your goal, you're much more likely to write some-thing many other teachers will want to read.

# Getting Response to Your Writing

Once you do have some drafts of writing, even if they are just a few pages recounting random incidents, you'll need to get some response from others. Before you send what you've written to a journal or book publisher, you should share it with at least a couple of close teaching friends and get their advice for what you should write next and what revisions are needed.

Who is the best person to respond? Brenda Ueland, in her classic and recently reissued book *If You Want to Write* (2010), explains who that person is:

> For when you write, if it is to be any good at all, you must feel free, free and not anxious. The only good teachers for you are those friends who love you, who think you are interesting, or very important, or wonderfully funny; whose attitude is: "Tell me more. Tell me all you can. I want to understand more about everything you feel and know and all the changes inside and out of you. Let more come out." (33)

Once you have that friend or colleague who will respond to your writing, here's the key question you'll want to ask: What's the story here? Where is the narrative thread that can hold this all together? Finding that narrative thread will help you figure out what needs to stay in the writing and what needs to go.

When you get response from others, stifle the urge to accept or reject their advice immediately. As Robert Frost said, "Thinking isn't agreeing or disagreeing—that's voting." Mull over the responses, negative and positive, and see what you can use from them to make the writing better. We also like Peter Elbow's (1997) advice about conferring over writing: "When you get conflicting reactions, block your impulse to figure out which reactions are right. Eat like an owl: take in everything and trust your innards to digest what's useful and discard what's not. Try for readers with different tastes and temperaments—especially if you don't have many readers" (118).

---

**Tips for Writing and Getting Published**

- The best way to start writing is to write as if you are writing a letter to a dear friend you've been out of touch with for a while. It's much easier to write a letter than it is to write an article. And before you know it, the imaginary letter will become the real deal.
- There is never a "good" time to write. Now is as good a time as any.
- Write every day, even if it's only a few words or phrases. Writing to and with your students counts, too.
- Get an outsider's view of the journal or publisher you want to work with: submission guidelines, upcoming themes.
- Get an insider's view of the journal or publisher you want to work with: tone of response, time for response, quality of response.
- Follow the rule of three: allow an article or proposal to be rejected at least three times before thinking seriously about revising it.
- A negative, hostile response from a journal says plenty about the insecurity of the editor and nothing about the quality of your writing.

---

If you're feeling courageous, ask someone outside of education to read something you've written. People with a little distance from the teaching culture can let you know immediately what jargon or phrasing gets in the way of the story you are trying to tell, and they can give you a sense of how wide an audience there is for your writing.

Many researchers we've worked with find the experience of presenting their work at a local in-service meeting, or a state or national conference, invaluable for drafting and improving their writing. Applying to present at a conference gives you a forced deadline for beginning to pull together a narrative.

Writing a proposal of one or two pages will get you organized for longer writing tasks. And presenting your work orally allows you to read cues from your audience. Their questions will push you forward in your thinking and help you go back to your classroom, writing, and thinking with an audience in mind. Noting when listeners seem engaged or bored can also help you decide what should remain in your writing and what should be cut.

**Tips for Organizing a Writing Retreat**

There is a long tradition of writers retreating from the busyness of their daily lives and carving out stretches of time where they can immerse themselves in their writing in a community of other writers. Many teacher-researchers are finding that weekends devoted to writing with a trusted group—and even better, weeklong summer writing retreats!—are a practical and enjoyable route toward making sense of their data and writing it up for their intended audiences. Many of the teacher-researchers in this book have found this a far more do-able alternative to rising at 4 a.m. to write, or trying to fit in time in the evening after responding to student work.

After taking part in several writing retreats ourselves, we're hooked. We encourage you to consider including at least a weekend with your teacher-research group that's devoted to writing and sharing your work. These tips, culled from teacher-researchers from Maine to Alaska, can help get you off to a successful start. Happy writing!

- Plan and organize. Choose your dates far enough in advance so that you can find times that will work for the most members of your group and that give you enough lead time to be working toward the goal of having the necessary data and books on hand.
- Choose a place away from school—an environment where you can be a writer. The place is important, which is another reason to plan ahead. This gives you a chance to poll friends and colleagues about possible cabins, off-season rates for retreat centers, and bed-and-breakfasts with reasonable rates, or even to write a small grant or request staff development funds. We've been at successful retreats at out-of-the-way bed-and-breakfasts, retreat centers, and the home of a group member who banned her family for a long weekend and scattered sleeping bags around the house.
- Have meals catered or provided by someone else. "Breaking bread together" is a central aspect of writing, talking, and thinking, but the preparation can really cut into your time. If your budget doesn't permit catered meals, you can enlist the support of a friend, family member, or even one member of the group who agrees to take on the responsibility on a rotating basis. It's an amazing gift to emerge from your writing cocoon to an already-prepared meal and colleagues ready to dig in and discuss your work in progress.
- Try for at least three days away. It can take a while to get started and into the rhythm of daily writing.
- Schedule long, unstructured blocks of writing time. It's easy to get sidetracked with lots of discussion. We have found it helpful to get together the first evening of the retreat and negotiate a tentative daily schedule, with at least two inviolate hours of writing time in the morning and another two in the afternoon. Some members might

want to plan on an early-morning walk to get the day started, a special time for reading before or after lunch, or conference times. Create a schedule that works for your group's needs. But keep the writing time central. It's surprising how much more writing you can accomplish when you are in the midst of a group of committed writers!

- Have set goals. Plan what will be accomplished before the retreat begins, and distribute these group and individual goals in advance.
- Bring lots of writing supplies. Make sure there's at least one printer that you can hook up to your laptop computers or tablets. Access to a copying machine is also a convenience, if possible. Bring pens, pads of paper, sticky notes, highlighters, and whatever else your writing rituals depend on; don't assume you can just pick them up on-site. And don't forget books—novels, poems, essays—whatever good reading you enjoy for that before-bed downtime and early-morning preparation for writing. We have found that the language of these novels and the good talk around texts finds its way into our final writing results.

You can often return to your research plan itself to give you a framework for your proposal. The origin of your research question is usually a good place to start. Another bonus of writing up a proposal is that the deadline forces you to consolidate your thinking and get it on paper and out the door.

You may want to present your work as part of a panel presentation (see Figures 7.1 and 7.2). This gives you a chance to plan together, talk through your ideas with others, and assemble a presentation that draws on the connections in your research. Some presentations are better suited to one person, with more time for in-depth explanations of the work or more audience participation, of course.

The accepted proposals in Figures 7.1 and 7.2 can serve as models for you as you think about presenting at a local or national conference. Both presentations allowed these teachers to talk their way through what they had learned from their research projects and what would connect them with a larger audience.

# Giving Response to Writing

Writers depend upon other writers for response. If you want to receive helpful response to your writing, you'll need to learn how to give useful feedback to colleagues. The process of responding to others will give you clues about what kind of response can be most helpful to you.

We've learned that vague comments can often lead to worse second drafts by researchers, and any initial response to writing needs to be tempered with a keen awareness of how much criticism the writer is ready and able to hear.

Figure 7.1 Presentation Proposal

---

### PROPOSAL TO NCTE NATIONAL CONFERENCE

*'Tween a Rock and a Hard Place: Supporting "Tweens" as They Navigate the Treacherous Waters of Accountability While Preserving the Joy of Literacy Learning*

The focus of this year's NCTE conference, Teachers and Students Together: Living Literate Lives, urges us to "dig deeply and think broadly" about the consequences of imposed mandates at the expense of students' creativity and authentic literacy experiences. More than two decades ago, writing instruction was revolutionized by the important work of Donald Murray, Nancie Atwell, and others who researched writing with children. Based on that research, together they created the philosophical foundations for what has become writer's workshop. On the surface, one would assume that teachers have held fast to their deeply held belief in writer's workshop. However, the impositions of curriculum mandates and accountability testing have isolated teachers and students by providing formulaic instructional guides and programs that ignore the necessary messiness of writing. The need for a community of writers in our profession and in our classrooms is lost at the expense of teaching to the test. Donald Murray (2007) argues, "To be an effective teacher of writing, you should grow your class plans out of your own experiences at your writing desk. When you are in class . . . you should understand the students' problems because you have met and solved them yourself."

Three teachers of "tweens" resolved to create a community of writers between themselves and their students. Instead of following the neatness of a prescribed curriculum, they chose to embrace the messiness of the writing process. Tim Gillespie (1985) says, "When teachers write, we become partners in a community of writers, full participants in our classroom writing workshop." These three educators will share the results of their journey in which they created a community of writers between their students and themselves.

Beth Lawson, third-grade teacher, and Katie Doherty, sixth-grade teacher, in their presentation "Write Like You Mean It," will share how they support students becoming emotionally invested in their writing by providing a model of teacher-as-writer. They realized the benefits that Katie Wood Ray (2002) advocated in her book *What You Know By Heart*: "We . . . pay attention when our co-teachers of writing talk about going through this process. . . . We need to know what they do because, whatever it is, it becomes something our students might do as well." In turn, Beth and Katie sought out a collaboration between their writing and that of their students. They tapped into the potential of creating a cross-age "tween" writing community where third and sixth graders shared their writing, offered meaningful feedback, and used shared mentor texts to hone their craft. The community learned to read as writers and to write authentically in the midst of both age groups feeling the pressure of district mandates and high-stakes test preparation.

Melanie Quinn, after six years in higher education, returned to the classroom and collaborated with Beth and Katie. In her presentation "Teach Like You Mean It," she will share the discoveries and disconnects she has experienced between best practice theory and the unintended consequences of the accountability movement in the classroom as well as in the profession. She will advocate for teachers to own curricular decisions in the classroom through the formation of collaborative communities that emphasize critical thought and value teacher autonomy.

This presentation will include photographs, artifacts, and video clips that showcase these communities at work. There will be opportunities for the audience to interact by sharing their own writer's workshop experiences and asking questions. Participants will receive resources that encourage building a community of writers in the classroom and with colleagues.

Figure 7.2  Presentation Proposal

---

**PROPOSAL FOR NATIONAL LITERACY CONFERENCE: EARLY CHILDHOOD STRAND**

*Creating a Literate Reality for Young Children*

Brief summary: Teachers play a critical role in helping young children see and believe that they are readers and writers. In this session, two teacher educators will share research and practice that fosters connection between young children and literature and ignites a passion for literacy that lasts a lifetime. Resources for early childhood educators, including the use of drama in creating literate environments, will be shared.

"Language . . . is not merely representational (though it is that); it is also constitutive. It actually creates realities and invites identities" (Peter Johnston).

Teachers of young children must work diligently to create classroom environments where young children can grow into literacy successfully. It is crucial that these teachers use language to intentionally influence the way children come to see themselves as readers and writers. Teachers must also use their knowledge of child development theory and current research in the field to meld together children from diverse backgrounds and cultures, who often have limited family literacy, into a caring community of learners passionate about reading and writing.

It is also necessary for teachers to understand the importance of honoring the family as the first teacher for children, and to support family literacy through the literacy of the child. In our presentation, two early childhood educators will share suggestions and resources for creating classroom environments that encourage all young learners to grow into the reality that they are successful readers and writers. Our goal is to provide concrete ways for other early childhood teachers to put research into action in the early childhood classroom, and to take away a practical repertoire of strategies and activities that will help them guide young children on their journey toward literacy.

First, Melissa Kolb will present "Environments of Expectation." Her presentation will provide a brief review of current literacy research in the field of early childhood, including what she has learned in her classroom on the importance of teacher language in creating a literate reality for children. She will discuss what she has discovered about the crucial role that environment plays, and provide examples of classroom structures that support literacy development. She will also discuss strategies she has employed for connecting with families and promoting family literacy development that complements classroom learning.

Next, Kelly Petrin will present "Strategies and Activities for Connecting to Literature." She will discuss strategies she has employed for helping children connect to literature and the process of becoming readers and writers. She will share multiple activities that have been successful in her classroom environment, including the incorporation of drama. The audience will have the opportunity to participate in a variety of dramatic activities.

The classroom examples are from low-income communities in a large urban school district, with a majority of students who are English language learners. The presentations will include a multitude of examples of classroom structures, environments, curriculum, activities, and suggestions for working with parents to nurture our young learners.

We will close by inviting the audience to share stories from their own classrooms and communities. There will be time for questions and comments.

Some years ago the editorial team for the *Teacher Research Journal* got together and compiled guidelines for reading and responding to writing by teacher-researchers. You can use these as a starting point for developing strategies for responding to writing within your own research community.

### Reading the Manuscript
- Read the draft at least twice. We have often been surprised by what we discover during the second reading. The first time through, try to get a sense of the whole piece without thinking about how to fix it.
- Note the areas of the draft you want to know more about. Jot down what strikes you, and indicate questions you have.
- Ask yourself questions as you read:
  > What am I learning?
  > What's new here?
  > Can someone on staff benefit from this piece?
  > What would other teachers learn?
  > Is this written in a teacher-to-teacher voice?
  > Is there any tension in the piece (rather than a tone of "I have seen the light!")?

### Responding to the Manuscript
We want these teachers to continue to research and share their discoveries. Frame your response so that the author will see what worked well in the draft and what worked less well. What would you say if you were going to have a writing conference with him or her? Try to keep in mind the kind of coaching that has been the most helpful to you as a writer.

- Be specific in your comments. Include direct quotes (with page numbers) in your examples of what worked and what didn't. Try to provide one or two concrete examples for every assertion you make, regardless of whether it's a strength or a weakness.
- Avoid educational jargon.
- Concentrate on the most important issues you'd like the author to address. You don't have to suggest ways to improve all aspects of the piece.
- If you wouldn't feel comfortable saying your comments to the author in person, don't write them.

We have found that if you schedule a time to share drafts in a group, the best starting point is to have the author tell the group what type of advice will be most helpful. Some authors will be in the final stages of writing, ready for copyediting and response about word choice; others will wither if they hear anything but the most global responses to what works and what doesn't in their initial drafts. If you ask first, you're more likely to give the author advice that will really be used.

# A Word About Rejection

We need to give a word of warning here about receiving responses to your writing from journals and book publishers. We've received much helpful advice from caring editorial board members and reviewers from publishers. But we've also received pages of snotty insults from reviewers that drove us to tears. A vicious or just plain lousy response to your work isn't a reflection on your writing—it's a reflection on the pettiness and unprofessionalism of the reviewer. We urge you to write to the editorial board of a journal or publisher if you think a review of your work crosses the line from critique to attack. We all have a responsibility to make our profession more caring and responsive to teachers' writing.

Even a kind rejection of writing hurts. It's hard to separate our classrooms and our psyches as teachers from the writing we do about them. Because we are all fragile as writers, it's helpful to know which journals have the most supportive editorial boards. Read journals you might submit your work to, and see if the tone of their published authors matches yours. We made the mistake early in our writing careers of submitting our work only to the largest journals in our field. We sometimes waited months for a response, only to get rejections with little or no editorial assistance for improving the draft.

It was only after we began submitting to regional and state journals in our field that we began to receive quicker, more positive responses to our writing. Consider submitting your work to smaller forums at the start—local newspapers as op-eds, a district newsletter, a state interest group's annual collection. As your confidence builds, progress to larger outlets for your writing.

It's ironic, too, that many of these organizations are accepting more writing for their Web sites, which may be a better venue for your writing anyway. If your writing is rejected by the print journal, publication on the Web can lead to a larger audience if it strikes a nerve and goes viral across teacher Web sites and blogs.

But the most important advice of all is to carve out some time to write. Though it can be daunting to start, writing will take you to deeper layers of meaning in your research and will transform your identity as a teacher and researcher.

---

## RESEARCH WORKSHOP

## Seeing What Is Not Seen: Another Reason for Writing Up Teacher Research

*Ruth Shagoury*

We sat together one evening in December, a group of teacher-researchers who had been conducting case studies in our classrooms. As we laughed and ate and prepared to share our final drafts with each other, we decided to reflect on what the process of writing up our research had been like. What emerged in our ten-minute free-writes was the discovery that what had helped most of us make sense of our data was the actual writing itself. We shouldn't have found this remarkable. As Donald Murray (1982) writes, "Your world is the universe you describe by using your own eyes, listening to your own voice—finding your own style. We write to explore the constellations and galaxies which lie unseen within us waiting to be mapped with our own words" (7).

During this process, some found surprises in the data, such as Jean, who wrote, "What I thought had been the focus of my study became just one piece after I began writing." Or Ann, who said, "As I was writing, I was surprised to hear myself writing that giving my students time to speak in class led to better writing."

Margie reflected on how writing had led her to see the pattern in her findings: "It wasn't until I laid out data, wrote and rewrote, that I could see a pattern—the real significance of the notes I had."

We decided that setting a deadline—having a date to bring our final (for now) published pieces to our group to share—had helped us analyze and bring together in new and unforeseen ways the piles of data we had collected. Besides providing a way to share what we knew with other teachers, writing our case studies had helped us discover what we knew. Writing up our research is an important tool for researchers, guiding us to insights that otherwise might have eluded us.

The words of the poet Diane Glancy can encourage teacher-researchers to turn to their data with a new vision. In her published journal, *Claiming Breath* (1992), she writes, "In writing, life sinks/rises like the moon with new visibility. Another dimension. Seeing what is not seen in a different way than if we'd seen it" (54).

Teachers who have found avenues into writing share their suggestions in the following paragraphs. Perhaps their insights can help you and the teacher-researchers you work with bring your work onto the page.

1.  Use writing to help you brainstorm what you know and what you still need to find out. After several weeks of collecting data on one student's learning, Monique Bissett found it helpful to give herself the goal of listing five things she knew about the student and five things she needed to find out. She wrote them in two columns in her teaching journal. When other teachers in her support group tried this strategy, they found it helped to point out themes that were emerging, as well as holes in the data.

2.  Make the time to write for ten minutes on what you are noticing and keep these anecdotal notes for later reflection. In reflecting on what had helped her conduct her case study, Tiffany Poulin noted, "The best thing I did was to take anecdotal notes early. Reviewing the narratives I had written at the end of one month helped me to remember in greater detail. In a sense, reviewing what I had written helped me to see what I had really been seeing." Lila Moffit agreed; she found that setting time for herself at the end of a school day works best: "Having a computer

and taking a few minutes each evening to 'revisit' Max gave me huge amounts of data with which to understand his literacy journey. I couldn't write in class. I needed time and quiet to discover the meaning of his contribution to my day."

Some teachers, such as Laura St. John, discover that in order to find that writing time, they need to set aside a few minutes within their teaching day. "What works in conducting my case study," Laura wrote, "is to specifically set ten minutes per day for writing. I remove myself from circulating and 'privately' do my work."

Find a way that fits your working style to write those brief anecdotal notes and reflections that can help uncover what you are seeing in your classroom.

3.  Write brief memos or narratives about the themes that you see emerging. "One surprising discovery I made in writing up my case study is that I associated the term *risk taker* with Max," wrote Lila. "I decided to center my write-up on that one literacy theme. Max was living it daily, expressing it in everything he did and said in the classroom."

    Memos might be two or three pages long, or as brief as a paragraph, like this memo Rick Osborn wrote that helped him bring together multiple data points to confirm a finding:

    > I was surprised at how well my initial interview with my case study prepared me for examining her writing. After talking to Stephanie about some of the basic or elemental things that she does in her writing, I am able to see the same patterns in her writing itself. For example, Stephanie talked about how she would always write some quick notes down before she stopped writing so that she could remember where she had left off and what her thought pattern was. In her paper, I can see right where she has done this. Then, when I interviewed her again, I was able to confirm this. Stephanie has really opened up to me and allowed me to see quite a bit of what she is thinking.

4.  Write a letter to a teaching friend about what you are learning. This can help put together what you are learning in new ways as you explain it to a new audience.

    Gina Brandt, a high school science teacher, complained that she was stuck when she tried to write up all that she knew about Mariah. To help herself get over this obstacle, she thought about a teaching friend who would be genuinely interested in the issues she was grappling with in working to understand the way Mariah learns, and she wrote that friend a letter. In her letter, she was able to write in her own voice about her concerns, delights, and surprises, and wonder on paper about how she could best meet her student's needs. When she finished the letter, she had a working draft as well as a letter to a friend.

5.  With your support group, experiment with writing different kinds of leads. The leads you find that work to start your paper will help give

you a frame for it and establish its tone. At one of our meetings, we brought in examples of anecdotal leads, "telling quotes," and setting up contrasts. In the ten-minute free-write that followed, social studies teacher Tom Ustach wrote the following anecdotal lead:

> I entered the rectangular room, sat at the rectangular table, and was introduced. The walls around me were as stale and white as the experts seated at the table. The psychologist opened the meeting by announcing, "Let's get this LDT going. Jim qualified LD, PS, handicapped over the past few years. How'd he do last week, Academic Specialist?"
>
> "His current WISC-III is verbal—73, Performance—98, and FSIQ—83. His academic results were Reading—7.6, Math—5.4, and Written—3.2. I've never seen a high school student score so low. He has problems calculating simple addition and subtraction. He can't do basic counting."
>
> "Speech Pathologist," the psychologist called.
>
> "Well, I'm embarrassed to say," answered an elderly woman wearing milk-yellow 1970s mineral rock jewelry, "I inaccurately calculated his score. I used the wrong birth date. I can go up and redo it real quick. Right now I got 74."
>
> "No, that's okay. If it's 74, then the new one will be even lower," said the psychologist. "Go on."
>
> "Well, his CELF-R was really low, too. I'll get it to you as well."
>
> "Where's his ERC case manager?" asked the psychologist.
>
> "Not here."
>
> "We'll get to him later, then, but I'll pass the B-5 around."
>
> Yes, these educational specialists are talking about my case study, who is not a lab rat or an astronaut, but a fifteen-year-old young man who is struggling with writing. He's really not struggling just with writing, but in surviving in a school system that structurally sets him up to fail. A working-class student, especially if he is a minority student, is rolling loaded dice each time he comes to class in today's public schools. My case study, Jim, has never hit a number in ten years of public schooling, and all the blame is placed on him.

When Tom shared his lead with our group, it was clear that he had found the way to frame his paper, drawing us all into his case study, which he went on to title "Playing the Numbers: Winning and Losing in Public High School."

Collect a range of examples of a variety of leads and experiment with them. As Ralph Fletcher (1993) writes, "The lead is more than the first step toward getting somewhere; the lead is an integral part of the somewhere itself. The lead gives the author his first real chance to grapple with the subject at hand. . . . The author writes for herself and she writes for her audience" (82).

Taking just ten or fifteen minutes to try a new lead and share it with your group or with a research partner can unearth new ways to frame your thinking, as it did for Tom. It's also a small enough task to put on a teacher-research group agenda and still leave time for lots of feedback that can help keep your writing going.

6. Set a deadline for a finished draft. This is perhaps the most important suggestion of all. Setting those deadlines forces us to use the writing to put our thoughts on paper for an audience. It gives us that all-important opportunity to think through our data, make choices, and find a focus.

## References

Fletcher, Ralph. 1993. *What a Writer Needs.* Portsmouth, NH: Heinemann.
Glancy, Diane. 1992. *Claiming Breath.* Lincoln: University of Nebraska Press.
Murray, Donald. 1982. *Learning by Teaching.* Montclair, NJ: Boynton/Cook.

## RESEARCH WORKSHOP

# Making Deadlines

*Julie Housum-Stevens*

I am an expert on deadlines. In fact, I am such an expert on them that I am writing this article on deadlines one week after missing my own. I couldn't find the turquoise notebook that had the notes I needed to write the article. That's a lie. I wasn't even sure which of the twenty-five binders and two hundred notebooks and legal pads scattered (neatly) all over my house and my classroom contained them, never mind what color the darn thing was.

If you never find yourself in this position, skip the rest of this article—you are way ahead of me. But if missed deadlines ever cause you to duck into the bathroom to avoid your principal, if you suddenly decide that you must clean your bureau and your closet instead of responding to that giant stack of journals, or if you can't even start doing your taxes because you've misplaced your W2s, I may be able to help.

At the very least, I can empathize. Setting and meeting deadlines are two of my biggest struggles, which means I am on a continuous quest for tips and tricks and tools that will both improve my organization and give me practice at meeting my goals—on time and in a reasonably sane state.

This past summer, I was with a group of teachers designing research studies to carry out in our classrooms this fall. As we were considering what kinds of support we would need to be successful, I said that I would need help setting and meeting deadlines to analyze my data and share my findings. Suddenly, everyone was recommending wonderful, simple, why-didn't-I-think-of-that ideas, which I frantically began scribbling down.

"These should be in an article!" I blurted, and just like that, I had a deadline to practice meeting. With thanks to my compatriots for sharing their good ideas, here they are:

1.  Post a large calendar where you will see it frequently, and write down due dates, and article, class, and grant deadlines.
2.  Break long-term goals down; put several smaller due dates on the calendar instead of one final one.
3.  Tell everyone you know about your deadline, especially nosy folks and your mom, all of whom will surely check up on you.
4.  Use deadlines you already have—the end of the quarter, for example.
5.  Tie as much of your work as possible to something you already do—a graduate class, a committee, and so on. Make integration work for you like it works for kids.
6.  Sign up to do a presentation as part of a group. This will force you to prepare, because you won't want to let your peers down, but you won't be alone.
7.  Do less regularly rather than more sporadically. Avoid setting yourself up for failure—start small and add.
8.  Avoid giving yourself an out or an excuse (such as losing your notebook). Self-sabotage doubles your misery.

These ideas may not seem like much, but my hope is that you will find them useful and doable, and that perhaps you will realize that no matter what you struggle with as a teacher-researcher, you are likely not alone. Write to me in care of Stenhouse if you have found tools around deadlines and organization that have been particularly helpful to you—I'm thinking of keeping this article going forever, or at least until I meet my deadline the first time around!

*If you're wondering where or how to start with your writing, you can follow the lead of scores of teachers who have started their own blogs in the last decade. Experienced teacher-researchers Mary Lee Hahn (author of* Reconsidering Read-Aloud*) and Franki Sibberson (coauthor of* Beyond Leveled Books*) have spent years collaborating on the popular children's literature blog A Year of Reading. They share a wealth of practical advice and encouragement for teacher-researchers who want to start their own blog.*

## FEATURED TEACHER-RESEARCHERS

## 5 Easy Steps for Starting a Blog

*Mary Lee Hahn and Franki Sibberson*

*Blog. Blog because it is reflective. Blog because we need you to share what you know with us. Blog because it is good to remember how it feels to be*

> *judged by others. Blog because you have a unique view on the world and*
> *by sharing it, we all have another piece of this puzzle that is life.*
> —iLearn Technology (http://ilearntechnology.com/?p=2938)

Who knew when we started our blog years ago what blogging would do for us? When we began our blog A Year of Reading (http://readingyear .blogspot.com/) in January 2006, we weren't really sure what we were getting into. We just knew that we wanted a place to have a conversation about the books we loved. We wanted a place to record our thinking and our conversations, but we soon realized that having a blog is about much more than writing. Blogs are about becoming part of a larger community of people who are interested in things that you are—building or becoming part of a new network of learners.

We started by learning from others. We had favorite blogs, such as Read Roger (http://readroger.hbook.com/) and Fuse #8 (http://blog.schoollibrary journal.com/afuse8production), which became our mentors for writing about children's books. We found Jen Robinson and her *Cool Girls of Children's Literature* blog (http://jkrbooks.typepad.com/blog/coolgirls .html). Her list inspired us to create 100 Cool Teachers in Children's Literature (http://readingyear.blogspot.com/2006/12/100-cool-teachers-in-childrens.html). Once we created that, we seemed to find our voices and began to write for the dependable audience that was emerging, people who were visiting the blog regularly.

Blogging is one of the best tools for collaboration that we know. Not only do we work together to create the blog, but we have connected with many other people who love children's books. These connections help our thinking about books, teaching, and reading grow.

## How to Begin

You've been hearing about blogs for quite awhile now, and you've caught yourself thinking, "Maybe *I* should start a blog." That's the first step you need to take if you want to blog.

1. **You need to *want* to blog.**
   This breaks down into the smaller steps of sharing your stories and thinking and learning from others.

- You love to write, or you at least want to work on your craft, and you're not afraid to go public with your work.
- You aren't afraid of work, because keeping up a blog and building a voice, a blogging identity, and a readership are hard work.

   We know that blogging often becomes addictive. When you get into the habit of writing regularly, you need time . . . and you need a topic that you won't tire of eventually.

   After you've decided to start a blog, there are a few steps to take before you jump in and get started.

2. **Find your niche.**
   Your blog doesn't have to be connected to your teaching. Maybe you have something else that you want to blog about: a passion, an interest, a hobby. A good friend of ours was inspired to start a cooking blog (Cooking With Aldo's Daughter, at http://cookingwithaldosdaughter .blogspot.com/) after a trip to Italy last summer. Another friend is a teacher whose blog is focused on English language learners (http://learnlovegrow.blogspot.com/). The I.N.K. blog (http:// inkrethink.blogspot.com/) focuses solely on great nonfiction for children. There are so many options out there!
   If you are going to blog about children's books (or teaching or coaching or cooking or whatever), what will make your blog unique? To help you figure this out, move on to the next step.

3. **Read lots of blogs of the type you want to start.**
   - Find yourself some "mentor blogs." Read them with a writer's eye. What is it that you like about them?
   - Start commenting on blogs so that bloggers from the corner of the blogosphere you plan to join will get to know you.
   - Gather contact information from the blogs you like so that when you launch your blog, you can let your potential readers know.
   - Start a Twitter account and follow your mentor bloggers. Twitter is a great place to get links to new blogs, and it will be a great place for you to publicize your blog, build a readership, and find your place in the blogging community you've chosen.

4. **When you know what you want to say and how you want to say it, you need to choose a blogging platform.**
   Try Blogger (www.blogger.com), Tumblr (www.tumblr.com/), LiveJournal (www.livejournal.com/), WordPress (http://wordpress .com/), or one of the many other blogging host services. Do some research: some are free, and others charge nominal fees.

5. **Name your blog.**
   Choose several names that reflect what you're planning to have as the theme or focus of your blog. You might not be able to use your first choice; you'll need to do a search on the Web of the names you've chosen to make sure there aren't any other blogs by that name.

All of this background work will pay off in the end. It's just like painting a room. Choosing the color, buying the supplies, moving the furniture, masking, laying down drop cloths, and priming all take up *way* more time than actually painting the room.

Now that you're *really* ready to start your blog, it's just a matter of following the directions, writing the first post, and hitting the "publish" button. Welcome to the blogosphere!

# Sustaining Research: Building and Extending Research Communities

*Community means different things to different people. To some, it is a safe haven where survival is assured through mutual cooperation. To others, it is a place of emotional support, with deep sharing and bonding with close friends. Some see community as an intense crucible for personal growth. For others it is primarily a place to pioneer their dreams.*
—CORINNE MCLAUGHLIN AND GORDON DAVIDSON

Marty Rutherford is a sixth-grade teacher-researcher in Arizona, and her students came from low-income and culturally diverse homes. More than half were bilingual. She tells a remarkable tale of realizing how little in common she had with many of her students:

> One Monday morning, a student in my classroom, Alzonia, asked me how my weekend went. "Not so hot—we got robbed," I replied.
>
> "Oh, what a coincidence!" Alzonia responded. "We got robbed too. What did they steal?"
>
> I told her the robbers took a bunch of little things, nothing of consequence. Alzonia expressed mild sympathy and explained that "her" robbers stole the family's Uzi. Quite taken aback, I asked if that might not have been a good thing—to which she calmly replied, "Marty, you will never understand my life." Of course she was right. (Goswami et al. 2009, 15)

This transformational moment came early in Marty's teacher-research study, and it made her realize the most important thing she needed to do was see the world through her students' eyes, a world where an Uzi is an essential and prized possession.

Think of the loneliness of an insight like this—the instant when a teacher-researcher realizes she really doesn't understand her students' culture. At the same time, the immersion in questioning, data collection, and analysis can distance you from the teaching community you're in. We're in a teaching culture where questions are often discouraged and data collection is limited to the instruments provided by others.

In Marty's case, the teacher-research community that helped her thrive came from two unlikely places: a group of teacher-researchers who gathered for summer study in Vermont as part of the Bread Loaf Teacher Network at Middlebury College and the Brookline (Massachusetts) teacher-research group that sponsored a conference she attended. She and a small group of colleagues working throughout the country stayed connected and built their community with data postings and ongoing messages on the BreadNet electronic bulletin board. Eventually, Marty founded a teacher-research group in her own school.

What's striking in Marty's experience of community building among teacher-researchers is the weaving of distant communication, connections through technology, and face-to-face meetings with colleagues near and far. Teacher-researchers have more opportunities than ever to connect with others grappling with classroom inquiry.

Whether your community is a colleague or two in your building, or a far-flung group of like-minded teacher-researchers you connect with annually at a national meeting, having the continuous support of kindred spirits is essential for any teacher-researcher who wants to sustain his or her work.

# Teacher-Research Groups and Professional Learning Communities: What's the Difference?

As we write this edition of the book, "professional learning communities" or PLCs, are pervasive throughout many schools and districts. If you are already part of a grade-level team or structured learning community in your school, it may be hard to see the difference between this community and an inquiry group. Yet there can be key distinctions that are crucial.

Many existing learning community groups are focused on analyzing assessment data and tackling deficiencies together. Although those are worthwhile goals, they are counter to what's at the heart of many teacher inquiry communities. We agree with Marilyn Cochran-Smith and Susan Lytle (2009):

> We are certainly not opposed to professional communities focusing on students' achievement nor to groups of professionals using students' progress to guide decisions about teaching, curriculum, and schooling. But when professional communities are urged to use assessment data and are strongly outcomes-oriented, they tend to focus on quick fixes and short term goals. (55)

Peter Block (2008) puts it even more bluntly:

> Communities are built from the assets and gifts of their citizens, not from the citizens' needs or deficiencies. (11)

If a collaborative group requires membership and attendance, if you have no say over the inquiry topic or agenda, and if there is no opportunity for others to join, then it really isn't a teacher-research community—at least the kind of teacher-research community that thrives as teachers question, collect data, and ponder their discoveries in the ways we've described in previous chapters. And it certainly doesn't feel like a place for pioneering dreams!

There is a special joy in our work when we see its connection to the work of others. If you look at any teacher-researcher who has sustained her work over time, you quickly see another person, or people, standing in the shadows. Virtually all teacher-researchers depend on a partner or a group who shares their passions and provides reassurance when a project bogs down. Often we see only the findings of research in publications, or the images of researchers working with students as they collect and analyze data. The power of collaboration is much less visible; the process of working through issues of collaboration is almost never documented.

JoAnn Portalupi (1994) describes the subtle ways collaboration changes and extends the work of teacher-researchers. She compares the effects of collaboration to the flow of volcano lava:

> On a recent trip to Hawaii, my husband and I drove from the top of Kilhauea Volcano down to the ocean where a current lava flow was emptying into the ocean. I didn't know what to expect. As we descended the hill, the water came in sight and I could see the head of steam where the hot lava hit the cool ocean. The expanding fountain of steam was the only evidence of flowing lava. We arrived as the sun was setting. As the night sky grew dark, the red flowing lava became visible. Of course it had been there all along, but it needed the contrast of the night sky to bring it out. When we bring colleagues into the landscape of our classrooms, their presence provides the contrast that heightens our self-evaluative tendencies and makes visible that which is previously unseen. (98)

In the dark days of your research, it is your research community that will show you the value of all you are learning and doing, especially when it is hard for you to see the value of your work at that moment. The community will provide heightened self-awareness but also a heightened awareness of the potential for your research to help others.

A wealth of research shows the positive benefits of social interactions—not just for teacher-researchers but for humans in general. Physical health is directly linked to how connected people are to other people, as Ornstein and Sobel (1987) write:

> People need people—not only for the practical benefits which derive from group life, but for our very health and survival. Somehow, interactions with the larger social world of others draws our attention outside of ourselves, enlarges our focus, enhances our ability to cope, and seems to make brain reactions more stable and the person less vulnerable to disease. (18)

Most teachers already belong to different communities—within their schools, within their towns, within their families. We know how important these communities are to our health and survival. The challenge for teacher-researchers is to realize that some of these communities will change and shift as research becomes a part of our professional lives. Trusted colleagues can be threatened by changes in the way you talk about your teaching, your students, and your classroom. Teachers often need to form new communities to sustain their research. This was true for Terri Austin (1994a), a teaching principal in Fairbanks, Alaska. She found she had to distinguish between "school" colleagues and "research" colleagues as her research became more important to her:

> My school colleagues reminded me daily that I was just a teacher. I was told again and again that my job was only "to teach between 8 a.m. and 3 p.m.—anything else was unnecessary and made everyone else look bad." In looking back, I believe they felt I tried new ideas to show off or stand out. What they never realized is that I tried new ideas because I genuinely wanted my students to become better learners.
>
> Teacher research is often not easy. There are many obstacles that get in the way, but there are zesty events also. A community is essential. Your research colleagues will keep you going. Make the time to seriously plan your project, talk about assessment issues and plan your year. But do silly things too, like make pizza in a hubcap, giggle together. Those moments will hold you together when things get rough. John Wayne said, "Courage is when you're afraid, but you saddle up anyway." It takes courage to be a teacher-researcher. (68)

Courage—and a community. One of the dark sides of teacher research that is rarely written or talked about is how wrenching it can be for teachers to see their professional friendships change as they become more involved and successful in their work. The change is often felt more keenly by women:

> One of the most important prerequisites of the creative process for a woman is the assurance that her work will not rupture the important connections of her life. Women are exquisitely sensitive to the possibility of such losses. . . . [They] are often looked at askance or asked if they've managed to write, or paint, or compose without harming someone else. We have to be quite tough to resist that sort of guilt. (Bolker 1997, 195)

Building a research community can be a way to increase that toughness and keep your sensitivity at the same time. For example, Terri worked with others to develop the Alaska Teacher Research Network (ATRN) two decades ago. Four teachers in the Fairbanks area decided they needed to get together with colleagues to talk about issues beyond bus schedules and lunch-duty rosters. From there, the group grew to include more than one hundred teacher-researchers throughout the state, linked through e-mail, phone, and regular local and statewide meetings.

The group spends a week in August at a retreat, talking about their research from the previous year and their plans for the next. The goal at the end of the week is for everyone to have a research question and some sense of how data will be collected. The Fairbanks group continues to meet monthly throughout the fall, with each meeting devoted to in-depth response to one member's research. In January, ATRN members meet again in Fairbanks to exchange research progress and plans. Research is brought to closure with a writing deadline of April 15—an easy deadline to remember because of taxes.

This group was able to continue its work because it had some clear goals and expectations. Other teacher-research groups form much more loosely, with goals emerging over time. Because it can be so difficult to build school-wide teacher-research communities, we want to take an in-depth look at how teachers at one small school have managed to build such a group, without clear distinctions between "school" colleagues and "research" colleagues. Their process may help you find ways to create a research community that can energize your work.

# The Evolution of One Teacher-Research Group

Teacher research finds a place in individual schools and teachers' lives in many different ways. For some teachers, a graduate course or inquiry group is the beginning of the research process. For others, reading professional literature and seeing the value of research in other teachers' classrooms provides an impetus for getting started. But at Mapleton Elementary School in Mapleton, Maine, the teacher-research group started in a more informal way—through jotted notes on the back of a restaurant napkin.

One evening some Mapleton teachers and their teaching principal, Gail Gibson, went out for dinner after an in-service presentation on reading. "We're always trying to figure out how to help readers in our school who are struggling. Teachers were feeling frustrated—they felt like they needed more information than what they were receiving from books and workshops," explained Gail. On that napkin, the group sketched out first thoughts for what became a two-thousand-dollar mini-grant from a federal agency to learn more about teacher research. Kelly Chandler Olcott, at the time a doctoral student at the University of Maine in Orono, was hired to help the group develop research skills over the next few months.

Gail found that involving an outside consultant in their case was critical for the group's success: "We are always trying new things on our own, but we've found that we sustain a project or new initiative better when someone comes in first and helps us get started with it. This need not be more than a couple of visits, and assisting us in finding the best materials to read and discuss, but it was essential with this project."

We wondered why the group chose reading as the research topic, given that Mapleton has very high Maine Educational Assessment scores in reading. An outsider viewing the scores alone might wonder how reading instruction could improve at the school. Gail laughed, and replied, "It doesn't matter how high the scores are. Every teacher has at least a couple of students in her class who aren't reading as well as they should, and this will always be something that concerns a good teacher." This is a clear example of the "careful gardener" metaphor for teacher research in action: until every student in every class thrives in reading, teachers will want to know more about how to best teach it.

Kelly found that the group had a few basic principles that sustained their work:

1.  *Every teacher was free to choose how much she wanted to become involved.* "I have the same attitude toward teachers as I do toward students—I try to respect where they are, and help them move to whatever is the next phase of their development," Gail explained. The Mapleton teaching staff is typical of staff in any small rural community: there are veteran teachers with empty nests at home, eager to take extra time after school to discuss their research findings. Other teachers have young children who need more time and attention. Gail and Kelly worked with the teachers throughout the project to let them know this was not a short-term project, but a long-term commitment on the school's part to building inquiry into the school day. The teachers were trusted to decide what level of participation made sense for them.

    "One teacher last year really struggled to attend meetings, and often she couldn't because she had a new baby and a lot on her plate," Gail said. "I respect that, because I've been there in my life, too. She came when she could and did what she could. This year, she's found more time to take notes, and even used some of her research notes to make a point at a district curriculum meeting this fall. I was so happy to see that—to help her see last year that it's all right to have other priorities for her life, and to see this year that when she does have more time for research, it's easy for her to integrate it into her professional life. When you tell teachers, 'Come in when you can, if you can,' there is a place for everyone, no matter what their personal situation is at the moment."

2.  *As part of the research, teachers observed each other and compared their notes to develop their observation skills.* For Gail, consistent and frequent visits by teachers and herself to other classrooms have become an essential element for fostering an environment where teacher development remains central in staff planning: "You know, there is so much pressure on teachers. We always expect them to do better, and even great teachers are expected to maintain that high level of terrific work at all times. It's remarkable what a difference it makes to teachers when they have colleagues who recognize and note in concrete ways the skills evident in their teaching. It makes them very willing to listen to suggestions for improvement."

3.  *The principal (Gail Gibson) was a full participant in workshops, reading discussions, and observational visits.* "Learning to take notes as a teacher-

researcher was important in maintaining a rapport with the teachers—I was very nervous about this, being a new principal when this project began," Gail said. "When I went to do observations of teachers, I found myself naturally scripting notes and then going through and color-coding three different themes or patterns I saw in each observation. Once teachers saw this was my process, and I was noticing so many positive things in their classrooms, they became very comfortable with my visits and looked forward to them."

4. *Money was budgeted to support the research throughout the year.* This dollar amount at Mapleton is small, but it's significant to Gail and the teachers. "I want to make the teachers feel cared for, and it's amazing what a boost it is to the staff when you surprise each of them with a small notebook of project planner paper [lined paper with a wide left margin] in their mailboxes," Gail said. "This week, I bought all twelve teachers a copy of a small new book on spelling they had expressed interest in—total cost with my professional membership discount was $112. When teachers know that a good article they read can be photocopied for their colleagues, or some money is available for Post-it flags for coding their notes, it sends a signal that research is valued here, and I value the extra work they are doing to learn research skills."

The focus of the research this year has shifted from reading instruction to spelling. "This was an obvious choice for us," explained Gail. "We have been yapping and yapping about spelling for years, so everyone was pretty eager to take a close look at the issues involved in teaching spelling."

Teacher research at Mapleton involves individual teachers taking extra time in their classrooms to gather data as well as time to meet together, visit other classrooms, and analyze the data. "Because it takes extra time, it's so important that it be something that the teachers really care about, that they can see as having an immediate effect on their practice and classroom needs," Gail said. "Spelling is also a topic that parents are concerned about, and they have many memories and experiences at home of standing at the sink washing the dishes at night, quizzing their kid on this week's words. It's something they want to understand, and they see it as part of their 'job' as a concerned parent to help in some way with it."

The change this year in the research agenda includes more awareness on the part of students of their role as both research informants and co-researchers. "We just did report cards, and I have students write comments to their parents about what they've learned," Gail said. "I noticed 75 percent said something about their spelling development—they have become so aware of their strategies and the research going on in the school around this issue. There is so much more talk in the teachers' room, too—a palpable change in the intellectual climate as teachers get more and more comfortable with talking about their research and comparing their findings with those of colleagues."

The research study *Inside the National Writing Project* by Ann Lieberman and Diane Wood includes a list of attributes of successful adult learning communities. These qualities are evident in the Mapleton research group, as well as any other teacher-research group we've worked with that has thrived:

- Approaching each colleague as a potentially valuable contributor
- Honoring teacher knowledge
- Creating public forums for teacher sharing, dialogue, and critique
- Turning ownership of learning over to learners
- Situating learning in practice and relationships
- Providing multiple entry points into the learning community
- Guiding reflection on teaching through reflection on learning
- Sharing leadership
- Promoting a stance of inquiry
- Encouraging participants to re-conceive their professional identity by linking it to their professional community (2003, 8)

Gail doesn't know where or when the spelling research will end, or how the teacher-research group will evolve, but integrating inquiry into Mapleton's daily agenda has already been a big success: "It's made every teacher aware of how much control they really have in their classrooms, and how much ability they have to make those classrooms better," she said. "It has increased every teacher's sense of autonomy and skill in this school, and the value of that to me is immeasurable."

The Mapleton teacher-research group raises important questions for any teacher-researcher who is thinking about forming an inquiry group. Teachers need to think first about what they want their community to be. Some view communities as a safe place to be nurtured in their work, with few expectations and demands; others require a set schedule and firm guidelines, with a goal of having the group keep them on task in their work. If you have a mix of researchers who want to socialize around research projects, and those who are very task-driven, conflicts will quickly emerge in your group. It's necessary to spend time at the beginning working through what group members expect from the group and how much time will be required to participate.

The following are some key questions:

1. *Are members allowed to float in and out of the group, missing meetings?* The more flexible the community at the start, the more participation you will have. But it can be difficult to sustain a group if attendance is too intermittent. Much time can be spent at every meeting orienting new members or those who missed the last meeting.

2. *Does the group have an end point or goals?* The goals for ATRN and the Mapleton group were very different, but each had goals and expectations. The Alaska researchers end their individual projects with writing in April; the Mapleton researchers have a new collective project each

year. You'll want to make sure to talk about how your group can balance individual and collective goals.

3. *Is there a leader for the group?* Who is responsible for organizing the group? Natural leaders can emerge, but there can also be tensions around who controls and sets the group agenda. Discussing the roles and responsibilities of group members at the start can bring unconscious issues of voice and ownership to the surface before they have a chance to fester and disrupt the community.

4. *Are you making time for "zest" in your group meetings?* The meetings should provide a chance to talk and laugh together as well as to focus on teaching and research. Because schools can be isolating places for teachers to work, there is often a tendency to spend meeting time on "teacher room talk." Venting can be therapeutic, but groups also need time to create a different culture for themselves, which can begin with setting a new tone for the meetings. The Portland [Oregon] Area Teacher Research Network varies its meeting places, choosing new cafés, neighborhood restaurants, or microbreweries to treat themselves to different environments. The participants consider their work serious and thoughtful yet joyful. Their meetings feel like gifts to themselves, adding that "zest" that Terri Austin recommends.

# District Support

A strong teacher-research group can help you bring energy back to your school and to your district, creating a culture of inquiry within them. The Clayton Action Research Collaborative, in Clayton, Missouri, is a fine example of a grassroots effort that has helped promote the kind of support teacher-researchers need districtwide. This committed group of teachers from across grade levels meets monthly to share their own projects and support each other's work, inviting any interested teachers and administrators to join them on an occasional or regular basis.

Each summer, they sponsor a one- to two-day summer institute, and they collaborate with the Clayton school district's staff development program to offer workshops throughout the year focusing on strategies, techniques, and resources for conducting classroom-based research. As part of one summer institute, the Clayton researchers sponsored an evening with administrators, staff development professionals, and university educators to discuss possible collaboration strategies and the genuine needs of teacher-researchers. Much of the meeting was a celebration of the quality of the district response. Teacher-researchers spoke with enthusiasm about the recent establishment of small grants, support for teacher research as part of the professional development process, and district willingness to provide time and materials They stressed that the most important support of all was the clear message from district administrators that the time teachers spend on classroom-based research is valuable and appreciated.

To continue to aid teachers new to research methodologies, members of the Clayton Collaborative act as "teacher-researcher team leaders" in the buildings in which they work, and they are paid a small stipend for the support and leadership they provide.

Erich Jantsch (1980) applies chaos theory to organizations and sees organizations growing in efficiency when people in them act as "equilibrium busters." No longer caretakers of order, they are the individuals who "stir things up and roil the pot" until work is reorganized in new and innovative ways. The teachers in the Clayton Action Research Collaborative show what is possible districtwide when "equilibrium busters" help redefine school structure from the inside out.

More recently, the concept of "walking out and walking on" as defined by Margaret Wheatley and Deborah Frieze (2011) explains the power of choosing to leave any traditionally defined community and building a new one with like-minded colleagues:

> The people you meet on this journey have walked out of a world of unsolvable problems, scarce resources, limiting beliefs, and destructive individualism. They've walked on to beliefs and practices that solve problems and reveal abundant resources. (47)

Certainly the national climate for schools is one of "unsolvable problems and scarce resources." The grassroots power of teacher-researchers building communities from the ground up is what can inspire hope that there are solutions, if only because kindness and support from other teacher-researchers are so abundant.

# Resources to Build Research Communities

As the teacher-research movement has grown in the last decade, so has the resource base to support school-based research. Teachers throughout the world have regional and national programs that can assist them as they work to develop research skills.

## *Regional Research Networks*

Many research partnerships have sprung up throughout the country to support teacher research. We hesitate to mention too many of these partnerships because most are short-term alliances that evolve and change as the needs of teacher-researchers change. The best way to find out if there is a regional teacher-research group near you is to call your local college or university and talk with the education professor who teaches research courses for teachers.

An example of an inquiry network that has been sustained for many years is the Western Maine Partnership, coordinated by the University of Maine at Farmington. This loose alliance coordinates inquiry groups throughout the western region of the state. Teachers meet regularly to discuss curricular and social issues, sharing data and strategies with others who grapple with the same concerns. The Western Maine Partnership also funds mini-sabbatical leaves for small teams of teacher-researchers.

In Maine, administrators call and receive information about the groups and distribute it to teachers. They provide release time for teachers to participate in regional research programs. Most important, this work counts for teachers as professional development.

At Texas A&M University–Commerce, the Department of Curriculum and Instruction has woven teacher-research communities into their work with students and across their faculty as well. Graduate and undergraduate students have built-in time in their courses to meet in teams to create "action research projects," creating networks of support that carry them beyond their time at the university. And their faculty members are able to share their own processes and experiences with support groups, serving as mentors for the potential that exists when colleagues work together.

Recently, interested faculty worked together on the Listo! Project, which focuses on strategies to help English language learning students. Faculty in different program areas from all age levels from Early Childhood through Secondary Education created teams to conduct action research on changes they had implemented in their curriculum to enhance instruction strategies for ELL students. For example, teacher-educators Carole Walker, Chris Greene, and Martha Foote's inquiry question was, What changes have occurred in preservice teachers' understanding of second-language acquisition and their perceptions of working with English language learners? and colleague Josh Walker explored, How is our collaborative partnership changing the nature of mealtime conversations with ELL students in a two-way immersion classroom in one elementary school?

Working on flexible teams like the faculty at Texas A&M can certainly be adapted for faculty at elementary, middle, or high schools. It makes sense for teachers to be able to substitute participation in an inquiry group or a professional research meeting for an in-service event that might not be as valuable for them. Regional and statewide collaborations are more likely to be sustained if administrators grant credit and support for meetings. If you're not sure if your principal would support your participation in a research group, just ask. In our experience, it is rare for a principal or superintendent not to support a teacher's desire to learn more about research.

Many other states sponsor annual conferences in support of teacher research. Most state and regional conferences sponsored by curricular groups (such as the National Council of Teachers of English and the National Science Teachers Association) have sessions devoted to presenting and fostering teacher research among participants. You can call the national office of any of these groups to find out if they have a special-interest group for teacher-researchers.

The International Reading Association and the American Association of Educational Researchers both have large, active special-interest groups for teacher-researchers.

## Conversations with Colleagues

Sometimes, case studies on the individual students we wonder about can lead us to a focus for our teacher research. A group of first-year teachers (and new teacher-researchers) decided they would each conduct a case study of one of their dual language learners, meet once a month, and discuss their inquiries. It became the perfect venue for their evolving questions.

One evening, Elsa began the conversation with her questions about Veronica. "I'm wondering, how does Veronica's difficulty with reading overlap with her being a second-language learner?" she pondered.

This wondering set an avalanche of questions in motion:

"I want to do all sorts of reading and writing interviews, study her written work . . . and . . . I'm wondering, did her mom pull her out of special ed? Because she's showing improved proficiency? Or is it social concerns?"

Melody's wondering, "Does she read in Spanish?" added more questions, and Elsa paused. "I don't know . . . She listens to Spanish radio and watches Spanish TV. . . . I need to do a lot of investigating."

Rachel prompted further, "I've got questions! Do the kids know that the books are at different levels? How do you handle that?"

Samae piggybacked, "What if we all had high expectations? Wouldn't they rise to that?"

This excerpt from a ten-minute clip of a transcript of their monthly teacher-research conversations shows the role of questions evolving. Elsa read her one-pager, full of insights and reflections of her case study of Veronica. Then the air was filled with the responses of colleagues who listened closely, ready to both support and to ask questions. These questions helped nudge them forward.

Melody wondered what Hung's real goal was as he worked in art while his new English skills blossomed.

Rachel asked herself, "How will Svetlana adjust to the other Russian speakers in her class? What will be the effect of my meeting with her to chart her growth?"

Samae wondered, "How can there be equity for all?"

Samae's story about discussing the issues of equity with all her students, DLL and English-proficient alike, sparked new questions: "Why aren't we talking about how all our students are in this together? Our more privileged students should be advocating for their fellow classmates. What would happen if the needs of classmates were less invisible to our students? If part of the curriculum becomes one of genuine inclusion?"

These first-year teacher-researchers found that their thinking about the real students in their classrooms was deepened and extended with the energetic, vibrant, and caring conversation, framed around their wonderings.

## Letters to Teacher-Researchers

"How strange that we, as teachers, are asked to share our knowledge with students but are rarely asked to share our knowledge with each other," Cindy

Quintanilla notes. "Having the opportunity to read what other teacher-researchers have written—and responding in a personal letter—was eye-opening for me. I was recently asked to write and publish some of the work my team and I are involved in, but my greatest concern was, Who will read this and what do they care? Yet now I know that someone out there will read it, and hopefully can find some useful thread to adapt to her classroom."

As we look for communities to help sustain our work, we can reach beyond our immediate local and regional networks and discover teacher-researchers who share our interests, research passions, and classroom tensions. And we can take it a step further and communicate with those distant colleagues, expanding our communities and supporting each other beyond geographic boundaries.

We have found that there are many benefits to taking the time to sit down and write to the teacher-researchers who have influenced our thinking or motivated us to make significant changes in our classrooms based on their research and classroom stories. The authors who receive the letters clearly benefit, too, of course: as Cindy says, it is important for teachers who write up their research to realize that, yes, their work and words have reached an audience, and their ideas have found a mark and made a difference.

When Annie Keep-Barnes first wrote the honest and wrenching story of her work with a seven-year-old boy (see Chapter 2), it was for her immediate research community, the Alaska Teacher Research Network. When they encouraged her to share it with a wider audience, she had no idea how much it would affect other teachers. A letter like the following one, written to her by high school teacher Bret Freyer, demonstrates the power of her words for teachers across grade levels:

> Dear Ms. Keep-Barnes,
> Thank you for your article entitled "Real Teachers Don't Always Succeed." You have helped me remember or realize several things about teaching and literature about teaching.
>
> I, too, have read too many "Teacher as Savior" books. Your fresh breath of reality in the beginning of your essay really rings true for me. In book after book, students are inspired, they make huge turnarounds, they even decide not to kill themselves after being in a dynamic English class. Should I be questioning my literature program? I don't think I've saved any lives. These models of English classrooms either make me say, "Oh, come on now," or "Geez, what am I doing wrong?"
>
> Thank you for reminding me when I present "language arts" to students, I need to show the excellent and the mediocre. I learned much by watching your struggles. I am reminded that I also need to show the struggles of readers and writers to my students. How else can they see that what we do is real? Real readers and real writers struggle with reading and writing. Because you showed me your frustrations and your difficulties, I recognized the reality of my students and myself in your teaching life. Thank you for reminding me that each teacher's story has something for me.

I, too, have not always been successful with my students. Sometimes I feel, as you did with Robert, that everyone is making excuses for a student or looking for someone to blame, but no one is really doing anything. I, too, have felt that maybe I am not pushing a student hard enough, or getting to know the parents well enough, or otherwise not doing my part soon enough or thoroughly enough. While it seems teachers often beat themselves up after the fact, I don't think you did. You simply reflected on Robert's situation with a hope of learning about yourself. That is what a good teacher does. You did for yourself what you would expect your students to do—learn from the lesson.

Thank you for reminding me that often success comes in small ways, like your success with Robert. If his desire to buy you flowers isn't a success, nothing is. He saw in you something positive about school. Because of that he probably listened more closely to you as you explained his "auditory channel" strength to him. He probably learned something about himself, because of the kind of person you are, that he would never have learned from the "demanding" teacher. I cherish moments like the time Ursula Winter ran into my class with her social studies paper claiming that practicing in English class was what really made her write an "A" social studies paper. Thank you for reminding me that I need to hug those memories tight.

I, too, feel the urgent need for success, not only for my students, but for myself—maybe even more so for myself. Maybe that is why those memories are so important. I used to think this was selfish, but I don't anymore. We are so much like our students, aren't we? We are prideful beings who measure ourselves against the myriad yardsticks we conjure for ourselves. We can't help it. I've stopped fighting it. I want to be good at what I do. I want to be good at it for me, and I want to be good at it for the students I teach. These are inseparable realities. I see memories of your experience with and research on Robert that you can hold onto. Thank you for reminding me that these selfish urges are alive in me. As I read, I found myself saying, "That's okay, Annie, that just means you are human" and "That's the mark of an excellent teacher!" We immerse ourselves so much in our work, that we are susceptible to drowning in the water of the burdens and responsibilities which envelop us. Maybe we need to be submarines, willing and able to bang around on the coral reefs of education. Those reefs can be destructive . . . and beautiful.

Were you hard enough on Robert? Only you can answer that. I think, though, that you are just hard enough on yourself. That you had the courage to share that will help me to be hard enough on myself.

Thank you for reminding me that this is okay—as long as I keep searching for the learning in the lesson.

Sincerely,
Bret Freyer

Bret's moving letter to Annie is the kind of detailed, thoughtful response to writing any author would appreciate hearing. On a deeper level, it is also the kind of more personal response that a letter format can offer, showing that Bret is really taking this opportunity to "talk" to Annie, person-to-person, letting her know the thoughts that went through his mind as he read her honest reflections and self-criticisms.

Bret's letter also demonstrates the power of the act of writing itself. In composing these words to Annie, Bret crystallizes the main messages he takes from her work and brings back to his own teaching the further resolve to "be just hard enough" on himself.

Teachers we know have written letters to teacher-researchers for a variety of reasons, often to thank them for their work and respond to their research on a personal level. Other times, the letters are a chance to share ideas and insights with a distant colleague who might be able to act as a sounding board or offer further resources.

Before beginning a teacher-research project, consider the research community you will be sharing your work with, and ask yourself these questions:

- Who will make up this community?
- When will we meet?
- How will we present our information?

In setting expectations and norms for your community, consider what is essential for any community to thrive. In *The Abundant Community* (2010), John McKnight and Peter Block identify these three properties of a competent community:

- Focus on the gifts of its members
- Nurture associational life
- Offer hospitality, the welcoming of strangers

In the selections that follow, you'll see how teachers and school leaders work together to build from strengths and create gracious inquiry communities where questions are encouraged.

*When teacher-research support groups get together, it helps to have plans for a variety of different ways to reflect on your practice and beliefs as well as share your works-in-progress. The following Research Workshops are examples of ways different groups we know have worked together during part of their meeting times.*

## RESEARCH WORKSHOPS

## "A Secret Hidden in Plain Sight": Reflecting on Life Experiences

"Good teaching requires self-knowledge," writes Parker Palmer (1998). "It is a secret hidden in plain sight" (33). As we rethink our identities in the classroom, we illuminate our sense of ourselves and our roles with our students, each other, and the larger education community. Without intentional attention, our evolution can go unexamined, and in the process, we can lose the opportunity for self-knowledge that can aid our teaching. Besides uncovering the hidden dimension in our changes in identity, it can be extremely helpful to dig back into our teaching roots: What drew us to teaching in the first place? What are the threads in our teaching lives and commitments that ground us and keep us teaching?

Veteran teacher-researcher Karen Gallas reflected on the role her background in anthropology played in her teaching life, noting that in retrospect it is one of those threads that stands out clearly:

> Now that I'm down the line a little bit, I see very clearly that it has [had an effect]. And it really has influenced the kind of work that I do. I find it interesting to look back on the choices that you make early in life. You know, you think you're doing them on instinct, and somehow or other, they seem to circle back and then begin to make sense in the larger picture. Those early interests come back. (Quoted in MacKay 2002, 140–141)

Like Karen, we can benefit from examining patterns in our lives and how they have shaped our identity—and how our identity continues to evolve. The following suggestions may help you begin a dialogue with colleagues about what has shaped, informed, and transformed your teaching life.

## I Used to . . . But Now I . . .

The ongoing cycle of action and reflection are at the heart of our journeys as teachers. One group of five teacher-researchers in Portland, Oregon, has been exploring questions such as, What drew us to teaching in the first place? What are the threads in our teaching lives and commitments that ground us and keep us teaching? How has our teaching practice evolved and changed?

Rather than exploring these reflections in isolation, they have found it helpful to write, and then use that writing to spark conversations with each other that lead them to insights and revitalized classroom agendas.

They found one simple structure for self-reflection that helped them focus on their professional changes. Using the format of parallel lists, they brainstormed what they used to do and what they now do.

High school English teacher Susan Tetrick was surprised to note how much her teaching practice had changed:

I used to
1. be a grammar and usage Nazi, proofing and correcting every tiny error on a student's final draft.
2. act as if mine were the only class for my students, giving lengthy reading assignments *and* papers.
3. have rigid deadlines with grades lowered one letter for each day late.

4.  give lots of "fix-it" comments and red-pen editorial marks, and few notes on what worked well.
5.  be strict about needing to keep a boundary between myself as a young(ish) teacher and adolescent students.

Now I
1.  grade one or two writing traits per paper and allow students (and myself) to break some rules and find a voice.
2.  assign shorter papers and assign short stories as well as novels to read.
3.  am more flexible with deadlines according to the needs of my students.
4.  focus much more on the positive when I give students feedback.
5.  allow myself to be more relaxed, smile a lot—and can still be in charge.

Nicole Hienlein works with younger children and also saw big changes in her expectations for her students—and for herself:

I used to
1.  expect children to work at their desks.
2.  expect children to all write on the same topic.
3.  expect kids to make friends and "behave."
4.  only rarely share my own writing.
5.  be afraid to challenge my students much or make work "too hard."
6.  sit back and listen passively at faculty meetings.
7.  expect to be a classroom teacher forever.

Now I
1.  encourage children to work everywhere in the room, wherever they need to.
2.  encourage children to choose to write on their own topics.
3.  model and teach what cooperation and being friends looks like.
4.  share my stories, poems, and all kinds of writing all the time.
5.  figure out what each of my kids can do, and set high expectations for their work.
6.  speak up and take action, volunteering to lead committees and advocate for new policies.
7.  am thinking about going into a leadership position in literacy and curriculum.

Nicole's reflection led to dialogue in their group about how changes in their teaching and evolving practices can help map out future directions for their work. Most important, group members report the rich conversations about classroom practice, stories from the classroom, and evolving plans. This turned out to be a great way to start their meeting time together.

If you and a trusted colleague or support group decide to try this out, depending on the amount of time you have, you might also use it as a closing reflection. Another option is to write your parallel lists at one session and open with the conversation about them at the next meeting.

## *Time Line of Professional Development*

Kathryn Mitchell Pierce brought a different kind of teaching life reflection to her teacher-research group—one that helped her look over her career, note patterns and evolving interests, and ultimately map out her future direction (see Figure 8.1). Kathryn's review of her teaching passions and interests came together as she forged her plans for continued work. And sharing her time line helped her colleagues think about their own. The time line needn't be a narrative. You could chart the highs and lows of your professional development on graph paper in a quick fifteen-minute session with teacher-research colleagues. It can be fascinating to share these, note similarities and differences, and use each other's graphs to help add to your own.

## *Reviewing Work and Reflections*

Your classroom is a veritable archive of historical information that can help you review your life as an educator. There are many data sources available to put you in touch with your experiences. You can

- reread teaching journals, class records, and notes;
- look back through the historical data in school newsletters, narrative assessments, and notes on planning, including lesson and unit plans;
- review previous end-of-the-year reflections and goal statements; and
- reacquaint yourself with student work that you have saved.

Figure 8.1
Teaching Life
Review

---

**Time Line of Professional Development**

*Early Career—Student Teaching/Early Teaching*
- Three-to-eight-year-old lab school, British infant school experiences. Watching children move up through the program beginning as three-year-olds and continuing through sixth grade—longitudinal look at children; upward influence of early childhood curricular experiences on the ways I thought about organizing elementary curriculum; working with multiage/multiyear groups of children and planning learning experiences that were based on "discovery learning" techniques.
- Concept webs for integrated curriculum planning. Developing a method for planning integrated curriculum units based on conceptual webs that began with a book, topic, or concept and then branched out to touch each subject area or different ways of studying the central focus.

*Mid-Career—University Teaching*
- Literature discussion groups, evaluation of literacy learning, collaborative curriculum inquiry. Opportunity to work with classroom teachers in their classrooms and on questions that affected their daily work and moved all of us ahead in our understanding of how to support student learning.

- Teacher study groups. Participating in and initiating/supporting teacher study groups in a variety of contexts and on a variety of literacy-related issues; learning experiences for child and adult learners focused on the value of small-group inquiry projects.
- Alternate sign systems. Studying alternate sign systems—semiotics—to gain insight into the reading and meaning-making process; helped me to value art, music, movement, drama, math, and language all as systems for making and sharing meaning and to seek ways of incorporating these into my own and my students' learning experiences.

*Current Career—Glenridge School*
Year One
- Reading teacher literature reviews. Collaborative experience with other classroom teachers, using and reviewing children's literature.
- Literacy committee. Developing and refining the literacy curriculum documents.
- Multiage. Working with others to create, support, and document the multiage pilot program at Glenridge.
- Curricular issues. Coming to terms with a mandated curriculum, re-creating professional understandings "from the inside out," from a classroom perspective.

Year Two
- Literacy curriculum implementer. Working with classroom teachers and creating support materials to strengthen the implementation of our new curriculum.
- Curricular issues. Multiage experiences within a grade-level curriculum, supporting inquiry and highlighting art as a sign system in inquiry, developing efficient strategies for documenting student work and growth.

Year Three
- Literacy committee. Struggling-reader document.
- Clayton Action Research Collaborative. Creating an ongoing group, developing strategies and structures to support others.
- Multiage. Focusing on multiyear plans for a mulitage classroom with specific emphasis on seeing math from an inquiry perspective and continuing to work against arbitrary grade-level divisions in the teaching and assessing of mathematical concepts.
- Curricular issues. Contained focus on art as a sign system; new focus on talking and learning in small groups in the math curriculum, particularly multiage math problem-solving groups.

*Future Career—New Questions, New Directions*
- Math problem solving. Taking a closer look at how children use small-group talk to explore and wrestle with complex math concepts; looking for ways to broaden consideration of math content beyond grade levels and to capitalize on vertical strands in development of mathematical thinking.
- Action research collaborative. Energized by the support of the collaborative, becoming more systematic in my own classroom inquiries and seeking ways of systematically documenting my work and sharing it with others.
- Role of art in inquiry. Using what I've learned about semiotics and the information available in the district on the Reggio Approach to early childhood curriculum that values art as one of the hundred languages of children; continue to refine the ways I support children in using art in their inquiry experiences.

### *Who Are the Teachers Who Have Shaped You?*

Remembering a teacher who made a difference in your life can help you reconnect with those mentors from the past. Parker Palmer (1998) often asks teachers to introduce themselves by telling a story about their mentors. "As these stories are told, we are reminded of many facts about good teaching: that it comes in many forms, that the imprint of good teachers remains long after the facts they gave us have faded" (21). He goes on to ask, "What is it about you that allowed great mentoring to happen?" In this way, you discover your qualities as a student that this teacher was able to draw out in you—a very revealing exercise.

When we discover the "secret hidden in plain sight"—our inner identities as teachers and learners—we are better able to work from a position of strength. We invite you to try these strategies as a start—and invent new ones—to help you reconnect with the teaching knowledge you already possess.

*Teachers who lead inquiry groups with colleagues can find it a daunting task. These groups need to evolve naturally, with agendas and goals developing organically from emerging research questions and needs. Yet at the same time, some structure and focus can help everyone stay focused and engaged. The next two pieces present sample activities and agendas inquiry group leaders can try to launch groups, or to energize colleagues when attention or commitment to inquiry starts to flag.*

## FEATURED TEACHER-RESEARCHER

## The Anticipation Guide: A Tool for Study Group Leaders

*Suzy Kaback*

When I was a fifth-grade teacher, a typical day ended with 101 important details that needed my attention: planning for the next day's classes, calling parents to talk about a struggling student, gathering books from the library for our new inquiry project—the list seemed endless. Among these preoccupations, faculty meetings and workshops were near the bottom. On an afternoon when I was expected at a grade-level meeting to review benchmark papers, for example, I usually arrived distracted, disorganized, and, therefore, minimally involved in the process. What I needed was the professional development equivalent of that fabled black dress that took a woman from the office to a cocktail party without missing a beat.

Unfortunately, I rarely found that adaptable outfit to help me move from one context to another in good cognitive shape. Now, as someone who is frequently leading those sessions with colleagues after school, I am sensitive to the transitional needs of the teachers with whom I work. Over the years, I have put together a "wardrobe" of ideas to help make classes, workshops, or study groups, as Janet Allen would say, "meaningful and memorable" right from the beginning.

One approach I use with success is the anticipation guide, a transition tool that's more Target than Saks Fifth Avenue on the bling index, but one that helps people move efficiently from the concerns of their daily teaching lives to what I hope is the renewing experience of a well-designed learning opportunity.

## *Anticipation Guides: An Introduction*

Anticipation guides were developed by J. E. Readence in 1986 as a way to engage readers with a text before, during, and after their reading. Formats differ, but the anticipation guide I'll describe here looks like a three-column chart. In the middle column are a series of statements about a topic. Statements can focus on the prior knowledge a student brings to the text, or on themes and essential questions posed in the reading. Students think about these statements before reading a text and decide if they agree or disagree with each one. By anticipating the content of a text, they are more likely to find connections between their existing background knowledge and new information, and as a result, their interest in the reading will grow.

While reading, students use the statements as a way to read purposefully, looking for sections that relate to the statements on the anticipation guide to help them decide whether they continue to agree or disagree with each one. After reading, they take another look at the statements to decide if they want to change any of their original opinions based on what they learned.

For example, if students were going to read about mollusks in their science books, an anticipation guide to accompany the reading might include statements such as, "A mollusk is a creature with a sturdy backbone" (not true—students should eventually disagree) or "An octopus is an example of a mollusk" (true—students should eventually agree). A well-written anticipation guide includes a variety of statements: those designed to test basic comprehension of content, and those intended to explore values or opinions that spark lively discussions. Here's an example of this latter type of statement, related to mollusks: "Having an exhibit of mollusks in a zoo would not be very interesting." Readers will not find clear-cut data to inform their thinking about this kind of statement. Instead, they need to make inferences and draw independent conclusions to decide whether to agree or disagree.

## *Using Anticipation Guides with Adults*

Using an anticipation guide to support readers' comprehension, and to prompt substantive discussions among students about a topic or issue, is what teachers find most valuable about this tool. The basic intent of the anticipation guide is easily transferred to different contexts with adult learners to achieve the same engaging effect with a topic. I know because when I use an anticipation guide to kick off a literacy workshop, teachers are hooked.

Below is an example of some anticipation guide statements I use when I'm hosting a workshop about content-area reading:

- I have so much content to cover in my classes, I have trouble finding time to teach reading skills.
- I'm not sure what it means to teach reading to kids who are supposed to know how to read already.
- All reading is not created equal: different kinds of texts require different ways of reading.
- I often choose to read nonfiction.
- Most of the reading and writing people do in the "real world" is nonfiction.
- I have some successful teaching strategies to help my students better comprehend their reading in my classes.

Each statement reflects a big idea I plan to explore during the workshop. As teachers think about each of these ideas, they are mentally preparing to engage with the content when we begin learning as a group. The statements are designed to be open-ended yet provocative so that people who arrive at the workshop distracted or ambivalent are easily absorbed into the fabric of this new context.

In addition to the transition benefits an anticipation guide offers, constructing this tool is invaluable for me. Deciding on statements to include in an anticipation guide requires me to think carefully about my goals for a workshop and how I want to evaluate its influence on teachers' thinking. Writing an anticipation guide also keeps me honest. I need to constantly revisit my guiding beliefs about well-designed professional development experiences when I strive to write thought-provoking statements.

The most meaningful and memorable workshops I've attended have tapped into the expertise I bring to the topic while inspiring me to confront perceived obstacles and figure out how to overcome them. As someone who now hosts workshops, I want to be sure I help teachers uncover their existing beliefs about the topic we're studying. I also want to honor the experience they bring to our workshop so I can tap into the many reservoirs of expertise that exist among colleagues. Finally, I am careful to design experiences that blend theory and research with practical applications that teachers can adjust to fit their instructional needs.

Ensuring attention to teachers' belief systems, their professional experience, and the potential application of new teaching ideas is a tall order for a workshop or study group that might last for only an hour. Anticipation guides help me maximize my time with teachers through the careful construction of statements and by "fitting" teachers with a tool that moves them effortlessly from the preoccupations and responsibilities of their daily teaching lives to the more global work of studying best practices.

## To Fart or Not to Fart? Reflections on Boy Writers

*Jennifer Allen*

Yesterday was the first meeting for our study group on boys and writing. Our study groups meet once a month for an hour after school and follow a predictable structure. (You can view the agenda at the end of this article.) Many of the teachers have been part of study groups exploring various topics over the past seven years.

I noticed right away that teachers who had been part of the group were making sure that everyone felt welcome and that they introduced themselves to new members. Our groups are a blend of teachers in grades three through five from two schools within our district. Typically I have had to make introductions at the start of our meetings to make sure that teachers at each building know the names of new staff.

There was energy and a sense of community in the group from the start. We began the session with reflections on our goals for the year. One of the fourth-grade teachers, Jill, whipped out a piece of paper and shared that she had a timely piece of writing. She started reading "Attack of the Llama" to the group, a piece written by a student in her class that day.

> **Attack of the Llama**
> In a place far away called Llama World, a young boy named "Keister"
> opened a gate . . . leading to evil. The llamas, they snorted, farted, and
> pooped the biggest poop ever! They scattered and farted some more. Then
> they said—"Keister" . . .

Jill finished reading and asked the group, "So what does anyone think?" Most of us laughed and giggled. The student writing sample launched us into a full-blown discussion of farting, farting noises, and a debate about whether to allow such writing in our classrooms. Jill shared her apprehension about this writing, yet we agreed that this was a skilled writer who presented his writing to the class with subtle sophistication. Another teacher, Sarah, responded, "And this is coming from the teacher who reads *Walter the Farting Dog* [Kotzwinkle and Murray 2001]?"

Not everyone around the table agreed that allowing students to write about farting was appropriate. The topic shifted from appropriate topics to how we each define "quality" in writing to strategies to motivate boys to write in the classroom. The conversation flowed naturally. Teachers disagreed with one another without any sense of tension. The conversation pushed all of us to think about the boundaries we establish within our classrooms and the gender stereotypes we have.

The issue of boundaries led me to read aloud the first two pages from the book *I Am Not Joey Pigza* by Jack Gantos (2007). In this excerpt, Joey's grandmother cuts the head off a chicken with an ax in front of him, to model that he acts like a chicken with his head cut off. Within a few paragraphs Joey's dog, Pablo, finds the carcass and is gnawing on it in Joey's bed. The writing is humorous and graphic.

As I read this excerpt, the entire table was cringing with horror and laughing at the same time. My own ten-year-old son had begged me to read the book aloud at home, and loves the story. So the question was raised, Would you use this book in the classroom as a read-aloud? Would you recommend it for independent reading? Would you select it as a mentor text?

I was thrilled with the level of discussion. I don't think we have ever had study groups launched in the past with such depth of conversation. I was most pleased with the ownership within the group. Of the ten members around the table, seven of the teachers had participated in study groups for more than five years. The other three were in their first few years of teaching. This meeting was also an induction for the new teachers to the world of our study groups. The new teachers listened attentively. I watched eyes shift to the speakers around the table. I wondered what they thought of such a lively, fast-paced discussion.

As we started talking about violent writing and what should be allowed, another teacher referred to the PBS video *Raising Cain* (Thompson 2006) that some of us watched last year while in a study group on the topic of boys. I asked the group if we should play a clip from *Raising Cain* so that we could look for insight into writing and so that everyone could refer to the same experience. They all agreed we should put off watching the planned video clip from *Conferring with Boys* by Max Brand (2006). Instead, we watched a clip on preschool students negotiating violent writing within their classroom. The video features researcher and author Thomas Newkirk. Our conversation then shifted to his work *Misreading Masculinity* (2002).

After seven years of organizing study groups, I've noticed a shift in their tone and style. Teachers take more ownership of the group and responsibility for the discussion. They share stories from their classrooms, refer to our core text, *Boy Writers* (Fletcher 2006), and bring writing samples from their classrooms without prompting from me. I didn't anticipate such a rich discussion. My role as facilitator is less dominant as teachers take more of a lead within these groups.

So should students be allowed to write about farting, pooping, and violent topics? We didn't even try to reach consensus. Rather, our time together pushed each of us to think a little harder about writing workshops and how we can support all student achievement and growth. I can't wait to look at more samples of student writing and see where our discussion leads us next month!

## Resources for Boy Writers Study Group

Brand, Max. 2006. *Conferring with Boys*. DVD. Portland, ME: Stenhouse.
Fletcher, Ralph. 2006. *Boy Writers: Reclaiming Their Voices*. Portland, ME: Stenhouse.

Thompson, Michael. 2006. *Raising Cain: Exploring the Inner Life of America's Boys.* DVD. PBS Home Video.

## *Additional Resources Referenced in Meeting*

Newkirk, Thomas. 2002. *Misreading Masculinity: Boys, Literacy, and Popular Culture.* Portsmouth, NH: Heinemann.

Gantos, Jack. 2007. *I Am Not Joey Pigza.* New York: Farrar, Straus and Giroux.

Scieszka, Jon. 2008. *Guys Write for Guys Read: Boys' Favorite Authors Write About Being Boys.* New York: Viking Junior.

### Agenda for Boy Writers Study Group

*October*

**Reflection Questions (10 Minutes)**
1. What are your thoughts about boys and writing?
2. What are your goals in the area of writing instruction for the year?

**Reading Excerpt (15 Minutes)**
1. Skim Chapter 2 of *Boy Writers,* "Failure to Thrive," pages 11–18.
2. Share thoughts on the chapter.

**Video Viewing: *Conferring with Boys* by Max Brand (20 Minutes)**
1. Two-column notes: What do you notice? / What do you wonder?
2. View video.

**Group Discussion (10 Minutes)**
1. Ralph argues that we must widen the circle and give boys more choice if we want to engage them as writers. React to this statement.
2. Look at your classroom through the eyes of your boys. What is and isn't working for them in your writing classroom?

**Putting Ideas into Practice (5 Minutes)**
1. What might you try? What are you thinking?

**Next Month**
1. We will discuss Chapters 3 and 4 from *Boy Writers: Reclaiming Their Voices,* by Ralph Fletcher.

# Epilogue
# Why Not
# Teacher Research?

*The problem is the solution. Everything is a positive resource; it is up to us to work out how we may use it as such.*

—BILL MOLLISON

Some years ago, a friend of ours who is a kindergarten teacher told us the story of setting up a dramatic-play area in her classroom. She decided the theme of the area for the first month would be a shoe store. The teacher threw herself into preparing the area for the children—she borrowed real foot-measuring tools from a local shoe store, got shelves from another outlet, and even had twenty boxes of old shoes, in a variety of sizes, neatly displayed.

During the first play period, the teacher told students they could do whatever they wanted in the play area. A large group eagerly congregated around the shelves and decided they would throw a pretend birthday party for a friend. They upended the foot-measuring device to use it as a cake stand and began to make greeting cards out of the shoe order forms laid out for their use. Their teacher gently, and then not so gently, began to nudge them toward other possibilities for the play area, with prompts like, "Gee, look at all these shoes! What else could you do here besides have a birthday party?" The kids blithely ignored her. After the birthday girl blew out the candles on the imaginary cake, each child one by one gave her a present to open. Not surprisingly, every present turned out to be a box of old shoes.

We think of this story when we think of the learning we've experienced in the past few years through working with teacher-researchers. We continue to have our notions of what teacher research is, or should be, upended by the actual work of teacher-researchers.

When we look at the history of our work with teacher-researchers, it's easy to see it being something like that play-area shoe store. For years, we have presented research strategies with what we thought were open-ended purposes, encouraging teachers to develop and use research strategies for their own needs, but teacher-researchers haven't really given us what we expected. This text is full of the surprises we've experienced in twenty-five years of learning from teacher-researchers. What we thought was a pretty open-ended conception of research in our early days was actually more constrained than we realized, or outside the realm of interest or need for many teacher-researchers.

For example, we find that for many teachers, writing up research in any kind of traditional or nontraditional way is often still a struggle. Teachers tend to concentrate on immediate, local needs for their research, even as we urge them to seek larger audiences so that teacher research can have more of an influence on our academic world.

The flip side is also true. Teacher-researchers come to university folks with grown-up needs, concerns, and expectations for their research and how we might help them. And in our eagerness to help them, we might still be staying within a pretty narrow conception of what it means to go public with research. In other words, teachers might come to us with quite sophisticated and unique purposes for audiences that demand diverse and creative approaches to going public—and university educators seem to be handing them box after box of old shoes.

After the kindergarten teacher got over her initial disappointment in the children's choices, she was amazed at the creativity and learning going on in her classroom. We, too, have had to get over disappointment as we've seen some of our hard work and assumptions about research challenged by teachers. More than anything, it's made us shift our thinking—from what university researchers can teach teachers, to what we might learn in the future from teachers as the teacher-research movement continues to grow. In the end, what endures is our wonder at and respect for the ways teachers integrate research into their lives.

At the heart of good teaching—and good teacher research—is the learning and growth of our students themselves. As state and federal legislatures one by one take on the task of challenging all of us—public school and university teachers alike—to account for the uses of our time and to teach to mandated, highly specific, and standardized curricula, there is a new sense of urgency about finding ways to show what happens when teachers search out new materials and tinker with their curriculum, design new challenges, and base their teaching decisions on the data they collect from and with their students. Teacher-researchers can show that our inquiries matter at all levels.

Many of the teacher-researchers you have met through the pages of this book are working to create restructured schools with the kind of supports that will energize their work and their students' learning. These teachers' advice points us to what is possible in schools.

High on their list of priorities is time. When asked what she would use funding for if there were no constraints placed on it, Terri Austin immediately responded, "I'd buy time! Time to visit other teachers' classrooms, time to write, time to buy a colleague some sub time so we could meet and discuss our data, time to plan together with my teaching team." Other teacher-researchers echo the need for more—or at least different uses of—time.

And they have proposals for how we might accomplish this. Terri, Rich Kent, and Linda Christensen suggest that professional organizations—and school districts, too—widen the parameters of what can be requested in grant budgets to include buying time for substitute teachers, for extended writing, and for visiting other classrooms.

Literacy researcher and advocate Jerry Harste echoes this call for creative ways of forming communities around inquiry, working together so that we are all "connected to the profession differently," as he puts it:

> One of the things researchers have to do is position themselves—and understand that position. I encourage teachers to make presentations, share their in-process thinking long before they ever think they're ready. It's important support to help them go to conferences, make sure they are on programs, and also to alter power positions, showing through my own process and behavior that I'm vulnerable. (Personal communication, 1998)

If there is one thing pre-K to grade twelve teachers and university professors will always share, it is that need to show that our work is relevant and to bring it to a larger audience. One of our biggest struggles as university professors assisting teachers is to respect the different agendas they have for presenting their research to wider audiences, especially when that presentation doesn't involve any writing. But whether through blogs, conference presentations, discussions with colleagues, or the written word in op-ed articles or reports of inquiry, we need to get our work out to other teachers. Teachers respond well to teacher-research studies because they are peppered with anecdotes from the classroom that connect with their own experience.

Teacher research challenges the writing conventions in much of education research, but we also believe that it has the potential to be the needed bridge between practitioners and university researchers. Teachers are demanding, in large part through their wallets, a research writing style and tone different from the scholarship that has dominated the research literature for decades.

At the same time, teachers beginning to complete their own research studies often need a new language to describe what they are seeing. What teachers scoff at as "jargon" before they begin their research sometimes becomes useful to describe learning events. They see their classrooms in a new light, and the language of research in a new way, after trying to describe their own findings accurately.

Part of the future work of developing research strategies and resources for teacher-researchers involves understanding the needs of teacher-researchers better. We are also thinking hard about how to channel our energies away from helping teachers write up their work for academic journals, and toward more political, proactive vehicles now available online. Teacher-researchers are coming to us sometimes with desperate needs as they see the good work of curriculum reform undone by state and federal mandates. We feel like we are in the midst of a shift right now, and teacher-researchers are helping us pivot toward a broader view of audiences for research at all levels.

Anne Lamott (1994), in considering writing, could just as easily be admonishing us about research when she says, "Writing is about learning to pay attention and to communicate what is going on. Now, if you ask me, what's going on is that we're all up to here in it, and probably the most important thing is that we not yell at one another" (97).

We are always "up to here in it" when we're talking about teaching and learning, no matter what the educational setting. The battles between different researchers, administrators, and politicians can be acrimonious and not always respectful. We are still often immersed in what Deborah Tannen (1998) calls "the argument culture," setting up one camp against another. This was evident to Glenda Bissex (1996), one of the pioneers in teacher research, when she applied for her first college teaching position. She recounts this experience:

> "And what does that prove?" one faculty member challenged me during an interview for my first full-time college teaching job. I had just finished telling him about my dissertation, a longitudinal study of my young son's writing and reading development. Nobody on my dissertation committee had asked me that question, nor had I asked it myself in all the years I collected and pored through data, searching for patterns. I was confronted with an alien view from which—I too keenly grasped—my research appeared worthless. . . .
>
> What had I proven? I hadn't set out with a hypothesis to test in order to prove something to somebody. I'd started out with a curiosity whetted by transcripts of children's talk. . . . I was fascinated by what I was seeing. I guess I was so busy learning that I didn't worry about proving anything.
>
> Here was this wonderful growth unfolding in front of my eyes, and I wanted to truly see it. I wanted to probe it in places so I could know more than was on the surface. I was constantly looking for patterns as I reviewed piles of writings, tape recordings, and notes. Again and again, I asked, "What does this mean?" . . . As I look at it now, the question of what I proved appears thin and pale and irrelevant beside the richness of all the meanings I discovered, of all that I learned. I wouldn't have had any trouble answering the question, "And what did you learn?" (142)

Bissex goes on to explain the fundamental differences in the aims of teacher-researchers compared with many educational reformers:

> The word *research* suggests the researcher is "proving" something, frequently to someone else. . . . While *research* has the right literal meaning—to look again—its connotations may be wrong for what teachers are doing. We are not researchers in other people's classrooms, looking for proofs and generalizable truths, but reflective practitioners in our own classrooms, searching for insights that will help us understand and improve our practice. That does not exclude us from finding generalizable truths, although we may not know when we have found them. (1996, 143)

We want to close with the idea that our work with teacher-researchers hasn't proved anything. Like Glenda Bissex, we are always brought up short when we're asked for concrete proof of why this work matters. We still haven't found those generalizable truths about what teacher research is or will become, but we continue to learn so much.

What we've always seen in our work with teacher-researchers is a fundamental kindness: teachers care about listening to students, their colleagues, and their gut instincts about how their research agendas need to change. And it is this kindness and concern that will continue to be an antidote to the hostility and tension in debates about education and funding today. As teachers take on the role of researchers, we hope their guidance can help us all write better, more strongly, and more widely about how schools need to change. We all need a voice in making these changes, and teacher research often brings the freshest perspective to old problems.

Most of all, teacher research is a gift: to the profession, helping us change the way we see old problems and bringing us new solutions; to research communities, showing us new research strategies and how to take risks in writing up research; to ourselves, reminding us of the energy and passion in learning that made us teachers in the first place. It is a gift that we're all working hard for, like the unmerited grace Annie Dillard (1989) writes of: "At its best, the sensation of writing is that of any unmerited grace. It is handed to you, but only if you look for it. You search, you break your heart, your back, your brain, and then—and only then—it is handed to you" (54).

No one in these pages has lied to you and told you that mixing teaching and research would be easy. The words of teachers in this book include many images of broken hearts and sore brains, but all in the larger context of gratitude for how research is transforming their professional lives.

No matter what questions you may be asking about your teaching and students, we challenge you to answer with a question: Why not teacher research? Why not learn, as the teachers throughout these pages have, to find a place for research in your life? Research may never give you all the answers you crave, but it may help you find joy in living the questions.

# Appendix:
# Teacher-Research Designs

## CATHERINE DOHERTY'S RESEARCH DESIGN

### Research Question

What happens when my students create their own essential questions for their social studies curriculum?

### Purpose for Research

Learning is all about engagement, and we are most engaged when we have ownership of what we are learning. When students read and discuss the authentic questions they have about a text, they are more apt to learn the material they are reading about. It is less "in one ear and out the other" because they are making the experience more meaningful; thus the experience and learning stick in their brains. In my reading classroom, we do this all the time with novels, short stories, poems, and even nonfiction articles. The kids come up with questions while they read, and share and discuss them in small groups or with the whole class, resulting in a deep discussion of text. Because of how engaged my students are with their reading class material, I want to carry this process over into their social studies class. We actually have a great text this year. *History Alive* is the name of the program, and it is very user-friendly. The text is accessible, with tons of visual aids and absolutely none of the dreaded questions at the end of the chapter. But I haven't been seeing my kids get as involved with the social studies text and curriculum as they are in their book clubs for reading class. My thinking is that if I give them the opportunity to create their own questions as they read, they will become more engaged with the text. I am also interested in any other outcomes from this little experiment. I am genuinely interested in simply seeing what happens with the kids, their learning, and our classroom environment.

### Subquestions

Do my students appear more engaged with the text?

Are all the students getting the opportunity to create questions and give input, or is it only a few?

### Data Collection

- Self-reflection and reflection of group progress at project halfway point
- Self-reflection and reflection of group progress after project and presentation
- Teaching journal (maybe more like a reflection of the process throughout and at the end)
- Photographs of groups at work (This will help me see if all kids are involved.)
- Anecdotal notes of groups working together
- Videotapes of groups working and groups' final presentations
- Questionnaire at end to gauge how the audience and groups learned from this method

### Data Analysis

- Self-Reflections
  a. The first set will be given and read at the halfway point so I can see if the kids need my help with any of the key points in the book. This will also help me get an idea of whether they understand the concept of "essential questions" and how they guide our learning.
  b. The final self-reflections written by the students will tell me how *they* thought the project went. They will tell me what they thought was good and bad, and also how their learning process was helped or hindered throughout the project.
  c. My own reflection of the entire process will really help me think through what worked and what did not. This will force me to sit and consider my question and what happened when my kids created their own essential questions.
- Photographs
  The photographs will be good to look at because they are brief glimpses into the groups while they work. I think I will have a pretty good idea of each child's engagement based on what he or she is doing in the photo and how he or she seems to be interacting with the others. I will also have at least one photo of each group each day of the project, so there will be several shots of each child.
- Anecdotal Notes
  My notes will be indispensable. Although similar to a photograph, they will be brief written snapshots of what I overhear kids talking about and doing. They will tell me how often a group seems to be off topic, who in the group is working well, and who might be having trouble contributing. I use these a lot in my classes already, so the kids are used to seeing me with my clipboard in hand, jotting notes about their progress in group work.

*Living the Questions, Second Edition: A Guide for Teacher-Researchers* by Ruth Shagoury and Brenda Miller Power. Copyright © 2012. Stenhouse Publishers.

- Video
    a. The video I take of the kids working with each other I hope will be a great resource in terms of getting some sound bites straight from their mouths. I think it will add a nice element to my research to rehear what specific kids were saying, as well as to see who was asking questions and contributing more than others.
    b. I also will ask questions about the stage the kids are in with their research, so I may be able to use some of that information to make some changes in the project if I use it again in the future.
    c. Filming the final presentations will be helpful so that I have the opportunity to really concentrate on several aspects of the project as a whole. I will be able not only to focus on the content presented, but also to take the time to notice which kids did what and perhaps make some connections with the rest of the research. This will also be at my disposal whenever I feel I need it, and because it is an actual account, I won't need to rely on my memory much!

### Tentative Time Line

This should take just a few weeks. I want the kids focused on the content, so I don't want to drag it out too long. They are not used to doing long-term projects, so I think they could get antsy if we keep at it for weeks and weeks. I think three weeks should be good. Kids can do some reading, come up with questions, and create a presentation. During the third week, the students will give presentations and write evaluations of themselves and of the groups.

We have seventy-minute blocks on an A/B day schedule. Social studies is taught on B-days. I will be taking anecdotal notes throughout, and videotaping once a week. I will take a few photographs each day as well so that I have a lot of data. At the end of the first week I will assign the first self-reflection. The final self-reflection will be assigned on the third day of presentations.

### Resources

Throughout this project I will be conversing with several other sixth-grade teachers. The other three teachers on my team, Doug Miller, Becky Buchanan, and Brian Arnold, are always ready to talk about kids and what we are doing in each of our classes. They see my kids in a different context and more often than not are able to share techniques that work for them with our large groups.

Kevin Topolski is a longtime colleague and partner-in-learning to whom I always go for advice. His teaching style and commitment to education are inspiring, and he is always handy for some great discussions about teaching and research.

### Bibliography

Hubbard, Ruth S., and Brenda Miller Power. 1999. *Living the Questions.* Portland, ME: Stenhouse.

Jacobs, Heidi H. 2006. *Active Literacy Across the Curriculum.* Larchmont, NY: Eye on Education.

Keene, Ellin Oliver, and Susan Zimmermann. 1997. *Mosaic of Thought.*
Portsmouth, NH: Heinemann.

## BITSY PARKS'S RESEARCH DESIGN

### Research Question
How does my "book club" format affect book selection and subsequent
reading in my second-grade classroom?

### Subquestions
Does it matter who chooses the books?
How do peers influence reading behavior?
How does time of day and time of year influence reading behavior?
How do my read-alouds and book introductions encourage reading?
How do my book displays and book talks encourage reading?
Does the amount of at-home reading affect in-class reading?

### Belief Statement
Second grade is a fun grade to teach because students are often able to read
when entering in the fall, yet their reading skills increase a lot within the
year—it's exciting to watch! I give students reading instruction in small-
group and whole-group settings, have a quiet reading time scheduled into the
day, have books on tape, offer a large and diverse classroom library, and read
aloud to them. Yet I always feel concerned about the amount of time that my
students actually spend reading. They are given plenty of time to read and
opportunities to choose their own reading books from the library and the
classroom library, and I assign twenty minutes of reading each night.
However, I think many of them don't use the time for actual reading. I
wonder how much time they are actually reading, as opposed to just looking
at pictures. I understand the importance of looking through choice books but
also want my students to have a structure within which they are practicing
reading at their level. I've implemented a "book club" format where students
choose a book to read, record it on a reading log, and confer (very briefly)
with me after finishing it. They seem to like the new format, but I wonder
what effect, if any, it's having on their reading behavior.

### Data Collection
- Student reading log: This is included in their book club folders and will
  help students and me track the books they read and brief conference
  notes from me. Ideally it will show a variety of books that increase in
  difficulty throughout the year.
- My conference journal and chart: This journal will give me a place to
  take notes about the reading behaviors I am noticing in each student. It
  will be a place to reflect on particular students, conferences, and my
  perception of the strategy as a whole. The conference chart is a class list

on a spreadsheet where I record the date each time I meet with a student. The chart gives me a quick reference for how often I confer with each one.

- Student reading survey: I will survey the students two to three times a year to gain information about their attitudes toward reading.
- Parent reading survey: I hope to gain information about at-home reading, such as topics parents are interested in reading about and the amount of time they spend reading. I also hope to learn of parents' perspectives on their students' school reading from any comments that students might share with their parents.
- Track seating arrangements: I will note this information in my conference journal as needed, if I think the seating arrangement is affecting students' book choices or focus on reading.

### Data Analysis

I will use the students' reading logs and my conference journal to look at the different levels and topics of books that students are choosing. I will also use my conference journal to note how well students are decoding and comprehending the texts they are choosing. Ideally with the two data sources I will be able to determine if students are reading by how often they meet with me to talk about their book, how well they understand the text, and how well they are choosing books appropriate to their reading level. I will also use the student and parent surveys to gauge whether student attitudes and habits around reading are changing. Together with the reading log and conference journal I hope to gain a clear picture of each student as an independent reader and determine the effectiveness of the book club format.

### Time Line

*August*

- Before school starts, prepare book club folders, logs, and teacher conference/observation journal. Meet with my principal and my school curriculum team to let them know what I will be working on.

*September*

- Survey students within the first week of school. Explain format to students, pass out book club folders and reading logs. Begin conferences as needed.

*November*

- Survey parents at conferences. Review parent surveys, student surveys, and conference journal. Meet with my principal and/or school curriculum team to get input into data analysis and effectiveness of the book club format. Determine if I will continue using the format into the second trimester and how I will modify it if necessary.

### Support/Resources

- Supplies: folders, reading logs, books (library and classroom library)

- School curriculum team (made up of three classroom teachers, the principal, and a district TOSA [Teacher on Special Assignment])
- Principal

### Bibliography

Atwell, Nancie. 2007. *The Reading Zone: How to Help Kids Become Skilled, Passionate, Habitual, Critical Readers.* New York: Scholastic.

Harvey, Stephanie, and Anne Goudvis. 2007. *Strategies That Work: Teaching Comprehension for Understanding and Engagement.* 2nd ed. Portland, ME: Stenhouse.

Keene, Ellin Oliver, and Susan Zimmermann. 1997. *Mosaic of Thought: Teaching Reading Comprehension in a Reader's Workshop.* Portsmouth, NH: Heinemann.

Routman, Regie. 2003. *Reading Essentials: The Specifics You Need to Teach Reading Well.* Portsmouth, NH: Heinemann.

## LARA MURPHY'S RESEARCH DESIGN

### Purpose

Our Title I school, with 70 percent of its students receiving free or reduced-price lunch, has built a school garden. Most of our 750-plus students live in apartments and have little experience with the earth and nature. Classes that are interested will care for a bed in the garden. They will maintain the bed and plant their choice of produce. Our goal is to connect students to the earth, teach them about sustainability and the environment, encourage them to try new vegetables and fruits, teach them about nutrition, and help them become more aware of how plants grow and where our produce comes from. I want to see how involvement in a school garden affects the choices students make.

### Question

How does being involved in a school garden affect the nutritional, educational, social, and physical choices students make?

### Subquestions

How do students view vegetables before and after growing a garden?

What kinds of vegetables do students eat before and after growing a garden?

How many students are inspired to have a garden at home after having a school garden?

Do students choose to play outside more often?

Do students choose to work in the garden during recess?

How do students interact with each other in the garden?

Do students write about nature?

Are students aware of the plants that are growing in their neighborhood?

Do students notice the little things in nature (ants, worms, budding trees, plants, sprouts, sounds, how things feel, and so on)?

How do students' classroom behaviors change as a result of working in the garden?

## Data Collection

*Parent and Student Survey*

- I will give the survey to them at the beginning of the year and at the end of the year.
  - ° They will be given the same questions both times.
  - ° I will look for changes in their answers.

Sample Questions

a. What vegetables and fruit do you eat at home?

b. What kinds of fruit or vegetables are your favorites?

c. Have you ever eaten a . . . ?

d. Have you ever eaten vegetables straight from a garden?

e. Have you ever grown vegetables in a garden?

f. Do you buy fresh, canned, or frozen produce?

g. What part of the carrot do you eat?

h. Do you like to weed?

i. Do you like to play outside?

j. Would you rather be inside watching TV or playing outside?

k. What activities do you like to do outside?

*Interviews with Students*

- I will ask questions after the first time they work in the garden.
- I will ask questions later in the year.
- I will look for changes.

Sample Questions

a. What did you like or dislike about being in the garden?

b. Did you notice anything interesting?

c. Draw what you saw today in the garden.

d. What did you notice about the plants?

*Student Garden Journals*

- Students will record observations about what they see in the garden.
- Students will draw pictures of plants and other things they notice.
- Students will keep a planting record and keep track of plant changes.
- They will make predictions about how long it will take plants to grow.
- Students will take notes on how they felt about being in the garden.

*Observations and Notes*

- I will observe students and take notes.

## Data Analysis and Time Line

- Review parent/student survey (beginning of year).
  - ° I will record observations and findings in my own journal.
- Take notes on individual interviews (three times during the year: September/March/June).
  - ° I will record findings and look for patterns.

- Take tallies several times throughout the year to keep track of how many students are choosing to work in the garden during recess (once a week each month of the year).
- Read students' garden journals and record observations. (Are students becoming more aware? Are they more detailed and descriptive? Are they using new vocabulary?)
  - ° I will read and take notes once a month.
- Take notes on individual interviews toward the end of the year. (Any changes?)
- Review parent/student survey (end of the year).
  - ° I will record findings. (Any changes?)

### Support
- Families
- Gardening materials (tools, seeds, starts, and so on)
- Recess-duty teachers (to record student involvement in the garden during recess)

### Bibliography

Louv, Richard. 2008. *Last Child in the Woods.* Chapel Hill, NC: Algonquin Books.

Stone, Michael K. 2009. *Smart by Nature: Schooling for Sustainability.* Healdsburg, CA: Watershed Media.

Waters, Alice. 2008. *Edible Schoolyard: A Universal Idea.* San Francisco: Chronicle Books.

## GLORIA TRABACCA'S RESEARCH DESIGN

### Question
How will the quality of student reading responses be affected when students analyze their peers' reading responses as well as their own?

### Purpose
I am interested in finding ways in which to expand both the variety and the quality of student reading responses. Although I have taught my students about the many ways in which they can respond to what they have read, very few have demonstrated that they understand what I have taught. I have included repeated modeling, as well as lists of questions in each category, to spark their thoughts, but often their reading responses are little more than summaries. A few students are able to write interesting responses that show they have thought about their reading, rather than just filling the required minutes of reading before filling the required three-quarter page. I enjoy reading the responses of engaged readers, but cringe at responses along the lines of "I read a story. It was about a boy and a dog. It reminded me of something that happened to me once. The end."

*Living the Questions, Second Edition: A Guide for Teacher-Researchers* by Ruth Shagoury and Brenda Miller Power. Copyright © 2012. Stenhouse Publishers.

Since my repeated lessons and modeling have not inspired these students, I wonder if they will be motivated by reading their peers' responses. Perhaps they will also enjoy reading the responses of engaged readers, and will aspire to mimic them in their own responses. Perhaps they will cringe, as I do, when they read the deadly boring words of students who are just filling space with words instead of thoughts, and will vow to never do the same. I do not know how they will react, but I wonder how the quality of student reading responses will be affected when students engage in the daily analysis of their peers' reading responses.

## Subquestions

If students' skills in writing reading responses improve, how will this affect other student writings?

Will students' skills be affected after analysis of their own writing or after analysis of peer writing?

Will student growth be more conscious or unconscious? For example, after they analyze peer work, will they say, "I want/don't want to write like this" or will it be more a process of osmosis?

Will students think they gain more from negative ("This is *not* how I want to write") or positive ("I'd like to try writing like this") models?

Will the students' level of reading enjoyment be affected by the process of writing and analyzing more varied responses?

Will student engagement in book group discussions change during the course of this research?

## Data Collection

- Analysis of current reading response categories
  I will begin by analyzing current reading responses, for diversity of subject. I will examine each response to determine the level at which the student has connected to the text. These will be coded as follows:

    Summary only—red dot
    Text-self—blue dot
    Text-text—green dot
    Text-world—orange dot

  These preliminary statistics will be recorded on the attached dated tracking sheet.
- Student analysis of personal and peer reading responses
  Once baseline information is recorded, students will begin examining their own responses. Each day, class time will be provided for students to determine what connection they have made in the previous night's response, color-coding it as above. I will collect journals once weekly (five journals daily, on a rotating schedule), compiling each student's weekly totals in the listed categories. Each week's data will be on a different tracking sheet. During this time, I will also read responses and respond to them as usual. I will note the accuracy of student analysis, reteaching the categories as needed.

After three weeks, our daily analysis time will begin by having students trade journals. I will change the pattern of exchange daily, so that students are exposed to many response models, both positive and negative. Students will read and code peer responses. Again, I will collect these once a week, recording results on a tracking sheet, dated and labeled as peer analysis.

Results will be recorded once weekly, student by student, on the attached tracking sheet.

- Reflective questionnaire
  I will give the students a self-reflective questionnaire, to determine the following:
  1. whether they think the quality of their responses has changed;
     1a. *how* they think their responses have changed;
     1b. *why* they think their responses have changed (negative or positive models); and
     1c. *what* evidence supports their position;
  2. which student they most enjoy trading responses with, and why;
  3. which student they least enjoy trading responses with, and why;
  4. which student's responses have helped them learn the most, and why;
  5. whether they noticed any changes in the reading responses of their peers;
     5a. *how* they think the responses have changed;
     5b. *why* they think the responses have changed (negative/positive, peer/teach models);
     5c. *what evidence* supports their position;
  6. before-and-after ratings of reading enjoyment;
  7. other comments, including things learned from peers or thoughts about the research.
- Field notes and reflective journal
  I will keep a journal noting lessons as well as comments, discussions, attitudes, and writings about in-class reading, including whole-group, small-group, individual, and read-aloud experiences. I will be especially interested to "listen in" on novel group discussions, to note any changes that may occur.

## Data Analysis

- I will compile three sets of reading response analysis: starting, self-analysis, and peer analysis, noting totals in each category. I will do this both for each individual student and for the whole group.
- I will make a line plot (three colors, one for each mode), beginning and ending for each type of response, to visually compare data.
- I will compile data from student reflective questionnaires, comparing student perceptions of change in reading response and enjoyment, with data I gather from response analysis.
- In addition, I will develop a sociogram, using information from student questionnaires (Questions 2-4), to determine if any individuals were

particularly influential as models of either positive or negative reading responses.

- I will gather information from my journal, comparing change in oral response with the data gathered about written responses.

### Time Line

I have completed the analysis of current response categories, confirming my impression that approximately one-third of my students write little more than summaries. Those remaining write predominantly text-self responses.

We will begin analysis of our own writings this week (April 9), and continue until the end of April. Beginning in May, we will begin peer analysis of reading responses, which I plan to continue until the end of the year.

Although informal analysis of data will occur as I record weekly data, I will probably not do a formal compilation and analysis until summer break. If I find this to be a successful model, I will introduce next year's students to it from the start.

### Support

- C. (colleague)—I can discuss plans and ideas with C., knowing she will be open and genuinely interested, perhaps wanting to join in my research, and definitely keep me on track. C. is someone who will point out problems in my research, as well as inquire often about my progress.
- L. (friend)—L. has retired from teaching grades K–5 as well as TAG (Talented And Gifted). He is always good about sharing his ideas. Since the challenges and successes of life are part of our daily conversation, I know L. will offer his thoughts and observations on the process.
- Grade-level team—Next year, I plan to ask my grade-level team to become involved in the process, as we have already met and they seem to be interested in working as a team. This would also provide a great research base.
- A. (reading coach)—A. is the reading coach at our school, and has been suggesting "action research." She would be supportive, and eager to hear about progress. She would also be in a position to talk about it with reading coaches at other district schools, which might result in parallel research.

### Permissions

At this time, this research is only for myself, but I am also thinking that I would like to repeat the process with next year's third-grade students. If I do, and decide I want to publish for a wider audience, I might find myself wishing I had permissions from this year's fifth-grade students. Therefore it might be wise to get permission to use their writings before they move on to middle school. Next year, I will introduce parents to my research at Back-to-School night, and gain permission from the very start by sending out the following letter.

Dear Parents/Guardians,

As a teacher, I am always looking for better ways to help your child learn. I am currently conducting research to determine if the quality of student reading responses changes when students analyze the reading responses of their peers.

At this point, my research is solely for the purpose of helping students better communicate their understanding of, and involvement in, the books and articles they choose to read. It is possible, however, that I may wish to publish my findings at some future date so that other teachers and students may benefit from what I have learned. In case I do publish my work, I would like to include copies of student work. All names would be changed to protect student identity.

I would appreciate your permission to include your child's work in any future articles or books I might write. If you are willing to grant permission, please sign and return the form below to me. If you have any questions, please do not hesitate to contact me.

Thank you so much for your help.

Sincerely,
Gloria Trabacca
\*\*\*\*\*

Yes, I grant permission for the use of material described above.
Child's name: _____
Signature of parent/guardian: _____
Date: _____

## Other Thoughts

- If I see more growth during the period of peer analysis, it will be impossible to tell if it is a result of peer modeling or of simply having had a longer period of experience with the process.
- I wonder if it would be useful to go into more detail. For instance, as Cris Tovani points out, text-text could be subdivided into text-book, text-music, and text-movie. That level of analysis might help students become more aware of the possibilities, but it might become unwieldy.
- It would be interesting to find out if certain students' writings are particularly influential as models, but tracking that would be difficult, and is more than I am ready for at this time. Perhaps this is a thought for the future.
- I wonder if teaching the skills needed to analyze responses will be as valuable as the analysis itself. Although it will be the same information students have seen in a lesson on writing responses, I wonder if seeing it from the perspective of an analysis of someone else's writing will allow them to be open to hearing the lesson. It will be impossible to separate the two, impossible to know which is most valuable, but it does make me wonder.

### Bibliography
Atwell, Nancie. 1987. *In the Middle: Writing, Reading, and Learning with Adolescents.* Portsmouth, NH: Boynton/Cook.

Hubbard, Ruth Shagoury, and Brenda Miller Power. 1999. *Living the Questions: A Guide for Teacher-Researchers.* Portland, ME: Stenhouse.

Pearson, P. David, Laura R. Roehler, Janice A. Dole, and Gerald Duffy. 1992. "Developing Expertise in Reading Comprehension." In *What Research Has to Say About Reading Instruction,* ed. S. Jay Samuels and Alan Farstrup. Newark, DE: International Reading Association.

Tovani, Cris. 2000. *I Read It, but I Don't Get It.* Portland, ME: Stenhouse.

## MOLLY TAYLOR-MILLIGAN'S RESEARCH DESIGN

### Research Purpose

I teach in a two-way bilingual immersion school. The main focus of my instruction is to teach the state standards through the other curriculum provided. Bilingual education offers minority language speakers the opportunity to learn their native language as well as to teach the nonminority learners. I want to know what happens when my students use sentence frames, language they've heard, and themselves to experiment with English conversations.

### Research Question

In a two-way bilingual immersion classroom, what happens when Spanish-speaking, English-language-learning students engage in weekly oral English discussion?

### Subquestions

Will they stick to the sentence frames provided or will they deviate from them and use their own language?

Will they take risks in their oral language?

What growth will my students make?

### Data Collection

- Starting at the beginning of the school year, once a week, I will record an oral group discussion.
- Using a rubric, I will "grade" the oral conversations weekly.
- Once a month, I will write out one class's conversation that was recorded that month.

### Data Analysis

- At the end of each week, I will review data that I begin to collect.
- I will review recorded oral conversations from group discussion.
- Using a rubric, I will "grade" the oral conversations weekly.
- Once a month, I will write out one class's conversations recorded that month.

### Time Line
*August*
- Begin to schedule and plan daily lessons for ELD (English Language Development).
- Create specific sentence frames for weekly discussions.
- Create oral rubric.
- Check in with Laura about September's sentence frames and new rubric.

*September–December*
- Begin using sentence frames with group.
- Start using rubric weekly.
- Record group discussion weekly.
- Complete one monthly listening and charting of recorded session.
- Check in with Laura monthly about group's data.

*January*
- Begin looking over all the data collected from the first term of school.

### Support/Collaboration
- Check in with Laura bi-monthly about data collection.
- Ask questions, make connections, and confer with her about data.

### Bibliography
Clay, Marie. 2002. *An Observation Survey.* Portsmouth, NH: Heinemann.

Hubbard, Ruth Shagoury, and Brenda Miller Power. 1999. *Living the Questions: A Guide for Teacher-Researchers.* Portland, ME: Stenhouse.

Krashen, Stephen. 1996. *Under Attack: The Case Against Bilingual Education.* Culver City, CA: Language Education Association.

Power, Brenda Miller, and Ruth Shagoury Hubbard. 2002. *Language Development: A Reader for Teachers.* 2nd ed. Upper Saddle River, NJ: Merrill Prentice Hall.

## LAURA MARTINEZ'S RESEARCH DESIGN

### Research Purpose
I have been teaching primary grades for the last eight years. Writing has always been an area of interest for me because I love the power of words. I have seen doors open for myself with college scholarships and recognition because of my writing skills. In both high school and college I wrote for student newspapers. I wrote spots in community newspapers and loved how my words could be shared with such a large audience. However, I could not tell you how I developed my own writing skills or my love for writing. I want to help my students become successful writers so they can feel successful and be proud of their work.

*Living the Questions, Second Edition: A Guide for Teacher-Researchers* by Ruth Shagoury and Brenda Miller Power. Copyright © 2012. Stenhouse Publishers.

In my school district, we use an adopted curriculum. Many teachers like myself have tried to implement it, but have found that it does not affect students' writing in a way that helps them achieve state standards. We are given professional autonomy and allowed to experiment with teaching to yield the most successful results. After trying out the adopted curriculum and having it fail, I have abandoned it and teach writing workshop in the style of Lucy Calkins. I have collaborated with writing researchers such as Penny Pavala and have found ways to infuse sheltered instruction for English language learners in my writing lessons. Students have found more success in their writing ever since I shifted my teaching. Now I want to build upon the changes I have started making.

I have worked with my colleagues and developed a writing workshop framework in my classroom. The design allows for me to teach mini-lessons and then allows students time to work on their writing. Mini-lessons allow me to model writing for my students and for us to work on a shared piece. In doing so, I can gradually release responsibility of writing to my students. From there, I must guide each one to become more proficient in all traits of writing. Individuals progress at their own rates and need different focal points to help them improve.

The process of identifying students' areas of strengths and weaknesses has driven me to ask my research question. I plan to confer with students weekly and analyze the effect of a focused conference on each one.

### Research Question

How does weekly conferencing and keeping records of conversations with first graders during writing workshop affect their independent writing?

### Subquestions

How is each student's independent writing responsive to teaching points the teacher and student focused on?

What class trends are noticeable (such as areas of strengths or weaknesses)?

What areas of writing need the most work for the majority of children? In which areas of writing are children already successful?

### Data Collection

- Work samples. During writing workshop students will work on writing narratives. They will keep their pieces of writing in individual folders, sorted by table group. Each week I will look at a piece of writing from every student to see what effect conferring had on their independent writing. I will look at Group 1 on Monday, Group 2 on Tuesday, and so on.
- Conference recording sheet. I will use a five-row, five-column recording sheet. Each child's name will be in one square. Once a week I will meet with each child and record the teaching point that the child and I discussed during our conference. I will compare this teaching point with the child's work sample to see if there was any effect. I will record this

by writing "TP (teaching point)" and a brief message about what was taught, along with any other notes of importance.

- Sticky notes. I will provide students with a sticky note as a visual written reminder of their conferencing goal. I will add an example of editing marks or a sketch if it applies to the child's goal.

### Data Analysis

- Once a month I will review two independent writing samples from each child. I will analyze them by comparing the child's conference goals to see if our conference points are reflected in the writing. For example, if I talked to a child about the need for a clear ending, I will look to see if the writing stops abruptly or a story wraps up with a clear ending. If a child worked on adding plurals, I will look for the child's writing to distinguish plural nouns with *s* endings.

    If a child's writing does not reflect growth toward conferencing goals, I will review the goals with the child again and scaffold him or her with more support such as a class or small-group mini-lesson.

### Support/Collaboration

I plan to do this research in my first-grade classroom. I will discuss it at monthly grade-level meetings. If I see good results such as students making progress, I will share my data-keeping tools and methods with my colleagues. I will encourage them to try data keeping while conferring. We have worked together for a couple of years, and I feel comfortable making teaching suggestions and improvements from the status quo. Our group has a collaborative nature, and we share ideas freely. If our conferring produces good results as a grade level, we might report our findings to our school during a staff meeting or staff development.

### Time Line
*September*
- Plan and teach lessons using Lucy Calkins and Abby Oxenhorn's book *Small Moments: Personal Narrative Writing*, parts 1–4.
- Collect baseline independent writing data at beginning of the month.
- Confer weekly with students and record data.
- Collect end-of-the-month writing data (two samples from each child) and analyze it.

*October*
- Plan and teach lessons on narrative writing.
- Confer weekly with students and record data.
- Collect end-of-the-month writing data (two samples from each child) and analyze it.

*November*
- Plan and teach lessons on narrative writing.
- Confer weekly with students and record data.

- Collect end-of-the-month writing data (two samples from each child) and analyze it.

*December*
- Plan and teach lessons on descriptive writing: focus on family traditions.
- Confer weekly with students and record data.
- Collect end-of-the-month writing data (two samples from each child) and analyze it.

*January*
- Plan and teach lessons on descriptive writing: snow buddies, Martin Luther King Jr.
- Confer weekly with students and record data.
- Collect end-of-the-month writing data (two samples from each child) and analyze it.

*February*
- Plan and teach lessons on expository writing: lobsters, whales, self-description.
- Confer weekly with students and record data.
- Collect end-of-the-month writing data (two samples from each child) and analyze it.

*March*
- Plan and teach lessons on expository writing: penguins, narratives.
- Confer weekly with students and record data.
- Collect end-of-the-month writing data (two samples from each child) and analyze it.

*April*
- Plan and teach lessons on narratives/expository how-to directions.
- Confer weekly with students and record data.
- Collect end-of-the-month writing data (two samples from each child) and analyze it.

*May*
- Plan and teach lessons on expository how-to directions.
- Confer weekly with students and record data.
- Collect end-of-the-month writing data (two samples from each child) and analyze it.

*June*
- Plan and teach lessons on poetry writing.
- Confer weekly with students and record data.
- Collect end-of-the-month writing data (two samples from each child) and analyze it.

### Bibliography

Anderson, Carl. 2005. *Assessing Writers.* Portsmouth, NH: Heinemann.

Calkins, Lucy, and Natalie Louis. 2003. *Writing for Readers: Teaching Skills and Strategies. Units of Study for Primary Writing: A Yearlong Curriculum.* Portsmouth, NH: Heinemann.

Calkins, Lucy, and Abby Oxenhorn. 2003. *Small Moments: Personal Narrative Writing.* Portsmouth, NH: Heinemann.

Calkins, Lucy, Amanda Hartman, and Zoe White. 2005. *One to One: The Art of Conferring with Young Writers.* Portsmouth, NH: Heinemann.

Fletcher, Ralph. 1999. *Live Writing: Breathing Life Into Your Words.* New York: HarperCollins.

Portalupi, JoAnn, and Ralph Fletcher. 2004. *Teaching the Qualities of Writing.* Portsmouth, NH: Firsthand.

## SAUNDRA HARDY'S RESEARCH DESIGN

### Research Purpose

I want to explore the writing process that elementary English language learners experience in a writing workshop. My desire for this exploration came about from my various teaching experiences, some of which were focused on passing the state writing assessment. In observing now as an ELL teacher in kindergarten to fifth grade, I am curious to know what makes ELL students most successful in writing. From my observations and conversations with colleagues, I know that ELL students in particular are not prepared to meet these state writing standards.

As I busily finish my master of arts degree in teaching with endorsements in language and literacy and English as a second language, I strive to implement language arts tools to better address the learning patterns of my diverse ELL student population. I want to build literacy strategies that incorporate listening, speaking, reading, and writing. Last year, I struggled within my classroom to establish a strong writing component to meet the needs of all my ELL students. I want to educate good readers to transition into good writers by incorporating good reading tactics into their writing. Also, I want to know how I can better support young ELL writers and make them successful by using the latest educational research.

### Research Question

How does participation in writing workshop affect elementary ELL students' writing?

### Subquestions

What things need to be in place to develop a writing workshop community?
Is there a certain time in the day when writing is more successful?
How can I incorporate good reading tactics into ELL students' writing?
How can I encourage ELL children to employ choice?

*Living the Questions, Second Edition: A Guide for Teacher-Researchers* by Ruth Shagoury and Brenda Miller Power. Copyright © 2012. Stenhouse Publishers.

*Living the Questions, Second Edition: A Guide for Teacher-Researchers* by Ruth Shagoury and Brenda Miller Power. Copyright © 2012. Stenhouse Publishers.

How can I help my ELL students organize their writing without limiting them?

What effect will a writing workshop have on my assessment process?

Will the ELL students eventually be able to assess themselves to become better writers?

### Data Collection
- Writing interviews (beginning and end of year)
- Conference notes
  - ° Teachers
  - ° Students
- Journals
- Writing portfolios
- Observation (after-the-fact) notes

### Data Analysis
- I plan to know ELL students as writers by investing in one-on-one writing interviews. I will take my interview notes and write short biographies on each ELL student at the beginning and end of the year.
- I plan to read over my ELL students' conference notes once a week to create mini-writing lessons for individuals or groups of students. I also will read over my observation notes during this time.
- I plan to cycle through my ELL student journals at least once each week and record observation notes.
- I plan to celebrate ELL students' writing successes in reviewing each student's portfolio before each bi-monthly student/teacher conference. Also, students will be invited to celebrate and share their writing at an end-of-year Writing Celebration with peers, parents, and staff.

### Tentative Time Line
*September*
- Permissions
- Prewriting interviews
- Student journals
- Create portfolio purpose.
- Observation notes

*October–February*
- Continue student journals.
- Hold bi-monthly student/teacher conferences.
- Continue portfolio collection.
- Continue observation notes.
- Meet with inquiry group.

*March–April*
- Continue student journals.
- Continue observation notes.

- Postwriting interviews
- Analyze student growth in portfolios.
    a. Student reflection
    b. Teacher reflection

*April–May*
- Share research findings with students and inquiry group.
- Invite ELL students to share writing at a Writing Celebration.
- Send invitations to the Writing Celebration to students, parents, and staff.
- Celebrate ELL student writing at the Writing Celebration.

## Support
- Observation notes
- Lewis and Clark inquiry group
- Molly Ennis—ELL teacher/teaching partner
- Aunt Jeanne
- Coffee's On (a local coffee shop)
- Principal

## Permissions
- Letter to parents/guardian
- Talk to principal.

## Bibliography

Cummins, Jim. 1979. "Cognitive/Academic Language Proficiency, Linguistic Interdependence, the Optimum Age Question and Some Other Matters." *Working Papers on Bilingualism* 19: 121–129.

Cushman, Doug. 2002. "From Scribbles to Stories." *Instructor* 111 (January–February): 32–33.

Donnelly, Ann, Janice Files, and Diane Stephens. 2000. "Inquiry Study into Understanding and Supporting Writers." *NCTE Reading Initiative*: 1–11.

Dragan, Pat. B. 2005. *A How-To Guide for Teaching English Language Learners in the Primary Classroom.* Portsmouth, NH: Heinemann.

Fay, Kathleen, and Suzanne Whaley. 2004. *Becoming One Community.* Portland, ME: Stenhouse.

Freeman, D. E., and Yvonne S. Freeman. 2001. *Between Worlds: Access to Second Language Acquisition.* Portsmouth, NH: Heinemann.

Furr, Derek. 2003. "Struggling Readers Get Hooked on Writing." *The Reading Teacher* 56 (6): 518–525.

Hurwitz, Nina, and Sol Hurwitz. 2004. "Words on Paper." *American School Board Journal* 191 (March): 1–5.

James, Leigh Ann, Mary Abbott, and Charles R. Greenwood. 2001. "How Adam Became a Writer: Winning Writing Strategies for Low-Achieving Students." *Teaching Exceptional Children* 33 (3): 30–37.

Kendall, Julie, and Outey Khuon. 2006. *Writing Sense: Integrated Reading and Writing Lessons for English Language Learners K–8.* Portland, ME: Stenhouse.

Krashen, Stephen. 1985. *Inquiries and Insights.* Haywood, CA: Alemany.
————. 2003. *Explorations in Language Acquisition and Use: The Taipei Lectures.* Portsmouth, NH: Heinemann.
Lieberman, Ann, and Diane R. Wood. 2002. "From Network Learning to Classroom Teaching." *Journal of Educational Change* 3: 315–337.
Parker, Emelie, and Tess Pardini. 2006. *"The Words Came Down!" English Language Learners Read, Write, and Talk Across the Curriculum, K–2.* Portland, ME: Stenhouse.
Peregoy, Suzanne F., and Owen F. Boyle. 2005. *Reading, Writing, and Learning in ESL: A Resource Book for K–12 Teachers.* 4th ed. Boston: Pearson.
Richgels, Donald J. 2003. "Writing Instruction." *Reading Teacher* 56 (4): 364–368.
Routman, Regie. 2005. *Writing Essentials: Raising Expectations and Results While Simplifying Teaching.* Portsmouth, NH: Heinemann.
Roy, Suzanne C. 2004. "Building Writer's Workshop: One Principal's Journey." *The Delta Kappa Gamma Bulletin* 70: 25–28.

## CHRYSTAL FREER'S RESEARCH DESIGN

How does freedrawing time affect students' imaginative (pretend) play? This question came about because I was looking at how to increase literacy instruction within my specialized preschool setting. I was wondering about how to do this when I was part of a discussion about letting students draw their ideas out. Knowing that my students have difficulty with pretend play, I began to wonder how they could draw pretend ideas if they couldn't pretend play. And then I began to wonder, If I give my students freedrawing time, will their pretend play expand? After some refining I came to my final research question: How does freedrawing time affect students' imaginative (pretend) play?

For my data collection on this research question I will use three forms of data:

- Video of the students drawing and pretend playing
- Anecdotal data of what I see while students are drawing and playing
- The students' drawings (Staff will ask students what they drew and write the students' descriptions on their drawings.)

I will take and analyze data over the course of the school year to determine the full effect of freedrawing time on students' imaginative (pretend) play. I will start the year by taking video and anecdotal data on students' pretend play without giving them freedrawing time. Then, starting the second month, I will provide them with five to ten minutes per class day to freedraw. During months two through nine I will videotape each class a minimum of once a month and take down anecdotal data a minimum of three times per month per student. Below is the form that I will use to analyze the data collected.

I will need to provide my students with drawing paper, crayons, and markers. They will need individual attention from a teacher or assistant to help them write a description of their drawing. I will also need to provide them with access to a variety of pretend-play items during their free-play time so that I can observe their pretend play. For my data purposes I will need to check out the Flip video camera from the office to take video and save it on my computer so that I can go back and look at it as the year progresses.

Books that may be good resources as this research project takes place:

Halle, Emese. 2009. "Mixed Messages: The Role and Value of Drawing in Early Education." *International Journal of Early Years Education* 17 (3): 179–190.

Smith, Melinda J. 2001. *Teaching Playskills to Children with Autistic Spectrum Disorder: A Practical Guide.* New York: DRL Books.

West, Sherrie, and Amy Cox. 2004. *Literacy Play: Over 300 Dramatic Play Activities That Teach Pre-Reading Skills.* Silver Spring, MD: Gryphon House.

| Chrystal's Data-Analysis Sheet | | |
|---|---|---|
| **Date** | **Drawing Topic** | **Pretend-Play Topic** |
|  |  |  |
|  |  |  |
|  |  |  |
|  |  |  |
|  |  |  |
|  |  |  |

## GABI MCGREGOR'S RESEARCH DESIGN

### Origin

Next year I will (I hope) be teaching in a classroom of my own, so I have been doing a lot of thinking about how I want to structure it. I strongly believe that children cannot achieve to their fullest potential in an environment that feels unsafe in any way. For this reason it is essential that I create a classroom climate that is safe, accepting, and meets the needs of all my students. I would like to research the effect of whole-class meetings and how they influence the classroom climate and interactions that students have with one another. Implementing classroom meetings where students are able to communicate their thoughts and needs will help to create an environment where everyone feels respected and responsible for their actions. I would like to hold classroom meetings on a weekly or as-needed basis. My role in classroom meetings is as facilitator; students will be expected to contribute and listen respectfully to the needs of others. We will work on problem-solving strategies, communication skills, and building a community where everyone is thoughtful of one another. Through my research I want to observe how students interact with each other, and how those interactions evolve as classroom meetings are introduced.

### Research Question

How do community-building classroom meetings affect students' interactions?

### Subquestions

How do different environments (such as PE, recess, and lunch) affect
  student interactions?
Do students who are pulled out of class have an effect on class meetings?
What kind of language do students use to interact with each other?
What kind of body language do students use while interacting, and how
  is the boys' body language different from the girls'?
How do student interactions evolve as the year progresses?
What observations have outside teachers made about how students in
  my class interact with each other?

### Data Collection and Analysis

- Student interviews about how they feel in the classrooms (at different times in the year)
  - This is an important piece of data to collect because I value students' thoughts and feelings. The ultimate goal is to have each student feel like a valued and respected member of our community, and interviewing classroom members is the best way for me to see if this goal is achieved.
    - Review student attitudes.
    - Compare how they have changed from the start of the year to the finish.

- Take pictures of students interacting.
  - ° The photographs will serve as data that is visually stimulating and will spark memories of things observed earlier in the classroom.
    - – Use pictures to help spark journal writing.
    - – Photographs will provide visual records of who students interact with and the body language they're using.
- Videotape one classroom meeting a month.
  - ° Videotaping classroom meetings occasionally will be a powerful tool students can use to critique how well the meetings are working. It will also be a great way to compare how classroom meetings have changed month to month.
    - – This will allow students to see themselves interact and reflect on the classroom-meeting process.
    - – Students will be able to discuss and write in their journals about what they learn.
- Audio-record one classroom meeting a week and transcribe it.
  - ° This will allow me to be present during classroom meetings, jotting notes only when I see fit.
  - ° I will transcribe and analyze the recordings after school and look for any trends that occur week to week.
- * Teacher journal and observations
  - ° Writing in my journal will allow me to reflect on the teacher-researcher journey, student observations, questions, and connections in student interactions.

### Time Line
*August*
- Get all materials and plans for classroom meetings organized and ready to go.
- Write letter to parents.
- Develop survey questions.
- Start teacher journal.

*September–October*
- Set up classroom procedures.
- Give students classroom community survey.
- Observe student interactions before classroom meetings are implemented.
- Continue teacher journal.

*November–December*
- Introduce classroom meetings.
- Continue teacher journal.
- Make and review audio recordings of classroom meetings once a week.
- Make and review video recordings of classroom meetings once a month.
- Photograph student interactions.
- Look for patterns.
- Talk with coteacher to share information.

*January–May*
- Analyze student growth in portfolios.
- Continue all of the above.

*June*
- Give students the final classroom community survey.
- Review the before and after surveys and compare differences.
- Draw conclusions from observations.
- Develop summary statement.

### Support/Collaboration
- Coteacher
- Principal
- Students

### Bibliography

Gathercoal, Forrest. 2004. *Judicious Discipline.* San Francisco: Caddo Gap.

Gibbs, Jeanne. 2006. *Reaching All by Creating Tribes Learning Communities.* Windsor, CA: CenterSource Systems.

Rosenberg, Marshall B. 2003. *Nonviolent Communication.* Encinitas, CA: PuddleDancer.

Styles, Donna. 2001. *Class Meetings: Building Leadership, Problem-Solving and Decision-Making Skills in the Respectful Classroom.* Portland, ME: Stenhouse.

## ELLIE GILBERT'S RESEARCH DESIGN

### Why Is a High School Teacher Interested in Preschool Literacy?

The short answer is, well, because I'm a mom. And I'm not just *any* kind of mom. No, no. I am the kind of mom who likes to Get It *Right*. What does that mean, exactly? My child's diet is gluten-free, dairy-free, all organic, and contains no high-fructose corn syrup. She washes her hair in shampoo that is free of chemicals and she brushes her teeth three times a day, thank you very much. From the day she was born—nay, even in utero—she has been read to. Reading aloud and together is part of our family's daily routine: we read in the afternoon after nap, we read together at the dinner table, and we read at bedtime.

Until my daughter turned three, I *knew* I was doing everything Right. Then my daughter started preschool. We had our first parent/teacher conference in the fall where my husband and I learned that our daughter was advanced in her reading skills. I was thrilled! Then confused . . . I thought, Wait, what does her teacher mean by "reading" skills? I mean, my daughter knows a couple of sight words, and she L-O-V-E-S books, but I'm not so sure that really makes her a "reader" yet.

I started worrying. If her teachers were already evaluating our daughter's reading skills, is merely reading aloud to her enough anymore? I'd always sworn that when she started kindergarten, she would be reading . . . but how does that happen, exactly? I, like most parents who are themselves readers, assumed my child would learn to read and that she would love it as much as I do. But when I was faced with actually making reading happen in my child, suddenly I felt like I was lost, behind, not getting it Right. Should I buy those *My Baby Can Read* DVDs? Should I be drilling her on sight words, or is a phonics regimen the way to go? (Queue the reel of me loading up my shopping cart at Costco with several hundred dollars' worth of teach-your-kid-to-read programs.)

I realized that my background as a high school teacher and as a corporate trainer had done next to nothing to prepare me for teaching reading. I wanted to encourage my daughter as a reader, but I didn't even know where to start. I needed more information:

- What skills should I be teaching her?
- What books should we be reading?
- Is there a best-known method for teaching reading?
- What *is* literacy in preschoolers anyway?
- Where can I find the information I need?

I'm not sure why, but I kept thinking about those one-page information sheets that pediatricians give to parents during routine wellness checkups. They list the milestones your child should reach between now and their next checkup, such as "be able to stack more than three blocks," or "can stand alone on one foot." I thought, Why don't they hand out a milestone sheet about reading development? There had to be an easier way for parents like me to access information about the emerging literacy in our preschoolers.

In the spring of my daughter's first year in preschool, I enrolled as a graduate student at Lewis and Clark and began to take courses toward my master's in education and reading specialist endorsement. WOW! I couldn't believe the wealth of information about early literacy that is out there. Suddenly, I was seeing my daughter's emerging literacy in a whole new light. I was so excited by what I was learning that I decided it was too good to keep to myself. So, I'm partnering with a classmate to create a workshop for parents of preschoolers that explores the multiple facets of preschool literacy and that gives strategies for fostering their children's growth as readers and as writers. I want to know if the workshop affects how parents view their child's developing literacy and how they try to encourage or shape it.

### Question

What happens to the literacy culture of a home after parents complete a workshop about literacy development in their preschool-age children?

### Subquestions

How do parents define preschool literacy before they take the workshop? Does this definition change once they have completed the workshop?

*Living the Questions, Second Edition: A Guide for Teacher-Researchers* by Ruth Shagoury and Brenda Miller Power. Copyright © 2012. Stenhouse Publishers.

How does the way in which parents define their child's literacy affect the way they teach their preschool children to read and write?

How do parents believe they are "encouraging" reading in their children? Does their approach change once they have attended the workshop? How?

How much time do parents spend reading to their children? Is this amount affected by attending the workshop?

What sorts of skills do parents teach their young readers?

Before they attended the workshop, did parents read in front of their children? Do they do so after completing the workshop?

## Data Collection

- Preworkshop survey
  - ° Everybody hates surveys, so I plan to make the survey the parent's entrance ticket to the workshop.
- Note taking during workshop
  - ° I'll jot down comments made by parents, capture aha moments, and consider having a historian to keep notes for me.
- Workshop response journals
  - ° Here's where I'll ask parents to delve a little more deeply into our topics, asking for their feedback and thoughts on the information we've just covered.
- Exit plans
  - ° As part of the requirement for leaving the workshop, I'll ask parents to draft an "exit plan," which will include their definition of literacy and identify which strategies they plan to use with their kiddos.
- Postworkshop interviews
  - ° I plan to follow up with workshop participants over the phone and in e-mail to get their feedback on the class and to ask how they are using their exit plans.
- Correspondence with workshop attendees
  - ° I'll collect any e-mail correspondence I may have with attendees.

## Data Analysis

- Each workshop session will have three folders: one for preworkshop interviews and response journals, one for notes, and one for exit plans.
- Forty-eight hours postworkshop
  - ° I'll go through workshop notes (kept by me and the historian) and follow up on any items that require immediate attention.
- One week postworkshop
  - ° I will review each exit plan and make notes about anything I think might need to be clarified. I will keep all the exit plans from each workshop session in a folder designated for that particular session. (For example, if there are six workshop session per year, there will be six folders of exit plans.)

- Two weeks postworkshop
  ° I will follow up via e-mail or phone with participants about if and how they are implementing their exit plans. I will make notes during the interviews about their plans.
  ° Preworkshop surveys, workshop response journals, workshop notes, and exit plans will be color-coded with highlighters for common themes that emerge.
- After every three workshop sessions
  ° I will enter emergent themes in my "master document" (an Excel spreadsheet) that tracks common ideas that surface during and after the workshop experience.

### Time Line
- Two weeks before workshop, send out preworkshop surveys via e-mail to registered participants.
- At beginning of workshop, collect surveys.
- Take notes during workshop.
- Make copies of exit plans before parents leave workshop.
- Two weeks postworkshop, conduct postworkshop interviews.

### Resources
- Partnership with Liz Limbird, cocreator of the workshop
- A location for the workshop that includes access to a copier
- Online survey service such as Survey Monkey for preworkshop survey
- On-site child care during workshop
- Fellow teacher-researchers to help me through the process of publishing my findings and determining whom to share them with.

### Bibliography

Cunningham, Andie, and Ruth Shagoury. 2005. *Starting with Comprehension: Reading Strategies for the Youngest Learners.* Portland, ME: Stenhouse.

Golinkoff, Roberta Michnick, and Kathy Hirsh-Pasek. 2000. *How Babies Talk: The Magic and Mystery of Language in the First Three Years of Life.* New York: Plume.

Golinkoff, Roberta Michnick, Kathy Hirsh-Pasek, and Diane Eyer. 2003. *Einstein Never Used Flashcards: How Our Children Really Learn—and Why They Need to Play More and Memorize Less.* Emmaus, PA: Rodale Books.

Miller, Debbie. 2002. *Reading with Meaning.* Portland, ME: Stenhouse.

National Endowment for the Arts. 2004. *Reading at Risk: A Survey of Literary Reading in America.* Research Division Report 46 (June).

Shagoury, Ruth. 2008. *Raising Writers: Understanding and Nurturing Young Children's Writing Development.* Boston: Allyn & Bacon.

Trelease, Jim. 2006. *The Read-Aloud Handbook.* 6th ed. New York: Penguin Books.

Wise, Jessie, and Sara Buffington. 2004. *The Ordinary Parent's Guide to Teaching Reading.* Charles City, VA: Peace Hill.

# Bibliography

### Professional Literature

Alinsky, Saul. 1971. *Rules for Radicals: A Pragmatic Primer for Realistic Radicals.* New York: Random House.

Anderson, Carl. 2005. *Assessing Writers.* Portsmouth, NH: Heinemann.

Ansay, A. Manette. 1996. *Sister.* New York: Morrow.

Anzul, Margaret. 1993. "Exploring Literature with Children Within a Transactional Framework." In *Journeying: Children Responding to Literature*, ed. Kathleen Holland, Rachael Hungerford, and Shirley Ernst. Portsmouth, NH: Heinemann.

Arbus, Diane. 1972. *Diane Arbus.* Millerton, NY: Aperture.

Ashton-Warner, Sylvia. 1963. *Teacher.* New York: Simon and Schuster.

Atwell, Nancie. 1987. *In the Middle: Writing, Reading, and Learning with Adolescents.* Portsmouth, NH: Boynton/Cook.

———. 1998. *In the Middle: Writing, Reading, and Learning with Adolescents.* Rev. ed. Portsmouth, NH: Boynton/Cook.

———. 2007. *The Reading Zone: How to Help Kids Become Skilled, Passionate, Habitual, Critical Readers.* New York: Scholastic.

Austin, Terri. 1994a. "The Well-Dressed Alaska Teacher-Researcher." *Teacher Research* 2 (1): 66–80.

———. 1994b. "Travel Together in Trust." *Teacher Research Journal* 1 (2): 122–127.

———. 1995. *Changing the View: Student-Led Parent Conferences.* Portsmouth, NH: Heinemann.

Ball, Arthena. 2009. "Teaching Writing in Culturally Diverse Classrooms." In *Telling a Research Story: Writing a Literature Review*, ed. Christine Feak and John Swales. Ann Arbor: University of Michigan Press.

Ballenger, Cynthia. 2009. *Puzzling Moments, Teachable Moments: Practicing Teacher Research in Urban Classrooms.* New York: Teachers College Press.

Barbieri, Maureen. 1995. *Sounds from the Heart.* Portsmouth, NH: Heinemann.

Bateson, Mary Catherine. 1994. *Peripheral Visions: Learning Along the Way.* New York: HarperCollins.

Bellack, Arno. 1966. *The Language of the Classroom.* New York: Teachers College Press.

Bennett, Sara, and Nancy Kalish. 2007. *The Case Against Homework: How Homework Is Hurting Children and What Parents Can Do About It.* New York: Three Rivers.

Berg, Elizabeth. 1993. *Durable Goods.* New York: Random House.

———. 1994. *Talk Before Sleep.* New York: Random House.

———. 1995. *Range of Motion.* New York: Random House.

———. 1997. *The Pull of the Moon.* New York: Random House.

Bernstein, Leonard. 1981. *The Unanswered Question: Six Talks at Harvard.* Cambridge, MA: Harvard University Press.

Berthoff, Ann. 1987. "The Teacher as Researcher." In *Reclaiming the Classroom: Teacher Research as an Agency for Change,* ed. Dixie Goswami and Peter Stillman. Upper Montclair, NJ: Boynton/Cook.

Bintz, William. 1997. "Seeing Through Different Eyes: Using Photography as a Research Tool." *Teacher Research* 5 (1): 29–46.

Bisplinghoff, Betty. 1995. "Reading Like a Researcher." *Teacher Research* 3 (1): 105–113.

Bisplinghoff, Betty, and JoBeth Allen. 1998. *Engaging Teachers.* Portsmouth, NH: Heinemann.

Bissex, Glenda. 1987. "Why Case Studies?" In *Seeing for Ourselves: Case Study Research by Teachers of Writing,* ed. Glenda Bissex and Richard Bullock. Portsmouth, NH: Heinemann.

———. 1996. *Partial Truths: A Memoir and Essays on Reading, Writing, and Researching.* Portsmouth, NH: Heinemann.

Bissex, Glenda, and Richard Bullock. 1987. *Seeing for Ourselves: Case Study Research by Teachers of Writing.* Portsmouth, NH: Heinemann.

Block, Peter. 2008. *Community: The Structure of Belonging.* San Francisco: Berrett-Koehler.

Bolker, Joan. 1997. "A Room of One's Own Is Not Enough." In *The Writer's Home Companion,* ed. Joan Bolker. New York: Owl Books.

Boushey, Gail, and Joan Moser. 2006. *The Daily Five.* Portland, ME: Stenhouse.

———. 2009. *The CAFE Book: Engaging All Students in Daily Literary Assessment and Instruction.* Portland, ME: Stenhouse.

Brand, Max. 2006. *Conferring with Boys.* DVD. Portland, ME: Stenhouse.

Branscombe, Amanda, Dixie Goswami, and Jeffrey Schwartz. 1992. *Students Teaching, Teachers Learning.* Upper Montclair, NJ: Boynton/Cook.

Bro, Elsa, Samae Horener, Rachel Reckord, Melody Rockwell, and Ruth Shagoury. 2006. "New Teacher Researcher Conversations: Understanding English Language Learners and Ourselves." In *New Horizons for Learning,* ed. Nathalie Gehrke. Olympia, WA: Antioch University.

Brown, Lynn, Carol Gilligan, and Amy Sullivan. 1992. *Meeting at the Crossroads: Women's Psychology and Girls' Development.* Cambridge, MA: Harvard University Press.

Buckner, Aimee. 2005. *Notebook Know-how.* Portland, ME: Stenhouse.

Burton, F. R. 1991. "Teacher-Researcher Projects: An Elementary Schoolteacher's Perspective." In *Handbook of Research on Teaching the English Language Arts,* ed. James Flood, Julie Jensen, Diane Lapp, and James R. Squire. New York: Macmillan.

Calfee, Richard, and Michael J. Chambliss. 1991. "The Design of Empirical Research." In *Handbook of Research on Teaching the English Language Arts*, ed. James Flood, Julie M. Jensen, Diane Lapp, and James R. Squire. New York: Macmillan.

Calkins, Lucy. 1983. *Lessons from a Child: On Teaching and Learning Writing.* Portsmouth, NH: Heinemann.

———. 2000. *The Art of Teaching Reading.* Portsmouth, NH: Heinemann.

Calkins, Lucy, and Natalie Louis. 2003. *Writing for Readers: Teaching Skills and Strategies. Units of Study for Primary Writing: A Yearlong Curriculum.* Portsmouth, NH: Heinemann.

Calkins, Lucy, and Abby Oxenhorn. 2003. *Small Moments: Personal Narrative Writing.* Portsmouth, NH: Heinemann.

Calkins, Lucy, Amanda Hartman, and Zoe White. 2005. *One to One: The Art of Conferring with Young Writers.* Portsmouth, NH: Heinemann.

Campbell, Kimberly. 1997a. "Celebrating 'Conscious Deliberate Thoughtfulness': An Interview with Deborah Meier." *Teacher Research* 5 (1): 11–25.

———. 1997b. "You're Invited." *Teacher Research* 1 (2): 57–62.

Cazden, Courtney. 1988. *Classroom Discourse: The Language of Teaching and Learning.* Portsmouth, NH: Heinemann.

Chambers, David. 1983. "Stereotypic Images of the Scientist: The Draw-A-Scientist Test." *Science Education* 67 (2): 255–265.

Chambliss, Michael J. 1991. "The Design of Empirical Research." In *Handbook of Research on Teaching the English Language Arts*, ed. James Flood, Julie M. Jensen, Diane Lapp, and James R. Squire. New York: Macmillan.

Chandler, Kelly. 1997. "Emergent Researchers: One Group's Beginnings." *Teacher Research* 4 (2): 73–100.

Cisneros, Sandra. 1989. *The House on Mango Street.* New York: Vintage Books.

Clark, Kelli. 1997. "Harvesting Potatoes." *Teacher Research* 4 (2): 182–183.

Clay, Marie. 2002. *An Observation Survey.* Portsmouth, NH: Heinemann.

Cochran-Smith, Marilyn, and Susan Lytle. 1990. "Research on Teaching and Teacher Research: The Issues That Divide." *Educational Researcher* 19 (2): 2–10.

———. 1992. "Student Teachers and Their Teacher: Talking Our Way into New Understandings." In *Students Teaching, Teachers Learning*, ed. Amanda Branscrombe, Dixie Goswami, and Judith Schwartz. Upper Montclair, NJ: Boynton/Cook.

———. 1993. *Inside/Outside: Teacher Research and Knowledge.* New York: Teachers College Press.

———. 2009. *Inquiry as Stance: Practitioner Research for the Next Generation.* New York: Teachers College Press.

Cooper, Harris. 2006. *The Battle Over Homework: Common Ground for Administrators, Teachers, and Parents.* Thousand Oaks, CA: Corwin.

Corsaro, William. 1981. "Entering the Child's World: Research Strategies for Field Entry and Data Collection in a Pre-school Setting." In *Ethnography and Language in Educational Settings*, ed. Judith Green and Cynthia Wallatt. Norwood, NJ: Ablex.

Cox, Dana. 1998. Interview. "Math by the Numbers: Seeing Is Believing." WQED, Public Broadcasting System, Pittsburgh, PA, May 27.

Cruz, Colleen. 2004. *Independent Writing.* Portsmouth, NH: Heinemann.

Cummins, Jim. 1979. "Cognitive/Academic Language Proficiency, Linguistic Interdependence, the Optimum Age Question and Some Other Matters." *Working Papers on Bilingualism* 19: 121–129.

———. 1997. "Metalinguistic Development of Children in Bilingual Education Programs." In *The Fourth Locus Forum,* ed. M. Paradis. Columbia, SC: Hornbeam.

Cummins, Jim, and Dennis Sayers. 1995. *Brave New Schools: Challenging Cultural Illiteracy Through Global Learning Networks.* New York: St. Martin's.

Cunningham, Andie, and Ruth Shagoury. 2005. *Starting with Comprehension: Reading Strategies for the Youngest Learners.* Portland, ME: Stenhouse.

Cushman, Doug. 2002. "From Scribbles to Stories." *Instructor* 111 (January–February): 32–33.

Daane, Mary C. 1986. "Review of 'If Not Now: Developmental Readers in the College Classroom.'" *Journal of Adolescent and Adult Literacy* 40 (3): 235–237.

Dana, Nancy, and Diane Yendol-Hoppey. 2009. *The Reflective Educator's Guide to Classroom Research.* Thousand Oaks, CA: Corwin.

Darling-Hammond, Linda. 1998. *The Right to Learn: A Blueprint for Creating Schools That Work.* San Francisco: Jossey-Bass.

Dewey, John. 1997. *Experience and Education.* New York: Macmillan.

Diaz, Rafael M. 1983. "The Intellectual Power of Bilingualism." Paper presented at the New Mexico Humanities Council, Albuquerque, NM.

Dickinson, Peter. 1992. *A Bone from a Dry Sea.* New York: Bantam Doubleday Dell.

Dillard, Annie. 1989. *The Writing Life.* New York: Harper and Row.

Donnelly, Ann, Janice Files, and Diane Stephens. 2000. "Inquiry Study into Understanding and Supporting Writers." *NCTE Reading Initiative*: 1–11.

Dorfman, Lynne. 2007. *Mentor Texts: Teaching Writing Through Children's Literature.* Portland, ME: Stenhouse.

Dove, Rita. 1997. "To Make a Prairie." In *The Writer's Home Companion,* ed. Joan Bolker. New York: Owl Books.

Dragan, Pat B. 2005. *A How-To Guide for Teaching English Language Learners in the Primary Classroom.* Portsmouth, NH: Heinemann.

Duffy, Gerald. 1998. "Teaching and the Balancing of Round Stones." *The Kappan* 79 (10): 777–780.

Early, Jessica Singer, and Ruth Shagoury. 2010. "Learning from the Lived Experiences of New Language Arts Teachers Working in Diverse Urban Schools." *Teaching and Teacher Education* 26: 1049–1058.

Edelski, Carole. 1996. *With Literacy and Justice for All.* Bristol, PA: Taylor and Francis.

Elbow, Peter. 1997. "Options for Getting Feedback." In *The Writer's Home Companion,* ed. Joan Bolker. New York: Owl Books.

Ellingson, Laura. 2009. *Engaging Crystallization in Qualitative Research.* Thousand Oaks, CA: Sage.

Erickson, Frederick, and Jeffrey Shultz. 1992. "Students' Experience of the Curriculum." In *Handbook of Research on Teaching,* ed. Peter Jackson. New York: Macmillan.

Fay, Kathleen, and Suzanne Whaley. 2004. *Becoming One Community.* Portland, ME: Stenhouse.

Fergusen, Charles. 1978. *Talking to Children: A Search for Universals.* Stanford, CA: Stanford University Press.

Fisher, Bobbi. 1991. *Joyful Learning: A Whole Language Kindergarten.* Portsmouth, NH: Heinemann.

Fletcher, Ralph. 1993. *What a Writer Needs.* Portsmouth, NH: Heinemann.

———. 1999. *Live Writing: Breathing Life into Your Words.* New York: HarperCollins.

———. 2006. *Boy Writers: Reclaiming Their Voices.* Portland, ME: Stenhouse.

Frazier, Charles. 1997. *Cold Mountain.* New York: Vintage Books.

Freeman, David E., and Yvonne S. Freeman. 2001. *Between Worlds: Access to Second Language Acquisition.* Portsmouth, NH: Heinemann.

Friedman, Bonnie. 1993. *Writing Past Dark.* New York: HarperCollins.

Frye, Sharon. 1997. "The Power of Deliberately Listening: An Interview with Maureen Barbieri." *Teacher Research* 4 (2): 42–58.

Fullan, Michael. 2007. *The New Meaning of Educational Change.* New York: Teachers College Press.

Furr, Derek. 2003. "Struggling Readers Get Hooked on Writing." *The Reading Teacher* 56 (6): 518–525.

Gallagher, Kelly. 2003. *Reading Reasons.* Portland, ME: Stenhouse.

———. 2004. *Deeper Reading.* Portland, ME: Stenhouse.

———. 2006. *Teaching Adolescent Writers.* Portland, ME: Stenhouse.

———. 2009. *Readicide: How Schools Are Killing Reading and What You Can Do About It.* Portland, ME: Stenhouse.

Gallas, Karen. 1994. *The Languages of Learning: How Children Talk, Write, Dance, Draw, and Sing Their Understanding of the World.* New York: Teachers College Press.

———. 1998. *Sometimes I Can Be Anything: Power, Gender, and Identity in a Primary Classroom.* New York: Teachers College Press.

Gathercoal, Forrest. 2004. *Judicious Discipline.* San Francisco: Caddo Gap.

Gibbs, Jeanne. 2006. *Reaching All by Creating Tribes Learning Communities.* Windsor, CA: CenterSource Systems.

Gillespie, Tim. 1993. "On Learning from the Inside: A Conversation with Glenda Bissex." *Teacher Research* 1 (1): 64–83.

———. 1994. "Interview with Dixie Goswami." *Teacher Research* 2 (1): 89–103.

Glancy, Diane. 1992. *Claiming Breath.* Lincoln: University of Nebraska Press.

Glaser, Barney, and Anselm Strauss. 1967. *Discovery of Grounded Theory: Strategies for Qualitative Research.* Hawthorne, NY: Aldine de Gruyter.

Goanos, Larry. 2011. "Standing Up for Natalie Munroe and the First Amendment." http://www.phillyburbs.com/blogs/opinions/intel/standing-up-for-natalie-munroe-and-the-first-amendment/article_3561c57b-17df-5ef3-8d6a-6029c10ef7e2.html.

Golinkoff, Roberta Michnick, and Kathy Hirsh-Pasek. 2000. *How Babies Talk: The Magic and Mystery of Language in the First Three Years of Life.* New York: Plume.

Golinkoff, Roberta Michnick, Kathy Hirsh-Pasek, and Diane Eyer. 2003. *Einstein Never Used Flashcards: How Our Children Really Learn—and Why They Need to Play More and Memorize Less.* Emmaus, PA: Rodale Books.

Goswami, Dixie, Ceci Lewis, Marty Rutherford, and Diane Waff. 2009. *Teacher Inquiry: Approaches to Language and Literacy Research*. New York: Teachers College Press.

Graham, Steven. 2008. "Research on Writing Development, Practice, Instruction, and Development." *Reading and Writing: An Interdisciplinary Journal* 21 (1 and 2): 172–183 and 210–221.

Graham Steven, and Jill Fitzgerald, eds. 2008. *Handbook of Writing Research*. New York: Guilford.

Graham, Steven, Charles A. MacArthur, and Jill Fitzgerald. 2008. *Best Practices in Writing Instruction: Solving Problems in the Teaching of Literacy*. New York: Guilford.

Graham, Steven, and Diane Perin. 2007a. "A Meta-analysis of Writing Instruction for Adolescent Students." *Journal of Educational Psychology* 99: 445.

———. 2007b. "What We Know, What We Still Need to Know: Teaching Adolescents to Write." *Scientific Studies of Reading* 11 (4): 313-335.

Graves, Donald H. 1994. *A Fresh Look at Writing*. Portsmouth, NH: Heinemann.

Hakuta, Kenji. 1986. *Mirror of Language: The Debate on Bilingualism*. New York: Basic Books.

Halle, Emese. 2009. "Mixed Messages: The Role and Value of Drawing in Early Education." *International Journal of Early Years Education* 17 (3): 179–190.

Halliday, Michael A. K. 1977. *Exploration in the Functions of Language*. New York: Elsevier North-Holland.

Harste, Jerome. 1990. "Foreword." In *Opening the Door to Classroom Research*, ed. Mary W. Olson. Newark, DE: International Reading Association.

Harste, Jerome, and Christine Leland. 2007. "On Getting Lost, Finding One's Direction, and Teacher Research." *Voices from the Middle* 14 (3): 7–11.

Harste, Jerome, Virginia Woodward, and Carolyn Burke. 1984. *Language Stories and Literacy Lessons*. Portsmouth, NH: Heinemann.

Harvey, Stephanie, and Anne Goudvis. 2007. *Strategies That Work: Teaching Comprehension for Understanding and Engagement*. 2nd ed. Portland, ME: Stenhouse.

Heard, Georgia. 1989. *For the Good of the Earth and Sun: Teaching Poetry*. Portsmouth, NH: Heinemann.

Heath, Chip, and Dan Heath. 2010. *Switch: How to Change Things When Change Is Hard*. New York: Crown.

Hillocks, George, Jr. 2008. "Writing in Secondary Schools." In *Handbook of Research on Writing: History, Society, School, and Text*, ed. Charles Bazerman. Mahwah, NJ: Lawrence Erlbaum.

Hitchcock, Graham, and David Hughes. 1989. *Research and the Teacher: A Qualitative Introduction to School-Based Research*. New York: Routledge.

Hord, Shirley. 1997. "Professional Learning Communities: What Are They and Why Are They Important?" *Issues About Change* 6 (1): 3–71.

Hubbard, Ruth, Maureen Barbieri, and Brenda Miller Power. 1998. *"We Want to Be Known": Learning from Adolescent Girls*. York, ME: Stenhouse.

Hubbard, Ruth Shagoury, and Brenda Miller Power. 1999. *Living the Questions: A Guide for Teacher-Researchers*. Portland, ME: Stenhouse.

————. 2003. *The Art of Classroom Inquiry: A Handbook for Teacher Researchers.* Portsmouth, NH: Heinemann.

Huberman, Miles. 1996. "Moving Mainstream: Taking a Closer Look at Teacher Research." *Language Arts* 73 (2): 124–140.

Hurwitz, Nina, and Sol Hurwitz. 2004. "Words on Paper." *American School Board Journal* 191 (March): 1–5.

Ingram, John, and Norman Worrall. 1993. *Teacher-Child Partnership: The Negotiated Classroom.* London: David Fulton.

Jackson, Phillip. 1968. *Life in the Classroom.* New York: Holt, Rinehart, and Winston.

Jacobs, Heidi H. 2006. *Active Literacy Across the Curriculum.* Larchmont, NY: Eye on Education.

Jalongo, Mary, and Joan Isenberg. 1995. *Teachers' Stories: From Personal Narrative to Professional Insight.* San Francisco: Jossey-Bass.

James, Leigh Ann, Mary Abbott, and Charles R. Greenwood. 2001. "How Adam Became a Writer: Winning Writing Strategies for Low-Achieving Students." *Teaching Exceptional Children* 33 (3): 30–37.

Janesick, Valerie. 1998. *Stretching Exercises for Qualitative Researchers.* Thousand Oaks, CA: Sage.

Jantsch, Erich. 1980. *The Self-Organizing Universe.* New York: Pergamon.

Johnston, Peter. 2004. *Choice Words.* Portland, ME: Stenhouse.

Kaback, Suzanne. 1997. "Digestion Not Digression: A Gourmand's Invitation to Teacher-Research Chat." *Teacher Research* 4 (2): 112–123.

Keene, Ellin Oliver, and Susan Zimmerman. 1997. *Mosaic of Thought: Teaching Reading Comprehension in a Reader's Workshop.* Portsmouth, NH: Heinemann.

Keep-Barnes, Annie. 1994. "Real Teachers Don't Always Succeed." *Teacher Research* 2 (1): 1–7.

Keffer, Ann, Debbie Wood, Shelly Carr, Leah Mattison, and Barbara Lanier. 1998. "Ownership and the Well-Planned Study." In *Engaging Teachers*, ed. Betty Bisplinghoff and JoBeth Allen. Portsmouth, NH: Heinemann.

Kempton, Sue. 2007. *The Literate Kindergarten.* Portsmouth, NH: Heinemann.

Kendall, Julie, and Outey Khuon. 2006. *Writing Sense: Integrated Reading and Writing Lessons for English Language Learners K–8.* Portland, ME: Stenhouse.

Kirby, Dan, and Carol Kuykendall. 1991. *Mind Matters.* Portsmouth, NH: Boynton/Cook.

Kohl, Herbert. 1990. *36 Children.* New York: New American Library.

Kohn, Alfie. 2007. *The Homework Myth: Why Our Kids Get Too Much of a Bad Thing.* Cambridge, MA: Da Capo.

Krashen, Stephen. 1982. *Principles and Practices in Second Language Acquisition.* Oxford, UK: Penguin.

————. 1985. *Inquiries and Insights.* Haywood, CA: Alemany.

————. 1996. *Under Attack: The Case Against Bilingual Education.* Culver City, CA: Language Education Association.

————. 2003. *Explorations in Language Acquisition and Use: The Taipei Lectures.* Portsmouth, NH: Heinemann.

Lamott, Anne. 1994. *Bird by Bird.* New York: Anchor.

Lieberman, Ann, and Diane R. Wood. 2002. "From Network Learning to Classroom Teaching." *Journal of Educational Change* 3: 315–337.

———. 2003. *Inside the National Writing Project: Connecting Network Learning and Classroom Teaching, Volume 3.* New York: Teachers College Press.

Lilburn, Pat, Peter Sullivan, and Toby Gordon. 2002. *Good Questions for Math Teaching: Why Ask Them and What to Ask, K–6.* Sausalito, CA: Math Solutions.

Lincoln, Yvonna, and Evon Guba. 1985. *Naturalistic Inquiry.* Beverly Hills, CA: Sage.

Linsky, Martin, and Ronald Heifitz. 2002. *Leadership on the Line: Staying Alive Through the Dangers of Leading.* Cambridge, MA: Harvard Business Press.

Lipton, Laura, Bruce Wellman, and Carlette Humbard. 2001. *Mentoring: A Practical Guide to Learning-Focused Relationships.* Arlington, MA: MiraVia Llc.

Louv, Richard. 2008. *Last Child in the Woods.* Chapel Hill, NC: Algonquin Books.

Lytle, Susan, and Marilyn Cochran-Smith. 1992. *Inside/Outside: Teacher Research and Knowledge.* New York: Teachers College Press.

MacKay, Susan. 1997. "Breaking in My Research Tools." *Teacher Research* 4 (2): 154–156.

———. 2002. "The Research Mind Is Really the Teaching Mind at Its Best: An Interview with Karen Gallas." In *Language Development: A Reader for Teachers,* ed. Brenda Power and Ruth Shagoury. Upper Saddle River, NJ: Merrill/Prentice-Hall.

Mair, Nancy. 1994. *Voice Lessons: On Becoming a (Woman) Writer.* Boston: Beacon.

McBride, Mekeel. 2006. "Inspiration's Anatomy." In *Dog Star Delicatessen: New and Selected Poems 1979–2006.* Pittsburgh, PA: Carnegie Mellon University Press.

McFarland, Katherine, and Janice Stansell. 1993. "Historical Perspectives." In *Teachers Are Researchers: Reflection and Action,* ed. Leslie Patterson and Carol Santa. Newark, DE: International Reading Association.

McKnight, John, and Peter Block. 2010. *The Abundant Community: Awakening the Power of Families and Neighborhoods.* San Francisco: Berrey-Koehler.

Michalove, Barbara. 1993. "Creating a Community of Learners in Second Grade." In *Engaging Children,* ed. Betty Shockley, Barbara Michalove, and JoBeth Allen. Portsmouth, NH: Heinemann.

Miller, Debbie. 2002. *Reading with Meaning.* Portland, ME: Stenhouse.

———. 2008. *Teaching with Intention.* Portland, ME: Stenhouse.

Miller, Donalyn. 2009. *The Book Whisperer: Awakening the Inner Reader in Every Child.* San Francisco: Jossey-Bass.

Mohr, Marian. 2011. "Casting Your Question." *Teacher Action Research.* http://gse.gmu.edu/research/tr/tr_process/tr_casting/.

Mohr, Marian, and Marion Maclean. 1987. *Working Together: A Guide for Teacher-Researchers.* Urbana, IL: National Council of Teachers of English.

Murray, Donald. 1982. *Learning by Teaching.* Upper Montclair, NJ: Boynton/Cook.

———. 1990a. *Read to Write.* Fort Worth, TX: Holt, Rinehart, and Winston.

———. 1990b. *Shoptalk: Learning to Write with Writers.* Portsmouth, NH: Heinemann.

———. 1996. *Crafting a Life in Essay, Story, and Poem.* Portsmouth, NH: Heinemann.

National Endowment for the Arts. 2004. *Reading at Risk: A Survey of Literary Reading in America.* Research Division Report 46 (June).

National Writing Project. *Guide to Ethical Issues in Teacher Research.* n.d. Available from National Writing Project, 5511 Tolman Hall #1670, University of California, Berkeley, CA, 94720.

Newkirk, Thomas. 2002. *Misreading Masculinity: Boys, Literacy, and Popular Culture*. Portsmouth, NH: Heinemann.

Newkirk, Thomas, and Patricia McLure. 1993. *Listening In: Children Talk About Books (and Other Things)*. Portsmouth, NH: Heinemann.

Nuño, Judith. 1998. "Draw a Scientist: Middle School and High School Students' Conceptions About Scientists." University of Southern California Rossier School of Education. www.jdenuno.com/Resume%20Web/DAST.htm.

Ohanian, Susan. 1992. "Who the Hell Are You?" In *Whole Language: The Debate*, ed. Carl Smith. Bloomington, IN: EDINFO.

———. 1993. "Counting on Children." *Teacher Research* 1 (1): 24–36.

———. 1996. *Ask Ms. Class*. York, ME: Stenhouse.

Ornstein, Robert, and David Sobel. 1987. *The Healing Brain*. New York: Random House.

Owston, Ron. 1998. *Making the Link: Teacher Professional Development on the Internet*. Portsmouth, NH: Heinemann.

Paley, Vivian. 1981. *Wally's Stories*. Cambridge, MA: Harvard University Press.

Palmer, Parker. 1998. *The Courage to Teach*. San Francisco: Jossey-Bass.

Pareles, Jon. 1993. "Pop and Jazz in Review." *New York Times*, February 24. http://www.nytimes.com/1993/02/24/arts/pop-and-jazz-in-review-898993.html.

Parker, Emelie, and Tess Pardini. 2006. *"The Words Came Down!" English Language Learners Read, Write, and Talk Across the Curriculum, K–2*. Portland, ME: Stenhouse.

Parks, Amy Noelle. 2009. "Can Teacher Questions Be Too Open?" *Teaching Children Mathematics* 15 (7): 424–428.

Pearson, P. David, Laura R. Roehler, Janice A. Dole, and Gerald Duffy. 1992. "Developing Expertise in Reading Comprehension." In *What Research Has to Say About Reading Instruction*, ed. S. Jay Samuels and Alan Farstrup. Newark, DE: International Reading Association.

Peregoy, Suzanne F., and Owen. F. Boyle. 2005. *Reading, Writing, and Learning in ESL: A Resource Book for K–12 Teachers*. 4th ed. Boston: Pearson.

Portalupi, JoAnn Curtis. 1994. "Three Conditions for Growth: Time, Talk and Texts." *Teacher Research* 2 (1): 98–103.

Portalupi, JoAnn, and Ralph Fletcher. 2004. *Teaching the Qualities of Writing*. Portsmouth, NH: Firsthand.

Power, Brenda. 1995. "Crawling on the Bones of What We Know: An Interview with Shirley Brice Heath." *Teacher Research* 3 (1): 23–35.

———. 1996. *Taking Note: Improving Your Observational Notetaking*. York, ME: Stenhouse.

Power, Brenda Miller, and Ruth Shagoury Hubbard. 2002. *Language Development: A Reader for Teachers*. 2nd ed. Upper Saddle River, NJ: Merrill Prentice Hall.

Ray, Katie Wood. 1999. *Wondrous Words*. Urbana, IL: National Council of Teachers of English.

———. 2002. *What You Know by Heart: How to Develop Curriculum for Your Writing Workshop*. Portsmouth, NH: Heinemann.

———. 2004. *About the Authors: Writing Workshop with Our Youngest Writers*. Portsmouth, NH: Heinemann.

———. 2006. *Study Driven: A Framework for Planning Units of Study in the Writing Workshop.* Portsmouth, NH: Heinemann.

Richardson, Laurel. 1994. "Writing: A Method of Inquiry." In *Handbook of Qualitative Research,* ed. Norman Denzin and Yvonna Lincoln. Thousand Oaks, CA: Sage.

Richgels, Donald. J. 2003. "Writing Instruction." *Reading Teacher* 56 (4): 364–368.

Rief, Linda. 1992. *Seeking Diversity.* Portsmouth, NH: Heinemann.

Rilke, Rainer Maria. 1995. "Starting on the Path." In *The Soul Is Here for Its Own Joy: Sacred Poems from Many Cultures,* ed. Robert Bly. Hopewell, NJ: Ecco. (Orig. pub. 1934.)

Rosenberg, Marshall B. 2003. *Nonviolent Communication.* Encinitas, CA: PuddleDancer.

Rosenblatt, Roger. 2011. *Unless It Moves the Human Heart: The Craft and Art of Writing.* New York: HarperCollins.

Routman, Regie. 2003. *Reading Essentials: The Specifics You Need to Teach Reading Well.* Portsmouth, NH: Heinemann.

———. 2005. *Writing Essentials: Raising Expectations and Results While Simplifying Teaching.* Portsmouth, NH: Heinemann.

Roy, Suzanne C. 2004. "Building Writer's Workshop: One Principal's Journey." *The Delta Kappa Gamma Bulletin* 70: 25–28.

Rudduck, Jean, and David Hopkins. 1985. *Research as a Basis for Teaching: Readings from the Work of Lawrence Stenhouse.* Portsmouth, NH: Heinemann.

Ryan, Kay. 1998. "Poetry Alive: Reading Before Breakfast." *Hungry Mind Review* 46: 14.

Schaef, Anne Wilson. 1992. *Women's Reality: An Emerging Female System.* New York: HarperOne.

Schaeffer, Carolyn, and Kristin Amundsen. 1993. *Creating Community Anywhere.* New York: Perigee.

Secor, Virginia, and Karen Lylis. 1990. *Developmental Guide to Early Literacy.* Available from Secor/Lylis, P.O. Box 98, St. Albans, ME, 04971.

Sega, Denise. 1997a. "Really Important Stuff." *Teacher Research* 4 (2): 174–175.

———. 1997b. "Reading and Writing About Our Lives." *Teacher Research* 4 (2): 101–111.

Selwyn, Doug. 2010. *Following the Threads: Bringing Inquiry Research into the Classroom.* New York: Peter Lang.

Shagoury, Ruth. 2008. *Raising Writers: Understanding and Nurturing Young Children's Writing Development.* Boston: Allyn & Bacon.

Shaughnessy, Susan. 1993. *Walking on Alligators.* New York: HarperCollins.

Shockley, Betty, Barbara Michalove, and JoBeth Allen. 1993. *Engaging Children.* Portsmouth, NH: Heinemann.

———. 1995. *Engaging Families.* Portsmouth, NH: Heinemann.

Short, Kathy G. 1990. "Creating a Community of Learners." In *Talking About Books: Creating Literate Communities,* ed. Kathy Short and Kathryn M. Pierce. Portsmouth, NH: Heinemann.

Silvia, Paul. 2007. *How to Write a Lot: A Practical Guide to Productive Academic Writing.* Washington, DC: American Psychological Association.

Singer, Jessica. 2005. "Finding and Framing Teacher Research Questions. Moving from Reflective Practice to Teacher Research." *The Journal of Natural Inquiry and Reflective Practice* 19 (3): 144–155.

———. 2006. *Stirring Up Justice.* Portsmouth, NH: Heinemann.

Smith, Frank. 1986. *Insult to Intelligence: The Bureaucratic Invasion of Our Classrooms.* Portsmouth, NH: Heinemann.

Smith, Melinda J. 2001. *Teaching Playskills to Children with Autistic Spectrum Disorder: A Practical Guide.* New York: DRL Books.

Stafford, Kim. 1997. *Having Everything Right: Essays of Place.* Seattle: Sasquatch Books.

———. 2003. *The Muses Among Us.* Athens, GA: University of Georgia Press.

Stafford, William. 1982. "Things I Learned Last Week." In *Glass Face in the Rain.* Portland, OR: Estate of William Stafford.

———. 1998. "You Reading This, Be Ready." In *The Way It Is: New and Selected Poems.* St. Paul, MN: Graywolf.

Stone, Michael K. 2009. *Smart by Nature: Schooling for Sustainability.* Healdsburg, CA: Watershed Media.

Streb, Marla. 2011. "7 Reasons Why Getting Lost Is the Path to Enlightenment." *Bike Magazine* 18 (4): 15.

Styles, Donna. 2001. *Class Meetings: Building Leadership, Problem-Solving and Decision-Making Skills in the Respectful Classroom.* Portland, ME: Stenhouse.

Sweeney, Diane. 2003. *Learning Along the Way.* Portland, ME: Stenhouse.

Tannen, Deborah. 1998. *The Argument Culture.* New York: Morrow.

Taylor, Jill M., and Carol Gilligan. 1995. *Between Voice and Silence: Women and Girls, Race and Relationship.* Cambridge, MA: Harvard University Press.

Terlecky, Karen. 2010. "Getting Started with a Teacher Blog" Choice Literacy. http://www.choiceliteracy.com/public/department84.cfm.

Thompson, Michael. 2006. *Raising Cain: Exploring the Inner Life of America's Boys.* DVD. PBS Home Video.

Tomlinson, Carol Ann. 2007–2008. "Learning to Love Assessment." *Educational Leadership* 65 (4): 8–13.

Tovani, Cris. 2000. *I Read It, but I Don't Get It.* Portland, ME: Stenhouse.

———. 2004. *Do I Really Have to Teach Reading?* Portland, ME: Stenhouse.

Trelease, Jim. 2006. *The Read-Aloud Handbook.* 6th ed. New York: Penguin Books.

Ueland, Brenda. 2010. *If You Want to Write: A Book about Art, Independence, and Spirit.* San Francisco, CA: Bottom of the Hill Publishing.

Vatterott, Cathy. 2009. *Rethinking Homework: Best Practices That Support Diverse Needs.* Alexandria, VA: Association for Supervision and Curriculum Development.

Wallace, James. 1997. "A Note from John Dewey on Teacher Research." *Teacher Research* 5 (1): 26–28.

Waters, Alice. 2008. *Edible Schoolyard: A Universal Idea.* San Francisco: Chronicle Books.

Weaver, Connie. 1994. *Reading Process and Practice.* 2nd ed. Portsmouth, NH: Heinemann.

West, Sherrie, and Amy Cox. 2004. *Literacy Play: Over 300 Dramatic Play Activities That Teach Pre-Reading Skills.* Silver Spring, MD: Gryphon House.

Wheatley, Margaret, and Deborah Frieze. 2011. *Walk Out, Walk On.* New York: Berrett-Koehler.

Whitman, Ruth. 1997. "Climbing the Jacob's Ladder." In *The Writer's Home Companion,* ed. Joan Bolker. New York: Owl Books.

Widmer, Lori. 2008. "Begging the Question." *Words on the Page.* http://loriwidmer.blogspot.com/2008/04/begging-question-continuing-on-our.html.

Wilde, Sandra. 1996. *Notes from a Kidwatcher: Selected Writings of Yetta Goodman.* Portsmouth, NH: Heinemann.

Wilhelm, Jeffrey. 1997. *You Gotta BE the Book: Teaching Engaged and Reflective Reading with Adolescents.* New York: Teachers College Press.

Williams, Martin. 1993. *The Jazz Tradition.* New York: Oxford University Press.

Wise, Jessie, and Sara Buffington. 2004. *The Ordinary Parent's Guide to Teaching Reading.* Charles City, VA: Peace Hill.

Wooldridge, Susan. 1996. *Poemcrazy: Freeing Your Life with Words.* New York: Clarkson Potter.

Wolcott, Harry. 1995. *The Art of Fieldwork.* Walnut Creek, CA: Altamira.

Zaharlick, Amy, and Judith Green. 1991. "Ethnographic Research." In *Handbook of Research on Teaching the English Language Arts,* ed. James Flood, Julie Jensen, Diane Lapp, and James R. Squire. New York: Macmillan.

## Children's Books

Blume, Judy. 1980. *Superfudge.* New York: Dutton.

Burnett, Frances H. 1988. *The Secret Garden.* New York: Viking.

Cleary, Beverly. 1975. *Ramona the Brave.* New York: Morrow.

Cowley, Joy. 1990. *The Ghost.* Bothell, WA: Wright Group.

Dorris, Michael. 1992. *Morning Girl.* New York: Hyperion.

Gag, Wanda. 1928. *Millions of Cats.* New York: Putnam.

Gannett, Ruth. S. 1948. *My Father's Dragon.* New York: Random House.

Gantos, Jack. 2007. *I Am Not Joey Pigza.* New York: Farrar, Straus and Giroux.

Glaser, Isabel J. 1995. *Dreams of Glory: Poems Starring Girls.* New York: Atheneum.

Kotzwinkle, William, and Glenn Murray. 2001. *Walter the Farting Dog.* New York: Puffin Books.

Lobel, Arnold. 1972. *Frog and Toad Together.* New York: Harper and Row.

Mowat, Farley. 1961. *Owls in the Family.* Boston: Little, Brown.

Paterson, Katherine Ann. 1978. *The Great Gilly Hopkins.* New York: Crowell.

Raschka, Chris. 1992. *Charlie Parker Played Bebop.* New York: Dutton.

Scieszka, Jon. 1992. *The Stinky Cheese Man and Other Fairly Stupid Tales.* New York: Viking.

———. 2008. *Guys Write for Guys Read: Boys' Favorite Authors Write About Being Boys.* New York: Viking Junior.

Shannon, David. 1998. *No, David!* New York: Scholastic.

Shreve, Susan. 1984. *The Flunking of Joshua T. Bates.* New York: Knopf.

Van Allsberg, Chris. 1992. *The Witch's Broom.* Boston: Houghton Mifflin.

Van Camp, Richard. 1998. *What's the Most Beautiful Thing You Know About Horses?* New York: Children's Book Press.

# Index

Page numbers followed by an *f* indicate figures.

## A

"after the fact" notes, 122–124. *See also* notes

Alaska Teacher Research Network (ATRN), 212–213, 221

Alexander, Audrey, 58–63, 59*f*–60*f*, 64*f*–66*f*, 167–168

Alexander, Wallace, 63–66

Alinsky, Saul, 91, 174

Allen, JoBeth, 144, 158

Alvarez, Julia, 174

American Association of Educational Researchers, 219

analysis of data. *See* data analysis

anticipation guides, 228–230

artwork, student artifacts in research, 115–118, 116*f*–117*f*

assessment
  audio and video recording, 129–133
  data analysis and, 162–167

attention deficit hyperactivity disorder (ADHD), 28–29

Atwell, Nancie, 6, 33, 79, 124, 163, 192

audio recording
  data analysis and, 149–150
  how to use in research, 107–108
  overview, 107–113, 109*f*

audit check, 143

Austin, Terri, 192, 212–213, 236–237

## B

background talk, 22–23

Ball, Arthena, 182–183

Ballenger, Cynthia, 6

Barbieri, Maureen, 173–174

Barratt, Carra, 153

Bateson, Mary Catherine, 72

Berg, Elizabeth, 8–9

bilingual education, 253–254

Bintz, William, 113

Bisplinghoff, Betty, 144, 158, 174

Bissett, Monique, 201

Bissex, Glenda, 238–239

Block, Peter, 210

blog writing, 188–191, 205–207

*Bone from a Dry Sea, A* (Dickinson), 19–20

"book club" format, 244–246

Boyer, Tonia, 24

boy writers, 231–233

Brandt, Gina, 202

Buckner, Aimee, 87

Burke Reading Inventory, 102

## C

Campbell, Kimberly Hill, 178–180

case study, 143

Casey, Katherine, 47

*Changing the View* (Austin), 192
Charney, Cristina, 47
Christensen, Linda, 107, 176, 237
Christenson, Sarah, 81–87, 140, 141*f*–142*f*,
    153–156, 154*f*, 155*f*, 156*f*
citations from readings
    examples of, 178–186
    overview, 171–174
    reading for pleasure and, 174–176, 176*f*
    writing and, 177–178
*Claiming Breath* (Glancy), 201
Clark, Kelli, 20
classroom environment, 263–265
Clayton Action Research Collaborative,
    217–218
coaching conversations
    data analysis and, 160–161, 161*f*
    writing and, 192
Cochran-Smith, Marilyn, 210
codes
    examples of, 249
    overview, 145–149, 146*f*, 147*f*
*Cold Mountain* (Frazier), 135–136
collaboration. *See also* research communities
    examples of, 251, 256
    mentors, 228
    research design and, 78
collection of data. *See* data collection
communities, research. *See* research
    communities
community-building classroom meetings,
    263–265
conference journal, 245. *See also* journals
confirmability, 143
constant comparison, 143
conversations, 22–23, 160–161, 161*f*
cooked notes, 148–149. *See also* notes
Cox, Dana, 142
Crews, Tracy, 103
Cross, Ally, 22
crystallization, 143, 151–153. *See also* data
    analysis
Csak, Nancy, 97–99, 98*f*, 99*f*
Cunningham, Andie, 111, 173
curriculum, standardization and, 15–16

**D**
data analysis
    Draw a Reader Test (DART) and,
        162–167
    examples of, 77–78, 80, 84, 88, 159–170,
        160*f*, 161*f*, 241–268
    language patterns, 159–162, 160*f*, 161*f*
    methods, 144–158, 145*f*, 146*f*, 147*f*, 154*f*,
        155*f*, 156*f*
    mini-inquiry projects and, 75
    overview, 3, 136–144, 138*f*–139*f*,
        141*f*–142*f*
    patterns in data, 135–136
    research design and, 55*f*–56*f*, 57–58,
        59*f*–60*f*, 60–63, 64*f*–65*f*
    terms and methods, 143–144
    unexpected findings and, 158–159
data collection. *See also* harvesting data
    examples of, 77, 79–80, 82–83, 88,
        241–268
    finding the time for note taking,
        120–124
    mini-inquiry projects and, 75
    overview, 3
    research design and, 55*f*–56*f*, 57–58,
        59*f*–60*f*, 60–63, 64*f*–65*f*
data presentation, 3, 61
Davidson, Gordon, 209
deadlines in writing, 204–205
*Deeper Reading* (Gallagher), 6
Department of Curriculum and
    Instruction, 219
design, research. *See* research design
Dewey, John, 4–5, 172
dialogue journals, 77–78. *See also* journals
Dickinson, Peter, 19–20
Dillard, Annie, 53, 190–191, 239
"distant teachers," 192
Dobash, Lynn, 96
Doherty, Katie, 100, 124–127, 125*f*,
    241–244
Doss, Wendy, 176
Draw a Reader Test (DART), 162–167
Draw a Scientist Test (DAST), 162–166
drawing in preschool, 261–262

**E**

Early, Jessica Singer, 91–92, 152–153, 180–185
Elbow, Peter, 194
Ellis, Maraline, 23–24
Emig, Janet, 20
engagement, 241–244
English language learner (ELL) students
    audio and video recording and, 111–112
    examples of, 258–261
    memos and, 150–151
ethical issues, research design and, 63, 66–69, 68*f*, 69*f*, 70*f*–71*f*
expectations, tension and, 23–24

**F**

Fcak, Christine, 182
Fels, Don, 100
field notes. *See also* notes
    cooked notes, 148–149
    examples of, 250
Fletcher, Ralph, 203–204
Foote, Martha, 219
Frazier, Charles, 135–136
freedrawing time, 261–262
Freer, Chrystal, 261–262
Freyer, Bret, 221–223
Friedman, Bonnie, 191
Frieze, Deborah, 218
Frost, Robert, 194
Frye, Sharon, 173–174

**G**

Gallagher, Kelly, 6
Gallas, Karen, 174, 224
garden, school, 246–248
gaze, 20–23
Gibson, Gail, 213–217
Gilbert, Ellie, 118–119, 135, 169–170, 265–268
Glancy, Diane, 201
Glazier, Debbie, 146–148, 147*f*
Goodman, Yetta, 172
*Good Questions for Math Teaching* (Lilburn, Sullivan, and Gordon), 47
Gordon, Toby, 47

Goswami, Dixie, 20
Graham, Steve, 182
graphing of data, 153–156, 154*f*, 155*f*, 156*f*. *See also* data analysis
Graves, Don, 159
Greene, Chris, 219
Gromko, Emily, 25, 79–81, 137–140, 138*f*–139*f*
grounded theory, 143

**H**

Hahn, Mary Lee, 205–207
"hanging around" activity, 72–74
Hardy, Saundra, 10–11, 176, 258–261
Harste, Jerome C., 53, 74–76, 237
harvesting data. *See also* data collection
    audio and video recording, 107–113, 109*f*, 129–133
    interviews, 100–102, 127–129, 128*f*
    journals and notes, 91–99, 95*f*, 98*f*, 99*f*, 120–124
    middle school readers' mid-year surveys, 124–127
    overview, 91
    photographic documentation, 113–115
    researcher's role and, 118–120
    student artifacts, 115–118, 116*f*–117*f*
    surveys and inventories, 103, 104*f*–106*f*, 124–127, 125*f*
Heard, Georgia, 123
Heath, Shirley Brice, 118
Heinlein, Nicole, 100–101, 225
Hillock, George, 184
home-school journals, 103, 144
Housum-Stevens, Julie, 204–205
hypothesis development, 31–32

**I**

*I Am Not Joey Pigza* (Gantos), 231–232
*If You Want to Write* (Ueland), 193
independent learners, wonder questions and, 50–51
*Inside the National Writing Project* (Lieberman and Wood), 216
*Inspiration's Anatomy* (McBride), 27–28
International Reading Association, 219

interviews
    examples of, 263–265
    getting started with, 102
    overview, 100–102
    student talk, 127–129, 128*f*
*In the Middle* (Atwell), 6, 192
"in the midst" notes, 121. *See also* notes
intuition, research project as a result of, 14
inventories, 103, 104*f*–106*f*

**J**
Janesick, Valerie, 152
Jantsch, Erich, 218
jargon, 16, 28–29
jazz, teacher research compared to, 13–15
*Jazz Tradition, The* (Williams), 15
*Journal of Mental Imagery*, 176–177
journals
    codes, 145–149, 146*f*, 147*f*
    examples of, 242, 245, 249–251, 259–260, 264, 267
    home-school journals, 103
    overview, 91–99, 95*f*, 98*f*, 99*f*
Justiss, Bridget, 67

**K**
Kaback, Suzanne, 16, 162–167, 175, 228–230
Kane, Katrina, 114–115
Kearns, Jane A., 12–15
Keep-Barnes, Annie, 40–45, 221–223
Kent, Rich, 237
Kingsolver, Barbara, 176
knowledge, research project as a result of, 14
Kohl, Herbert, 37
Kulak, Andy, 108–111, 109*f*

**L**
Lamott, Anne, 176, 187, 192–193, 238
Larsen, Lee Anne, 145, 158
learning disabilities
    example of using research questions and, 40–45
    refining research questions and, 28–29
Leland, Christine, 53, 74–76
letters to teacher-researchers, 220–223. *See also* research communities

Libby, Barbara, 107–108
Lieberman, Anne, 216
Lilburn, Pat, 47
Lipton, Laura, 161
Listo! Project, 219
literacy acts, figuring out the questions and, 32–33
literature review in research. *See also* citations from readings
    examples of, 178–186
    overview, 171–173
    reading for pleasure and, 174–176, 176*f*
    research workshop, 178–180
    writing and, 177–178, 180–185
Lytle, Susan, 210

**M**
MacKay, Susan Harris, 33–40, 93–94, 97
magnification, data analysis and, 159–160, 161*f*
Maher, Jan, 135
Mariechild, Diane, 8
Martinez, Laura, 254–258
McBride, Mekeel, 26–28
McGregor, Gabi, 263–265
McLaughlin, Corinne, 209
McLure, Pat, 121
meaningful research, 29
member check, 143
memos, 150–151, 202
*Mentoring Matters: A Practical Guide to Learning-Focused Relationships* (Lipton and Wellman), 161
mentoring teachers, 184–185, 228
mentor texts, 182–183
Michalove, Barbara, 144, 158
Miller, Debbie, 6, 50
mini-inquiry projects, 74–76
Mitchell, Lucy Sprague, 172
Moffit, Lila, 201–202
Mollison, Bill, 235
Munroe, Natalie, 189
Murphy, Lara, 246–248
Murray, Donald, 177
*The Muses Among Us* (Stafford), 92

**N**

narratives, 144. *See also* writing
Neary, Stacy, 113
needs of students. *See* student needs
neti neti, 45–46
Nihart, Heather, 108, 109*f*
notes
    codes and, 145–149, 146*f*, 147*f*
    cooked notes, 148–149
    examples of, 242, 259–260, 267
    finding the time for, 120–124
    overview, 91–99, 95*f*, 98*f*, 99*f*
Nye, Naomi Shihab, 171

**O**

Ohanian, Susan, 142–143
Olcott, Kelly Chandler, 213–217
online writing, 188–191, 205–207
Osborn, Rick, 202
Ostrow, Jill, 15–17

**P**

Palmer, Parker, 223–224, 228
Pareles, Jon, 14
parents. *See also* permissions
    sharing assessment data with, 130
    surveys and inventories and, 103,
        104*f*–106*f*, 247
    video recording and, 113, 130
Parks, Amy Noelle, 46
Parks, Bitsy, 96, 244–246
Pastan, Linda, 174
permissions
    examples of, 251, 252–253, 259, 264
    overview, 67–68, 68*f*, 69*f*
    research design and, 63, 66–69, 68*f*, 69*f*
Peters, Robert L., 53
Petrin, Kelly, 115–118, 116*f*–117*f*
photographic documentation, 113–115,
    242
Pidhurney, Susan, 103
Pierce, Kathryn Mitchell, 226, 226*f*–227*f*
Piercy, Marge, 174
planning research design, 69, 71
Portalupi, JoAnn, 30–33, 211
Poulin, Tiffany, 201

Power, Brenda Miller, 72–74, 120–124
preschool
    freedrawing time, 261–262
    literacy and, 265–268
process of teacher research, 15–17
professional development, 226, 226*f*–227*f*
"professional learning communities,"
    210–213. *See also* research
    communities
pronoun preferences, 161–162
*The Pull of the Moon* (Berg), 8–9
*Puzzling Moments, Teachable Moments:
    Practicing Teacher Research in Urban
    Classrooms* (Ballenger), 6

**Q**

questions
    art of questioning, 45–48
    audio and video recording and, 107, 108,
        109*f*
    cooked notes and, 148–149
    examples of, 76, 79, 81–82, 87–88,
        241–268
    mini-inquiry projects and, 75
    origins of, 19–23
    refining, 28–29
    research design and, 55*f*, 57–58, 59*f*, 64*f*
    strategies for working toward, 30–33
    tension and, 23–24, 26–28
    value of subquestions, 24–26
    wonder questions, 49–51
Quinn, Melanie, 185–186

**R**

Rader, Heather, 45–48, 159–162, 160*f*, 161*f*
raw notes, 148. *See also* notes
Raymond, Bekah, 101
Readence, J. E., 229
*Readicide* (Gallagher), 6
reading
    overview, 171–178
    preschool literacy and, 265–268
*The Reading Zone* (Atwell), 79, 163
reading instruction, 29
reading responses, 248–253
*Reading with Meaning* (Miller), 6, 50

reading workshop. *See also* workshops
   data analysis and, 167–168
   examples of, 244–246
   refining research questions and, 29
reflection, 224–225, 226
rejection, 200
research citations. *See* citations from
    readings
research communities. *See also* collaboration
   anticipation guides, 228–230
   district support and, 217–218
   evolution of, 213–217
   examples of, 213–217, 223–224, 228–233
   letters to teacher-researchers, 220–223
   mentors, 228
   overview, 209–213
   professional development and, 226,
    226*f*–227*f*
   "professional learning communities" and,
    210–213
   reflection and, 224–225
   resources to build, 218–224
research design
   ethical issues, 63, 66–69, 68*f*, 69*f*, 70*f*–71*f*
   examples of, 54–63, 55*f*–57*f*, 59*f*–60*f*,
    64*f*–66*f*, 76–89, 241–268
   "hanging around" activity, 72–74
   mini-inquiry projects and, 74–76
   overview, 8, 53–54
   permissions and, 63, 66–69, 68*f*, 69*f*
   planning, 69, 71
   pleasure and, 69, 71
researcher's role, 118–120
research questions. *See* questions
research workshop, 178–180
resources
   boy writers, 232–233
   examples of, 86, 243, 245–246
   figuring out the questions and, 31
   research communities and, 218–224
Richardson, Laurel, 151–152
Rosenblatt, Roger, 191
Rutherford, Marty, 209
Ryan, Kay, 174, 175
Rylant, Cynthia, 86

**S**
Salisbury, Carey, 94–95, 95*f*
Schaef, Anne Wilson, 172
Schardt, Michelle, 76–78, 110
school garden, 246–248
Sega, Denise, 25
self-reflection, 224–225
Seneca, 158
Shagoury, Ruth, 26–28, 185–186, 200–204
Sibberson, Franki, 16, 205–207
Silvia, Paul, 189
Smith, Andrea, 49–51, 129–133
sociogram, 144, 156–158, 250–251. *See also*
    data analysis
Sorley, Nicole, 103
special-needs students, 28–29
Stafford, Kim, 92, 97
Stafford, William, 10, 120, 174
standardization, curriculum and, 15–16
Stenhouse, Lawrence, 5, 6
Streb, Marla, 173
student artifacts, 115–118, 116*f*–117*f*
student needs
   examples of using research questions
    and, 33–45
   overview, 16
   research design and, 53
*Students Teach Me Things* (Hardy), 10–11
student surveys. *See* surveys
student talk, 127–129, 128*f*. *See also*
    interviews
subquestions. *See also* questions
   examples of, 76, 79, 81–82, 87, 241–268
   research design and, 55*f*, 64*f*
   value of, 24–26
Sullivan, Peter, 47
surveys
   examples of, 247, 267
   middle school readers' mid-year surveys,
    124–127, 125*f*
   overview, 103, 104*f*–106*f*
   research design and, 79–80
Swales, John, 182

**T**
Tannen, Deborah, 174, 238

Taylor-Milligan, Molly, 253–254
teacher-research community. *See* research communities
teacher research in general
    endurance of, 7–8
    examples of, 178–186
    history of, 5–7
    overview, 2, 3–5, 235–239
    reading and, 171–178
teaching journal, 96. *See also* journals
*Teaching with Intention* (Miller), 6
technology, 8, 188–191
*Telling a Research Story: Writing a Literature Review* (Feak and Swales), 182
tension
    research questions and, 23–24
    turning into research questions, 26–28
Terlecky, Karen, 190
Tetrick, Susan, 175–176, 176*f*, 224–225
thick description, 144
*Things I Learned About Research*, 12
*Things I Learned Last Week* (Stafford), 10
*Things I Learned This Week About Teaching*, 11
Toll, Cathy, 47
Tomlinson, Carol Ann, 165, 166–167
Trabacca, Gloria, 248–253
transferability, 144
triangulation, 144
tunneling, 32
Turner, Patrice, 54–58, 55*f*–57*f*
Tyler, Anne, 174

**U**
Ueland, Brenda, 193
Ustach, Tom, 203–204

**V**
value-laden words or phrases, 28–29
Van Camp, Richard, 185–186
video recording
    data analysis and, 169–170
    examples of, 129–133, 243, 261–262, 263–265
    overview, 107–113, 109*f*
Vygotsky, Lev, 175

**W**
Walker, Carole, 219
Walker, Josh, 219
Wallace, Anne, 111
Wallace, Christina, 86–89
Web sites, writing and, 188–191
Wellman, Bruce, 161
Welty, Eudora, 172–173
West, Rebecca, 169
Western Maine Partnership, 218–219
*What's the Most Beautiful Thing You Know About Horses?* (Van Camp), 185–186
Wheatley, Margaret, 218
Widmer, Lori, 100
Williams, Martin, 15
Winterbourne, Nancy, 112
Wolcott, Harry, 92
wonder questions, 49–51. *See also* questions
Wood, Diane, 216
Woodhouse, Leslie, 111–112
Wordle, 159–162, 160*f*, 161*f*
working hypothesis, 144
workshops. *See also* reading workshop; writing workshop
    overview, 15–17
    refining research questions and, 29
writing. *See also* journals; notes
    blog writing, 188–191, 205–207
    boys and, 231–233
    deadlines and, 204–205
    "distant teachers" and, 192
    examples of, 200–207
    importance of, 192–193
    narratives, 144, 202
    organization and, 190–191
    overview, 187–188
    presentation proposals, 196, 197*f*–198*f*
    publishing and, 194
    reading like a researcher and, 177–178
    rejection and, 200
    research communities and, 220–223, 224–225
    response to, 193–199, 197*f*–198*f*
    self-reflection and, 224–225
    starting, 188–190
*The Writing Life* (Dillard), 190–191

writing retreats, 195–196
writing workshop. *See also* workshops
    examples of, 254–261
    harvesting data and, 129–133
    overview, 15–17
    research design and, 86–89
    video recording and, 129–133

**Y**
Young, Sherry, 127–129, 128*f*, 145, 158
*You Reading This, Be Ready* (Stafford), 120

# Published Article List

## Articles from *Teacher Research: The Journal of Classroom Inquiry*

Alexander, Wallace. 1996. Research Plan and comments. *Teacher Research* 4 (1): 112–115.

Allen, Jennifer. 1997a. "Letting Inventories Lead the Way." *Teacher Research* 4 (2): 159–162.

————. 1997b. "Reflections as a Teacher-Researcher: Exploring Literature Through Student-Led Discussions." *Teacher Research* 4 (2): 124–139.

Bisplinghoff, Betty Shockley. 1995. "Reading Like a Researcher." *Teacher Research* 3 (1): 105–113.

Bradshaw-Brown, Judith. 1995. "We Have Met the Audience and She Is Us: The Evolution of Teacher as Audience for Research." *Teacher Research* 2 (2): 18–31.

Campbell, Kimberly. 1997. "You're Invited." *Teacher Research* 1 (2): 57–62.

Chandler, Kelly. 1997. "Emergent Researchers: One Group's Beginnings." *Teacher Research* 4 (2): 73–100.

Glazier, Debbie. 1997. "Teacher-Researcher Extensions: Coding." *Teacher Research* 1 (2): 14–16.

Harste, Jerome, and Christine Leland. 1998. "Testing the Water with Mini-Inquiry Projects." *Teacher Research* 5 (1): 123–127.

Housum-Stevens, Julie. 1997. "Making Deadlines." *Teacher Research* 5 (1): 161–162.

Hubbard, Ruth Shagoury. 1993. "Seeing What Is Not Seen: Another Reason for Writing Up Teacher Research." *Teacher Research* 1 (1): 143–147.

Kane, Katrina. 1998. "A Quick Guide to Using Photography in Research." *Teacher Research* 5 (1): 99–101.

Kearns, Jane. 1996. "Teaching and Researching Riffs." *Teacher Research* 3 (2): 1–4.

Keep-Barnes, Annie. 1994. "Real Teachers Don't Always Succeed." *Teacher Research* 2 (1): 1–7.

Larson, Lee Ann, and Sherry Young. 1998. "Home-School Journals." *Teacher Research* 5 (1): 10–14.

Libby, Barbara. 1998. "How to Use Audiorecordings in Research." *Teacher Research* 5 (1): 15–17.

MacKay, Susan. 1997. "Real Magic: Trusting the Voice of a Young Learner." *Teacher Research* 4 (2): 13–21.

Pidhurney, Susan. 1996. "Home-School Literacy Connections: Research Brief." *Teacher Research* 4 (1): 117–119.

Pierce, Kathryn Mitchell. 1998. "Timeline of Professional Development." *Teacher Research* 5 (1): 31–41.

Portalupi, JoAnn. 1993. "Strategies for Working Toward a Research Question." *Teacher Research* 1 (1): 58–63.

———. 1994. "The Trickle-Down Effect of Teacher Research: Students Adopting a Research Stance." *Teacher Research* 1 (2): 145–148.

Turner, Patrice. 1998. Research Plan and comments. *Teacher Research* 5 (1): 44–45.

Young, Sherry. 1997. "Focusing on Student Talk." *Teacher Research* 4 (2): 22–27.

Note: The following teacher-researcher essay is used in the text, but not as a Featured Teacher-Researcher:

Clark, Kelli. 1997. "Harvesting Potatoes." *Teacher Research* 4 (2): 182–183.

## Articles from Choice Literacy

"To Fart or Not to Fart? Reflections on Boy Writers" by Jennifer Allen

"Middle School Readers' Mid-Year Surveys" by Katie Doherty

"5 Easy Steps for Starting a Blog" by Mary Lee Hahn and Franki Sibberson

"The Anticipation Guide: A Tool for Study Group Leaders" by Suzy Kaback

"The Draw a Reader Test: Informal Assessment Supporting Teacher Inquiry" by Suzy Kaback

"Process Versus Product" by Jill Ostrow

"What's the Most Beautiful Thing You Know About . . . ?" by Melanie Quinn and Ruth Shagoury

"Language Patterns: Reflecting with Transcripts and Wordle" by Heather Rader

"You Get What You Ask For: The Art of Questioning" by Heather Rader

"Assessment: Inside and Outside Views" by Andrea Smith

"The Power of Wonder Questions" by Andrea Smith